Contributions to Management Science

The Faculty of Economics, Business Administration and Information Technology of the University of Zurich hereby authorizes the printing of this Doctoral Thesis, without thereby giving any opinion on the views contained therein.

Zurich, April 1 2009 The Dean: Prof. Dr. Dr. Josef Falkinger

Jan Pfister

Managing Organizational Culture for Effective Internal Control

From Practice to Theory

Physica-Verlag
A Springer Company

Jan Pfister
Lancaster University
Management School
Dept. Accounting & Finance
Bailrigg, Lancaster, LA1 4YX
United Kingdom
j.pfister@lancaster.ac.uk

Dissertation for the University of Zurich, April 2009

ISSN 1431-1941
ISBN 978-3-7908-2339-4 e-ISBN 978-3-7908-2340-0
DOI: 10.1007/978-3-7908-2340-0
Springer Dordrecht Heidelberg London New York

Library of Congress Control Number: 2009926051

Cover design: SPi Publisher Services

Printed on acid-free paper

Physica-Verlag Berlin Heidelberg (www.springer.com)

"To my parents Anthonia and Alexander and my siblings Alexandra and Georg"

Foreword

This book has been developed in association with the Center for Financial Reporting & Management (CFRM) at the Haas School of Business, University of California, Berkeley. As Jan Pfister's sponsoring faculty member at the Haas School of Business, I take great pride in contributing the opening piece of his publication. To my knowledge, this is the first in-depth interdisciplinary and theory-building study that addresses how organizational culture can be managed to enhance effective internal control.

Having served as senior finance officer at several major corporations for more than 14 years, it is clear to me that organizational culture needs to be addressed, particularly from an accounting and control perspective. As a native of India, I believe the need for considering cultures is accentuated even further in the internal control of international and global companies, where different national cultures come together. Thus it is the role of the control environment to address these issues in light of the internationalization of corporations.

Being on the cusp of current issues in practice and research, Pfister's work makes a significant leap in this direction, emphasizing the control environment. In any organization, the *culture* influences our behavior to some extent, which accounts for how the design and execution of internal control is encouraged. An example is the current financial crisis, which demonstrates clearly the need to develop cultures in which long-term rather than short-term thinking is ingrained. Pfister's approach distinguishes itself from other accounting and control research efforts as culture here is seen as a social "construct" that can be influenced by control. Hence, in this study, not only does culture provide the context for control, but any control mechanism also influences organizational culture.

This study is an excellent example of the thesis that accounting and control research can and should go beyond numbers and formal systems, and that there is a need to accept the study of accounting and control, not only in quantitative but also in qualitative terms. In fact, many senior corporate officers of large corporations contributed willingly and shared their valuable experiences through private interviews, which are incorporated within this book. The qualitative data provides unique evidence that many quantitative accounting studies cannot match. In addition, the interdisciplinary aspect of this study is so relevant and so timely that the theoretical grounding of Pfister's work was awarded "Best Paper by a PhD Student" at the 12th Annual Ethics Research Symposium of the American Accounting Association in 2007. The theory and the interviews form an original bridge between innovative academic research and professional practice to respond effectively to a current need.

I am convinced that awareness of organizational cultures with regard to internal control adds value to the quality and performance of every business. This book offers valuable new insights for academics, professionals and many other groups. I enthusiastically recommend this book to you.

February 2009

Solomon N. Darwin
Executive Director
Center for Financial Reporting & Management
Walter A. Haas School of Business
University of California at Berkeley

Acknowledgments

This is a wonderful opportunity for me to express my gratitude and respect for the many people who supported the successful completion of this study. Professor T. Flemming Ruud from the University of Zurich inspired me to study internal control, encouraged me early on in my doctoral studies to approach this international research focus, and gave me the necessary freedom to tackle this project. Professor Andreas Georg Scherer from the University of Zurich provided me with detailed feedback and encouraged me to follow the interdisciplinary and theory-building research design, which was crucial for the outcome of this study. Professor Gary Weaver from the University of Delaware readily agreed to being part of my doctoral committee and also gave me detailed comments and new perspectives on culture. Professor Solomon N. Darwin from the University of California, Berkeley provided me a welcoming research environment and was always available for inspiring discussions and advice.

My special thanks go to all the senior-level people who agreed to support this research project. The interviewees gave their valuable time for the interview, reviewed their quotes, and provided me with unique insights. The following 21 companies have contributed to this study:

Adecco SA	Ernst & Young	Levi Strauss & Co
Advanced Micro Devices	Genentech	Microsoft
Charles Schwab Corporation	Google	Motorola
Ciba Speciality Chemicals	Hewlett Packard	Novartis
Credit Suisse Group	Intel	Pacific Gas & Electric Corp.
Deloitte	KPMG	Sirf Technology Holdings
eBay	Leadis Technology	SureWest Communications

I wish to thank Helmut Willke from the University of Bielefeld, and Holly Ashbaugh-Skaife from the University of Wisconsin-Madison, for their detailed comments on my earlier working papers. I also gratefully acknowledge Allan Hansen, Hans ten Rouwelaar, James Lincoln, Jan Mouritsen, Jennifer Chatman, Manfred Piwinger, Nicole Johnson, Roland Spékle, Urton Anderson, William Kinney, and participants of the Annual Meetings of the European Accounting Association in Lisbon 2007 and Rotterdam 2008, the Ethics Research Symposium of the American Accounting Association in Chicago 2007 and the Workshop on Accounting as Social and Organizational Practice in Paris 2008 for their insightful comments and suggestions. I would like to thank my colleagues at the Institute for Accounting and Control at the University of Zurich and Felix Reichert, Michèle Rüdisser, and Shqiponja Isufi, in particular, for detailed feedback, Maximillian Müller for collecting data, and Esther Bannwart and Jochen Kühn for their mental support over the years. I also wish to thank John Bird and Jessica Villat for helping with editing and giving valuable suggestions, and Mara Luning for her assistance in transcribing interviews. Christian Früh, Eric Halverson, Katharine Brewer, Nicole Gehrmann, Rich Wong and Steven Holden provided me with invaluable assistance to help open doors to many renowned companies. Financial support from the Swiss National Science Foundation (Project no. 112729) and the Janggen-Pohn Stiftung is gratefully acknowledged.

Finally, I would like to thank my family and friends for their support all along the way – it was motivating and helped me to achieve my goal. In particular, I gratefully acknowledge my parents, Anthonia and Alexander, and my siblings, Alexandra and Georg, to whom I dedicate this study. Their continuous encouragement and support in various ways was invaluable.

February 2009

Jan Pfister
Zurich

Contents

Abbreviations

AAA	American Accounting Association
ACCA	Association of Chartered Certified Accountants
ACFE	Association of Certified Fraud Examiners
AIA	American Institute of Accountants
AICPA	American Institute of Certified Public Accountants
BCBS	Basle Committee on Banking Supervision
BIS	Bank of International Settlements
BSC	Balanced Scorecard
CEO	Chief Executive Officer
CFO	Chief Financial Officer
CICA	The Canadian Institute of Chartered Accountants
COBIT	Control Objectives for Information and Related Technology
CoCo	Canadian Criteria on Control Board
COSO	Committee of Sponsoring Organizations of the Treadway Commission
EFQM	European Foundation for Quality Management
ERP	Enterprise Resource Planning
EU	European Union
FCPA	Foreign Corrupt Practices Act of 1977
FEE	Fédération des Experts Comptables Européens
FEI	Financial Executives International
HKICPA	Hong Kong Institute of Certified Public Accountants
ICAEW	Institute of Chartered Accountants in England and Wales
IFAC	International Federation of Accountants
IIA	The Institute of Internal Auditors
IMA	The Institute of Management Accountants
ISACA	Information Systems Audit and Control Association
ISO	International Organization for Standardization
KPI	Key Performance Indicator
MD&A	Management Discussion and Analysis
OECD	Organization for Economic Co-operation and Development

PCAOB	Public Company Accounting Oversight Board
R&D	Research and Development
SA	Securities Act of 1932
SEA	Securities and Exchange Act of 1933
SEC	Securities and Exchange Commission
SOX	Sarbanes-Oxley Act of 2002
US GAAP	United States Generally Accepted Accounting Principles
US	United States
UK	United Kingdom

List of Figures

List of Tables

Chapter 1
Introduction

1.1 Need for the Study

1.1.1 Current Issues in Practice

Investment bank Lehman Brothers filed for bankruptcy protection on September 15, 2008. Three major British banks – the Royal Bank of Scotland, HBOS, and Lloyds TSB – relied on a rescue plan from the British government on October 13, 2008. At the same time, Iceland's stock market plunged 76%, bringing that state to potential national bankruptcy.[1] As a consequence of the worldwide financial crisis, a stream of struggles and failures from financial institutions around the world has resulted. These events are rooted in failures which, as will be seen in this study, can be linked to internal control and organizational culture. Before relating these failures to this study, internal control and organizational culture should be defined:

- *Internal control* is a process effected by an entity's board of directors, management, and other personnel, designed to provide reasonable assurance for the achievement of organizational objectives in regard to effectiveness and efficiency of operations, reliability of internal and external reporting, and compliance with applicable laws, regulations, and internal policies.[2]

[1]*Guardian*, October 15, 2008: Pressures on G7 as financial chaos continuous.

[2]This definition of internal control is based on the combination of the definitions from the US Committee of Sponsoring Organizations of the Treadway Commission (COSO 1992) and the Canadian Guidance on Control Board (CoCo 1995), which are two commonly accepted control frameworks from practice. The definition of internal control will be further discussed in Sect. 2.1.1 and the two frameworks will be presented in the literature review in Sect. 3.2. This interpretation of internal control includes the more focused definitions of internal control (often then also called accounting controls), which are defined by Simons (1995, p. 84) as the "detailed, procedural checks and balances". Internal control *differs from management control* because it is not about management decisions itself. Instead internal control provides integrity for any control systems by assuring information quality and the safeguarding of assets so that reasonable assurance for the achievement of the objective categories operations, reporting and compliance can be achieved (see also Sect. 2.1.2).

J. Pfister, *Managing Organizational Culture for Effective Internal Control*, Contributions to Management Science,
DOI: 10.1007/978-3-7908-2340-0_1, © Springer Physica-Verlag Berlin Heidelberg 2009

- *Organizational culture* is a pattern of basic assumptions that a group has invented, discovered, or developed in learning to cope with its problems of external adaptation and internal integration, which is represented in a system of shared values defining what is important, and norms, defining appropriate attitudes and behaviors that guide each individual's attitudes and behaviors.[3]

This study explores the interrelations between internal control and organizational culture. In general, internal control is effective if it provides reasonable assurance for the achievement of the three objective categories (see above: operations, reporting, and compliance) and is free from any material control weaknesses.[4] Although internal control is about "technical" checks and balances such as the maintenance of data bases, record keeping, or segregation of duties, these aspects of information handling all rely on the effort, trustworthiness, and discipline of the people involved. Pfaff and Ruud (2007, p. 23) highlight the importance of a culture that promotes control awareness throughout the organization because only then can all the benefits of effective internal control be reached. While positive examples of cultures with effective internal control find relatively low public attention, negative examples are found in abundance. For instance, in regard to the current financial crisis, the Association of Chartered Certified Accountants (ACCA), a global body representing accountants and finance professionals, identifies the roots in excessive short-termism and sees a lack of accountability within financial institutions. In more detail, the association sees a failure:

> to appreciate the influence of cultural and motivational factors such as rigidity of thinking, lack of desire to change. An attitude of 'it is not my problem', inappropriate vision/drivers and, perhaps most importantly, human greed, lack of training to enable management to understand underlying business models, leading to poor managerial supervision, lack of rigorous challenge by non-executive directors possibly caused by poor understanding of the complexities of the business and bad habits and complacency after a prolonged bull market.[5]

When reading news about the collapsed investment banks and other financial institutions, their cultures are described with the words: "swashbuckling", "combustible", "detached", "a climate of opulent pay", "lax oversight", and "blind faith".[6] These attributes recall the Enron and WorldCom scandals of the early 2000s which, in the former case, installed complicated off-book partnerships and special-purpose entities in order to hide the real financial conditions and, in the latter case, institutionalized a process named "closing the gap" which was about systematically

---

[3]The definition of organizational culture is a combination from the definitions of O'Reilly and Chatman (1996) and Schein (1990). The combination of these two definitions will be discussed in more detail in Sect. 2.2.1.

[4]Material weaknesses will be discussed in more detail in Sect. 2.1.3.

[5]*BusinessDay*, October 12, 2008: Climbing out of the credit crunch.

[6]*BusinessWeek*, October 7, 2008: Reining in Wall Street's Rainmakers: How excessively risk-taking corporate cultures and unbalanced reward practices have contributed to the current financial crisis.

altering the numbers to meet analysts' forecasts.[7] What all these examples demonstrate is the cause-and-effect between culture and control. For example, an attitude of "it is not my problem" is a cultural aspect that is likely to enhance the omission of necessary data entries, which are part of control. "Poor managerial supervision" can lead to control deficiencies simply because people will not give adequate attention and effort when executing controls. Although the influence of culture on control seems to be omnipresent in an organization, it is difficult to capture culture systematically because it often relies on interpretation. *Consequently, one challenge of this study is to capture the influence of organizational culture on internal control effectiveness.*

Companies that have major control failures often replace their senior-level people. Then, the new senior-level people have the task of changing the culture and assuring effective controls. An example is the Swiss bank UBS, which experienced huge financial losses as a result of its investments in the US subprime market. The new Chairman, Peter Kurer, explained the reasons for the losses as a problem of a culture "without brakes" based on a strong, growth strategy. Traders, being keen on achieving performance goals, invested in positions without analyzing the whole complexity behind them. Simons (2000, p. 5) points out: "Managers can fool themselves into thinking that because the business is profitable, controls must be adequate". A "full-speed" culture "without brakes" leads to inadequate emphasis on proper risk and control management and put its long-term financial performance at risk.[8] Another example of an organization whose controls failed and is now attempting to change the culture is Siemens. Europe's most renowned engineering group experienced one of the largest bribery scandals in business history. Despite their established code of conduct and clear rejection of bribery as business practice, several hundred senior-level people from the company engaged in bribery, mostly between 1998 and 2006.[9] Even though they had all formally signed the business code of conduct, bribes were informally accepted and sanctions were not carried out. Peter Löscher, the new CEO, officially explained the failures as an issue of culture and leadership responsibility, and he now is attempting to change Siemens' culture by holding people accountable through sanctions and rewards.[10] What these examples indicate is that not only does culture influence control, but control also influences culture. New senior-level people attempt to change the culture by applying typical control mechanisms such as declaring tighter policies and reemphasizing that accountability will be enforced. *Hence, another challenge of this study is to capture how control mechanisms influence organizational culture.*

In sum, these practical issues indicate that there is a two-way relationship between control and culture, and understanding how the two influence each other is of high practical importance. Both internal control and organizational culture are

[7]For more details on Enron and WorldCom see Brickey (2006), Curall and Epstein (2003), Rockness and Rockness (2005), Sims and Brinkmann (2003), Stewart (2006).

[8]For more details see UBS (2008): Shareholder Report on UBS's Write-Downs.

[9]*Economist*, March 6, 2008: Stopping the rot.

[10]*Financial Times*, January 20, 2008: Scandal puts Siemens to the test.

not only relevant to failures, but are also of daily importance anywhere people work in an organization.[11]

1.1.2 *Stage of Research*

Research in management accounting and control gives surprisingly incomplete answers to questions on the relationship between control and culture. While the impact of culture on control has been addressed in research, how control affects culture has not been comprehensively addressed. As the more detailed literature review will follow in Chap. 3, in this section the stage of research and the main issues from the literature are briefly summarized.

Research in *internal control* can be divided into a focused, more traditional accounting-oriented view and a comprehensive business view of internal control.[12] While traditional accounting controls are widely studied primarily in auditing research,[13] the comprehensive view of internal control, which includes controls in operations and compliance, is promoted by practical-oriented internal control frameworks, but finds less attention in research. Kinney (2000b, p. 83) clarifies that despite its relevance for the public at large, the comprehensive view of internal control is relatively unexplored by researchers. A reason why management accounting and control researchers have not afforded much attention to the comprehensive view of internal control might be the similarly appearing definitions of internal control and management control. These similarly appearing definitions blur the fact that the two concepts have a different purpose in supporting the achievement of organizational objectives.[14] While management control is primarily concerned with controlling people in order to achieve the organizational objectives, the focus of internal control is to provide information quality and safeguard assets in order to provide integrity for any other control system in the organization (including management control systems).[15] Hence, although addressing partially similar phenomena,[16] the purpose of internal control differs clearly from management control.

[11]The subject of this study is of interest for anybody associated with any type of organization – whether the organization is for profit or not for profit, whether it is a start-up or established, local or international, or whether it is family owned, private, public, or governmental.

[12]An alternative classification offers Maijoor (2000) who divides research on internal control into an economics, an organization theory and an external auditing perspective. Maijoor's economics perspective contains agency-theory and analyzes top-level control problems such as reward systems, bonus plans, and monitoring mechanisms that are investigated with regard to effects of uncertainty and costs of monitoring. While his second and third categories reflect the comprehensive and focused view taken in this study, the economics category is excluded here because these aspects are related to the broader organizational governance and not specifically to internal control.

[13]For example, Ashton (1974), Bower and Schlosser (1965), Mock and Turner (1981).

[14]See the definitions of internal control and management control in Sect. 2.1.2.

[15]See Sect. 2.1.2.

[16]For example, "management override" is similarly discussed in internal control and management control research (see also Merchant and Van der Stede (2007, p. 82) and Sect. 2.1.4).

While field-study research in management control is common,[17] focusing *on internal control* in an in-depth field visit study, such as this study here, is a relatively new approach in the accounting and control area.

In contrast to the comprehensive view of internal control, *organizational culture* is a topic that has a long research tradition. Culture has been studied from various perspectives such as anthropology,[18] sociology,[19] and psychology.[20] As will be discussed in more detail in Sect. 2.2, researchers have explained organizational culture through factors such as values, group norms, climate, embedded skills, habits, symbols, and rites,[21] and have investigated its relation to various topics such as socialization, change, functioning, and competitive advantage, to name just a few.[22] Having a plethora of research on organizational culture, little consensus has been reached on a general theory of organizational culture as well as whether culture can be measured.[23] While some researchers see measuring as problematic,[24] others interpret culture as measurable based on a set of variables.[25]

In the accounting and control area the *link between internal control and organizational culture* has been considered in practical-oriented internal control frameworks, but barely in research. Therefore, the focus of the literature review has been broadened to the general field of management accounting and control research. In this stream of research, culture has been introduced and explored in various ways. As will be discussed in more detail in Chap. 3, from the literature review in the management accounting and control area, five broad issues have been identified that this study attempts to address:

- Typically, culture is studied as a contextual factor that influences specific accounting and control practices. In other words, culture is seen as an independent variable that influences accounting and control outcomes.[26] Other disciplines, however, demonstrate that culture can be influenced and changed over time.[27] *Therefore, how can culture be captured as a construct that is being influenced by control?*
- In management control frameworks[28], culture is often interpreted as being part of specific types of controls, standing next to other more technical "behavioral"

[17]See Ahrens and Chapman (2004), Mikes (2008), Simons (2005).

[18]See Kroeber and Kluckhohn (1952).

[19]See Lincoln and Kalleberg (1990).

[20]See Hofstede (1983), O'Reilly et al. (1991), Schein (2004).

[21]For an overview of definitions of organizational culture see Sect. 2.2.1.

[22]For example, Chatman (1991), Barney (1986), Hampdon-Turner (1990), Schein (1985), Wilkins and Ouchi (1983).

[23]Denison and Mishra (1995, p. 207).

[24]For example, Alvesson (2002), Siehl and Martin (1990).

[25]For example, Alexander (1978), O'Reilly et al. (1991), Sørensen (2002).

[26]See Bhimani (1999), Birnberg and Snodgrass (1988), Dent (1991), Efferin and Hopper (2007), Hopwood (1983).

[27]See O'Reilly and Chatman (1996), Schein (2004), Wiener (1988).

[28]These frameworks will be discussed in Sect. 3.3.

types of controls (e.g., cultural controls stand next to action controls and result controls).[29] Other disciplines teach that culture is a pervasive concept that is established and expressed through all types of aspects in a setting.[30] *Thus, how can culture be captured as a transcendental concept in the context of control?*

- Culture is often discussed through the degree of formality and seems to be captured through the so-called "social controls."[31] These social controls are possible because culture exists, but culture is similarly reflected in formal controls. Although the degree of formality is important in the context of culture, it is probably not of primary interest. *Therefore, what other concepts exist in order to capture culture?*
- While there is an understanding for both control and culture, there is a lack of understanding on the processes between culture and control behavior.[32] Drawing and explaining these processes in between provides a better understanding of how culture can optimally be influenced. *How can cultural processes and its impact on behavior be theoretically explained?*
- Research in management control has spent much attention on distinguishing different types of control and relating them to specific organizational settings.[33] A more recent tendency in research has recognized that the interrelation between controls and their simultaneous use are important.[34] *How can organizational culture contribute to explaining the interrelations of different types of controls?*

These five issues from the literature represent open questions to be addressed in this study. The current issues in practice and the stage of research demonstrate the need for studying internal control and organizational culture and provide the foundation for this study's objective, which is defined in the next section.

1.2 Research Objective

This study aims to link internal control with organizational culture in order to build a theory to explain the causal interrelations between control and culture. More specifically, this study attempts to answer the following overall research question:

> *How do management principles and practices affect organizational culture in a way so that organizational culture positively impacts internal control effectiveness?*

---

[29]For example, Merchant and Van der Stede (2007), Simons (1995).

[30]See Alvesson (2002), Schein (1990).

[31]See Collier (2005), Nixon and Burns (2005).

[32]See Bititici et al. (2006).

[33]See Eisenhardt (1985), Govindarajan and Fisher (1990), Ouchi (1979), Rockness and Shields (1984).

[34]See Bititici et al. (2006), Efferin and Hopper (2007), Simons (2005).

In order to address the issues identified in the literature, the purpose of this study is to develop an alternative terminology to common control frameworks from research.[35] An alternative terminology means to develop a framework for control and culture that sees culture as mediator[36] which is influenced by specific control influences and, in turn, influences specific control outcomes. Thus, the viewpoint differs from common research in the accounting and control field[37] by viewing organizational culture as a construct that can be influenced.[38]

The purpose of this study is to contribute to both research and practice. For research, the study attempts to potentially contribute "for making significant advances in the conceptual development of a managerially relevant phenomenon".[39] As was summarized in the last section, the study addresses a research gap for three reasons: (1) internal control itself, (2) the relation between internal control and organizational culture, and (3) the influence of control on culture in general are all relatively unexplored topics in management accounting and control research. As the issues identified are of practical relevance, the study attempts to contribute by advancing research in all of these three related areas.[40]

For practice, the study attempts to provide a deeper knowledge of the relationship between internal control and organizational culture. As the practical issues demonstrated, the subject of this study has high importance for any business. Knowing more about how culture can be influenced in order to achieve effective controls, potentially supports the protection of future failures. The research can contribute to board, managers and employees, internal and external auditors, and other parties by providing explanations in how culture can be captured and addressed in the context of internal control.[41]

Unlike research on the determinants of internal control deficiencies,[42] the aim of this study is not to provide quantitative results on the relationship between internal control and organizational culture – nor is the purpose to compare company cultures such as it is done in other action research.[43] In alignment with Wilkins and Ouchi (1983), who question the importance of an organization-wide culture, the study attempts to develop a general framework that is applicable to any organizational setting (e.g., team, department, and organization) and can be specified and transferred to specific research questions. Thus, the study focuses on the relationship between internal control and organizational culture in a normative way.

---

[35]See Chap. 3.

[36]For a discussion on the role of mediation in accounting research see Gerdin and Greve (2004).

[37]While considering internal control-related areas such as organizational governance, risk management, operations management, and internal and external auditing, the study's primary focus and emphasis is the management accounting and control area.

[38]Typically, in accounting and control research culture is seen as an independent variable.

[39]Bruns and Kaplan (1987), quoted after Mikes (2005b, p. 7).

[40]The academic contribution of this study will be discussed in more detail in Sect. 9.2.

[41]The practice-oriented contribution of this study will be discussed in more detail in Sect. 9.2.

[42]For example, Ashbaugh-Skaife et al. (2007) and Doyle et al. (2007).

[43]For example, Ahrens and Chapman (2004), Dent (1991), Mikes (2005b).

1.3 Research Design

As the literature review confirmed, the relation between internal control and organizational culture is still relatively unexplored to date. To achieve the overall research objective, the study takes an exploratory and theory-building research design. Such an approach needs to be distinguished from common theory testing design approaches. As illustrated in Fig. 1.1, while a theory-building design generally starts with observations and builds a theory from those observations, a theory-testing approach starts with a theory, then tests that theory based on observations. Starting with observations and employing inductive reasoning with the intent to make sense of observations, a theory-building design moves from the particular to the general and intends to make sense of observations.[44]

In order to develop ideas, definitions, and propositions, which are useful in developing theoretical patterns, this study builds on two pillars:

1. The first pillar consists of an exploratory field study based on semi-structured interviews with 31 senior-level people from 21 companies in order to gather an empirical grounding on internal control and organizational culture.[45]
2. The second pillar consists of insights from knowledge outside the accounting and control area such as sociology and social psychology in order to analyze the role of organizational culture for internal control.[46]

These two pillars will be presented in Parts II and III of the study, and finally are included in the synthesis in Part IV. Combining the findings from the field with existing theory from other disciplines in order to build new insights for a specific topic, is a common research method in the accounting and control field. A renowned representative of such an approach is Simons, who builds on both multiple

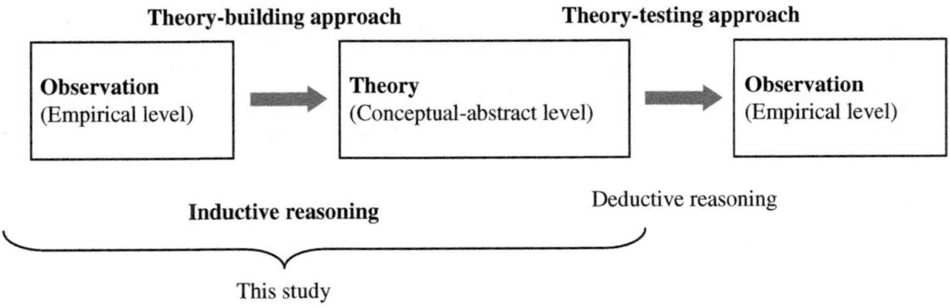

Fig. 1.1 Theory-building versus theory-testing.
Source: Adapted from DeVaus (2001, p. 6)

[44]Kerlinger (1986, p. 9), also quoted in Gray (2004, p. 5).

[45]See Chap. 4.

[46]See Chaps. 5–7.

interactions within the field and existing theories from other disciplines in order to develop new theoretical patterns.[47]

This study is based on the typical steps in qualitative research such as those presented in Fig. 1.2. As a first step, the research project started based on a broad research question.[48] In the second step, senior-level people from large companies (listed in the US) were selected as a source of data.[49] In the third and fourth steps, preliminary data from semi-structured interviews was gathered and interpreted. The interpretation of these preliminary materials further defined the research question, which led to an iterative process between further specifying the research focus, data gathering, and conceptual and theoretical work. This approach makes sense from the observed patterns by combining the field material with adapting theories from other fields to internal control.[50] As a result, a theoretical framework makes sense from the field observations.

Epistemology represents the researcher's philosophical background, which determines what type of knowledge is legitimate and adequate. Epistemology is important because it determines the researcher's attitude toward what type of knowledge is adequate. For example, objectivist epistemology separates reality from consciousness, arguing that there is one objective truth, and research is about discovering this objective reality.[51] With regard to culture, an objectivist epistemology would imply

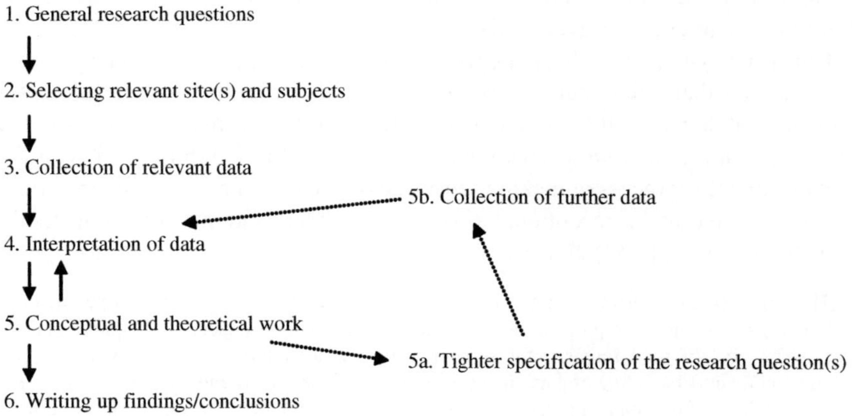

Fig. 1.2 Steps in qualitative research.
Source: Bryman and Bell (2003, p. 283)

[47]See Simons (1995, 2005).

[48]A first attempt in the field was to identify practical issues in internal control ("Where are current issues in internal control from a professional perspective?"). See also the overview of interview questions in Appendix D.

[49]Saunders et al. (2000, p. 150). Taking a theory-building and exploratory design approach implies the use of qualitative research methods. By searching the literature and talking with experts, this study applied two major methods in exploratory research.

[50]Bryman and Bell (2003, p. 283), Gray (2004, p. 8).

[51]Gray (2004, pp. 16-17).

that researchers perceive the same cultural and organizational setting in similar ways because only one objective truth exits. In contrast, the standpoint of a constructivist epistemology is that researchers can perceive the same cultural situation differently.[52] Gray (2004, p. 17) describes the constructivist stance as follows: "Meaning is *constructed* not discovered, so subjects construct their own meaning in different ways, even in relation to the same phenomenon". The constructivist epistemology takes the stand that there is not one exact world that everyone understands in the same way. Instead, there are an infinite number of realities based on the experiences and backgrounds of the observers.[53] For example, whether a certain organizational setting is seen as trivial or non-trivial relies on the particular observer and his or her attitude toward the subject.[54] This study is based on a constructivist view because the researcher beliefs that the interaction with the field as well as the selections to be made in a research study rely significantly on the researcher's background and interests, and will influence the research outcome. This stance taken, however, does not follow the *radical* constructivism, which would imply that there is no objective truth at all. Instead, the researcher believes that some general cause-and-effect relationships seem not only be convergent between different observers, but might reflect some common truth. This truth, however, is, to some extent, biased by the observers. Consequently, in alignment with field research in the accounting and control area this study underlies the constructivist (but not radical constructivist) epistemology.[55]

Constructivist epistemology supports the theoretical approach of interpretivism, which argues that individuals or groups (or any other cognitive system) do not act upon the influence of their immediate reality but on the image they reproduce, based on their interpretation and knowledge of that reality.[56] Johnson (1987, p. 206) explains that this process of making sense can be seen as a process of interpreting in the light of a particular reception: "to know is to understand in a certain manner".[57] And Bailey (2007, p. 53) clarifies:

> Thus, the researcher using an interpretive paradigm asks what kinds of things people do, how they do them, what purposes activities serve, and what they mean to the participants. ... The goal of field research for scholars who use an interpretive paradigm involve empathetic understanding of participants' day-to-day experiences and an increased awareness of the multiple meaning given to the routine and problematic events by those in the setting.

---

[52]Baecker (2006, p. 137), Quattrone (2000, p. 137).

[53]Rusch (1987, p. 218).

[54]Von Foerster (1994, p. 252).

[55]The constructivist epistemology is widely accepted in accounting and control research (for example, Ahrens and Chapman 2006; Efferin and Hopper 2007; Hopwood 1983; Quattrone 2000).

[56]Schwandt (1994, p. 125) even argues that constructivism and interpretism appear to be similar. Regarding interpreting the reality, Mitnick (1994, p. 114) says that in order to create order out of confusion, people select and order abstractions of phenomena that are said to grant understanding.

[57]Johnson (1987, p. 206).

As Brunnson and Sahlin-Andersson (2000, p. 721) note, it is important to consider what researchers construct as a certain type of reality, can differ from interpretations of professionals.[58] Therefore, to ensure that this research is close enough to practice and addresses professionals' issues,[59] research design and method were chosen in a way to ensure that adequate practical input could be given.

Building theory is a challenging procedure because it is based on an iterative process of repeatedly evaluating the match between data and presentation.[60] Alternative results based on the same phenomena could have been found by another researcher with another background.[61] Also, other people participating in the field study might have brought different results. Although the results of this study might apply to any type of organization, the primary reference and source of empirical evidence comes from companies in the US and Switzerland, most of which operate internationally.[62] The text therefore primarily addresses medium and large, international operating organizations, and does not give specific consideration to small companies (except where they are mentioned in specific contexts). Because the field research is limited to in-depth interviews with 31 professionals from 21 companies, the results cannot be used to make universal generalizations. Nevertheless, the study combines empirical evidence from various functions and industries with existing theories, and as a result provides strong indications that the ideas and concepts presented provide both academic and practical relevance. This study here is an in-depth qualitative approach to support further quantitative approaches that can test ideas, concepts, and relationships developed in this study. In this sense, for the purpose of this research issue and stage of research, the chosen research design was found to be adequate for this study.

1.4 Organization of Study

Based on the research design, the further study is divided into four parts (see Fig. 1.3).

Part I addresses the *groundwork* of the study. The *basics* of each internal control and organizational culture are described. Moreover, the bridge is built between control and culture by a *literature review* from the accounting and control perspective. Derived from the literature, this part concludes with a set of theses that build the starting point for the own contribution in the further course of study.

Part II presents the *field study*. The observations from the field summarize 25 principles and practices that senior-level people perceive as drivers for internal

---

[58]Brunnson and Sahlin-Andersson (2000, p. 721).

[59]Osterloh and Frost emphasize that professionals should be involved in the theory-building process to say whether the theory addresses what is important in their work or not (Osterloh and Frost 2007, p. 17).

[60]Mikes (2005b, pp. 6-7).

[61]See Bryman and Bell (2003), Lincoln and Guba (1985).

[62]For more details about the field study setup see Sect. 4.2.

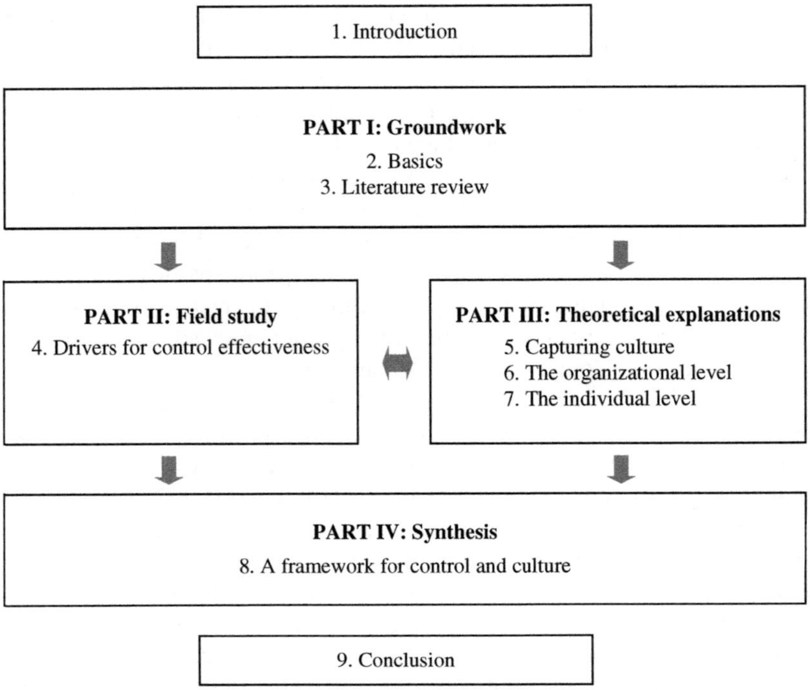

Fig. 1.3 Organization of study

control effectiveness. Representing empirical data from multiple renowned organizations, the results provide not only an empirically grounded input for the further theory-building process, but also a practice-oriented tool.

Part III provides *theoretical explanations* for how control can influence culture and vice versa. A brief setup discusses whether *culture* should be *captured* as a variable or as a root metaphor. The further analysis on the *organizational level* applies the theory of social systems to organizational culture, while the analysis on the *individual level* applies the value theories in order to derive implications for the further course of study.

Part IV terminates the study in the *synthesis* of field work and theories. A *framework for control and culture* is presented, which explains under what conditions organizational culture positively impacts internal control effectiveness, and how drivers for control effectiveness can be mixed to achieve these cultural conditions. By seeing culture as being impacted by control practices, the framework clearly distinguishes itself from common control frameworks in the accounting and control area.

The study concludes with a discussion of the key results, contribution, and generalization. It also proposes future research opportunities and terminates with final remarks.

Part I
Groundwork

Chapter 2
Basics

2.1 Internal Control

2.1.1 Definition

This chapter introduces both internal control and organizational culture in order to provide a basic understanding for the two topics. Before addressing organizational culture in the second part of this chapter, the focus is set on internal control. A wide range of control concepts exist in the management accounting and control literature: strategic control, management control, internal control, and control systems, to name just a few of the major themes. The variety of concepts, their different purposes in closely related areas, and particularly the different interpretations from the various authors, generate many overlaps between concepts.[1] As a result, differences in terminologies often cause miscommunication and misguided expectations among the parties involved.[2] To understand the reason for the variety of definitions of internal control itself, the term will be embedded in its historical evolution and divided into a focused and a comprehensive view of internal control. In addition, internal control will be discussed and integrated with strategic control, management control and control systems in order to provide a holistic understanding of the fundamental role of internal control for any business. Spending adequate time for defining internal control provides the basis for investigating the role of organizational culture for internal control throughout this study.

---

[1]Merchant and Otley (2007) provide an overview of different control areas in their review of the literature on control and accountability.

[2]Additional misunderstandings on the term control are more linguistic in nature. For example, while in the English language the term 'control' covers proactive (e.g., directive, preventive controls) and reactive controls (e.g., detective and corrective controls), in the German language the term 'Kontrolle' is usually understood only as reactive control (Ruud and Jenal, 2005, p. 456).

J. Pfister, *Managing Organizational Culture for Effective Internal Control*, Contributions to Management Science,
DOI: 10.1007/978-3-7908-2340-0_2, © Springer Physica-Verlag Berlin Heidelberg 2009

2.1.1.1 Brief Historical Sketch

During the last 15-20 years, a shift in focus from the accounting and finance orientation of internal control to a much broader governance and business perspective has taken place.[3] The term internal control developed in the accounting and auditing discipline, and was traditionally interpreted as "accounting controls", limited to the system that auditors test as part of their assurance on the reliability of financial reporting.[4] Therefore, internal control was often discussed in the context of the external auditor's work. While the detection of fraud as an audit objective has a long history, internal control (as a subject) was not recognized until the twentieth century.[5] According to Brown (1962, p. 696), the difference between no recognition and slight recognition of internal control was found in a 1905 publication entitled *Auditing* by Lawrence Dicksee, an English audit specialist. In his study, originally published in 1892, Dicksee does not mention the term internal control itself, but addresses internal control by explaining that the object and scope of an audit has three parts to it: "the detection of fraud, technical errors, and errors in principle".[6] From approximately 1905 to 2004, Heier et al. (2005, p. 41) show that the debate and definitions, interpretations and applications of internal control have emerged as a reactive evolution. Often these changes of definitions, interpretations and applications happened as "a reaction to a major change in the economic situation of a country as a whole or to the actions of individual firms within the economy".[7]

Most recent and prominent examples of such events and their reaction are a series of company failures in the early 2000s associated with the scandals at Enron and WorldCom.[8] As a major legislative reaction, the US Congress introduced the Sarbanes-Oxley Act of 2002 (SOX), which brought about a series of new requirements for domestic and foreign companies that are listed on US stock exchanges.[9]

---

[3]Maijoor (2000, p. 105). See also Power (1997).

[4]For example, the Securities Act of 1933 addressed internal control and the audit process in the following words: "In determining the scope of the audit necessary, appropriate consideration shall be given to the adequacy of the system of internal check and internal control" (Early Regulation SX Rule 2-02 (b) of the 1933 Act, quoted after Ferald Fernald (1943, p. 228). A later and broader approach by the American Institute of Accountants (AIA) defined that "Internal control comprises the plan of organization and all of the co-ordinate methods and measures adopted within a business to safeguard its assets, check the accuracy and reliability of its accounting data, promote operational efficiency, and encourage adherence to prescribed managerial policies" (AIA 1948, quoted after Heier et al. 2005, p. 48).

[5]Brown (1962, p. 696).

[6]Dicksee (1892, p. 6), quoted in Heier et al. (2005, p. 42).

[7]Heier, Dugan, and Sayer discuss internal control in the context of auditing and its impact on audit engagements.

[8]For example, Brickey (2006), Rockness and Rockness (2005), Stewart (2006).

[9]At that time, in the US regulation addressing internal control was limited in scope as the Foreign Corrupt Practices Act of 1977 (FCPA) represented the only regulatory requirement for internal control reporting. The purpose of SOX was to restore public confidence in the capital markets by enhancing the reliability of financial reporting and the effectiveness of corporate governance by addressing management's responsibility for financial reporting as well as the scope and nature of the audit (Ge and McVay 2005, p. 139).

With regard to internal control, a major and cost-intensive provision from SOX is Section 404, which obliges management to assess and report on the effectiveness of internal control over financial reporting.[10] SOX is just one example of a reaction to significant events. Heier, Dugan, and Sayer explain that the stock market crash of 1929, the economic boom after World War II, the revelation of bribery of several 100 US companies (including well-respected firms such as Exxon) in the aftermath of the Watergate affair in the 1970s, and corporate failures at the beginning of the 1980s, are earlier examples of events that had an impact on internal control regulation and interpretation. These events led either to more regulation and mandatory disclosure of internal control aspects and/or to a broadening of the interpretation of internal control in public policy documents.[11] From these historical developments, a more focused view and a more comprehensive view on internal control can be distinguished.[12] The focused view sets internal control equal to the "checks and balances" in accounting systems, while more recent approaches place more emphasis on a more holistic approach to internal control, emphasizing operational effectiveness and efficiency and compliance with laws, regulation, and internal policies. Internal control is then an integrated part of organizational governance. The focused and comprehensive view of internal control will be discussed subsequently.

2.1.1.2 Focused View of Internal Control

A focused and traditional view of internal control (also referred to as accounting controls[13]) is offered by Simons (1995, p. 84) as the "detailed, procedural checks and balances". They are designed to safeguard (tangible and intangible) assets from

---

[10]Coates (2007, p. 96) and Mintz (2005, p. 595). In Europe, the extraterritorial influence of SOX was discussed and debated critically. In the European Union the Eight Directive addresses internal control and risk management as well. As most European countries take a more principles-based approach, the European approach is less detailed. In Switzerland, as a non-EU member, a new regulation requires the auditor to prove the existence of the internal control system.

[11]An early example of such a discussion on the broadness of internal control can be given with the question whether administrative controls should be part of the audit or not. The American Institute of Certified Public Accountant (AICPA 1958, pp. 66-67) states that "[administrative controls] ordinarily relate only indirectly to the financial records and thus would not require evaluation". However, in the event these controls have "an important bearing on the reliability of financial records", then the auditor should consider including these controls in the assessment. Thus the discussions in the 1950s are still accounting oriented but already were concerned about the broadness of internal control. As will be discussed in this section, the debate about a broadening of the interpretation of internal control will be continued later in the twenty-first century.

[12]A similar distinction is taken by Jenal (2006, p. 3) who divides definitions on internal control into a focused view (focusing only on financial reporting) and a comprehensive view (focusing on operations, financial reporting and compliance).

[13]Throughout this study the terms internal control, internal controls, and controls are treated as synonyms.

misappropriation and ensure that accounting records and information systems are reliable.[14] According to Simons, these checks and balances concern three categories:

- *Structural safeguards* include an active audit committee of the board, an independent internal audit function, segregation of duties, defined levels of authorization, and restricted access to valuable assets.
- *Staff safeguards* include adequate expertise and training for all accounting, control, and internal audit staff, sufficient resources, and rotation of key jobs.
- *System safeguards* include complete and accurate record keeping, adequate documentation and audit trail, relevant and timely management reporting, and restricted access to information systems and databases.[15]

Standing for the detailed procedures and safeguards for information handling, transaction processing, and record keeping, internal control is critical in ensuring that accounting records and information systems are reliable. Internal control relies on "staff groups", which design and execute controls, and on internal and external auditors who assess periodically whether controls are reliable.[16] Although the focused view of internal control emphasizes the technical aspects such as databases, record keeping, and segregation of duties, it is clear that these aspects of information handling rely significantly on the effort of staff.[17] That is why organizational culture is important for internal control. Culture influences the common behaviors in an organization and the efforts of each individual.[18] However, this view of internal control is focused because it limits the responsibility for internal control to the finance and auditing area and places little emphasis on the fact that internal control is a part of operations and compliance as well and is of concern to all people within an organization.

2.1.1.3 Comprehensive View of Internal Control

Business and accounting scandals in the 1980s challenged the adequacy of financial reporting systems.[19] To investigate the causes of fraudulent financial reporting and make recommendations to reduce its likelihood, in 1985 the US established the National Commission on Fraudulent Financial Reporting, known as the Treadway Commission.[20] The Commission's recommendations led to a task force, which was

---

[14]See Kinney (2000a).

[15]Simons (1995, pp. 84-85).

[16]Simons (1995, pp. 85-86).

[17]See Kinney (2000a), Pfaff and Ruud (2007), Pfaff et al. (2007), and Simons (1995).

[18]See O'Reilly and Chatman (1996).

[19]Ge and McVay (2005, p. 139). In the late 1980s the collapse of Bank of Credit and Commerce International (BCCI) caused a financial panic spanning four continents and involved the Bank of England (see Mintz 2005).

[20]The Treadway Commission addressed internal control aspects such as the control environment, code of conduct, audit committees, and internal audit. It also called for additional internal control standards and guidance, and suggested that all listed companies should be required to include a report on internal control in their annual reports (COSO 1992, p. 96).

built under the auspices of the Committee of Sponsoring Organization of the Treadway Commission (COSO). This commission created the 1992 COSO-control framework for the purpose of providing broadly accepted criteria for establishing, monitoring, evaluating and reporting on internal control.[21] COSO (1992, p. 3) takes a comprehensive approach and defines internal control as:

> a *process*, effected by an entity's board of directors, management and other personnel, designed to provide *reasonable assurance* regarding the achievement of objectives in the following categories:

- *Effectiveness* and *efficiency* of operations.
- *Reliability* of financial reporting.
- *Compliance* with applicable laws and regulations.[22]

Kinney (2000b, p. 84) remarks that the COSO definition is widely accepted in practice, as can be seen through the application of similar conceptual definitions by other relevant groups around the world.[23] For instance, the definition from the Canadian Guidance on Control Board (CoCo)[24] explains internal control as "all the resources, processes, culture, structure, and tasks that, taken together, support people in achieving those objectives". Approaching the subject more broadly, the CoCo definition explicitly mentions internal elements such as "internal reporting", "information within the organization", and "internal policies" as part of internal control. The Institute of Chartered Accountants in England and Wales (ICAEW)[25] emphasizes the importance of responding to risk and, relevant to the focus of this study, states that internal control has to do with "behaviors". The European Federation of Accountants (FEE) sets internal control in relation to governance and describes internal control as going "beyond procedures" and includes "elements such as corporate culture, systems, structure, policies and tasks".[26] Despite minor differences in accentuation, all these definitions support the COSO definition.

---

[21]COSO (1992, p. 97). The COSO framework is summarized in Sect. 3.2.2.

[22]Emphasis added.

[23]Pfaff and Ruud (2007, p. 19). A reason for this broad acceptance might be that there is generally more awareness for the fact that internal control is more than finance and accounting, but is pervasive throughout all areas of the organization. The COSO definition has a broad foundation in the US as the Treadway Commission was established as a collaborating sponsorship among the relevant institutions in accounting, control and auditing, including the American Institute of Certified Public Accountants (AICPA), American Accounting Association (AAA), Financial Executives International (FEI), The Institute of Internal Auditors (IIA) and the Institute of Management Accountants (IMA).

[24]The Guidance on Control Board is associated with the Canadian Institute of Chartered Accountants (CICA) and issues the CoCo control framework (see CoCo 1995b and Sect. 3.2.3).

[25]The internal control definition of the ICAEW is from the Turnbull report, which is part of the Combined Code – A mandatory guideline for listed companies in the UK (see ICAEW 1999 and Sect. 3.2.4).

[26]See FEE (2005). A more specialized group such as the Information Systems Audit and Control Association, which provides the IT-governance-framework called COBIT (Control Objectives for Information and Related Technology), offers a more technical interpretation and distinguishes between preventive, detective and corrective control (see ISACA 2007). The Basle Committee on Banking Supervision describes control as something that is "continually" going on at all levels in a bank and also highlights the importance of an "appropriate culture". BCBS is responsible for the international banking regulation and is associated with the Bank of International Settlements (BIS) and Basel II (see BCBS 1998).

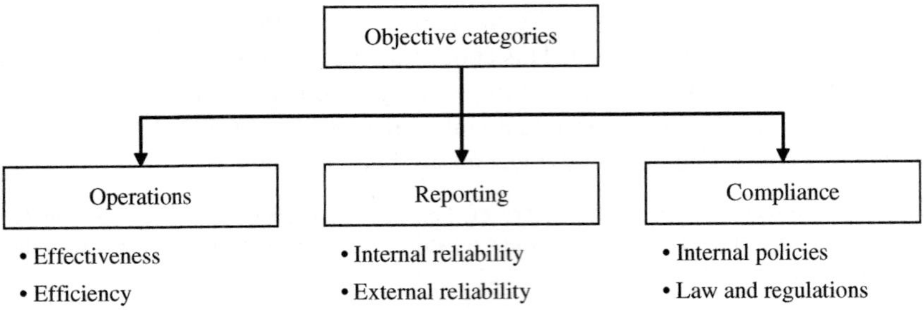

Fig. 2.1 Objective categories

This study applies the comprehensive view of internal control. The broad view includes the focused view. *Internal control* safeguards assets and provides reasonable assurance for information quality so that the organization can achieve its objectives regarding effectiveness and efficiency of operations, reliability of internal and external reporting, and compliance with laws, regulations, and internal policies. Internal control is effected by board, management, and other personnel, "by what they do and what they say".[27] Figure 2.1[28] illustrates the three objective categories operations, reporting and compliance of the comprehensive view of internal control.

2.1.1.4 Specifying the Comprehensive View

This comprehensive view of internal control is seen as an integrated concept within organizational governance. The OECD (2004, p. 11) defines organizational (corporate) governance[29] as:

> a set of relationships between a company's management, its board, its shareholders and other stakeholders. Corporate governance also provides the structure through which the objectives of the company are set, and *the means of attaining those objectives and monitoring performance are determined*. Good corporate governance should provide proper incentives for the board and management to pursue objectives that are in the interests of the company and its shareholders and should facilitate effective monitoring.[30]

As the definition from the OECD illustrates, compared to internal control, governance puts a stronger emphasis on the discrepancies between the interests of

[27]COSO (1992, p. 14).

[28]The figure is based on the COSO categories, complemented with CoCo's "internal reporting" and "internal policies".

[29]The OECD uses the term *corporate* governance (instead organizational governance). Organizational governance is broader than corporate governance as it can include any type of organization and not only corporations.

[30]Emphasis added.

organizational in- and outsiders.[31] The primary interest is on whether board and top management work in alignment with the interests of shareholders and other stakeholders. The OECD definition contains the words: "means of attaining those objectives", which is in alignment with the definition of internal control.[32] Therefore, one interface between governance and control is the objective setting process. While organizational governance "provides the structure through which the objectives of the company are set",[33] internal control represents the means to achieve the organization's objectives.

Pfaff and Ruud (2007, p. 21) clarify that internal control consists of a series of actions that are integrated with business activities and conducted throughout the organizational units and functions. As illustrated in Fig. 2.2, Porter (1985, p. 46) divides business activities into primary activities that generate value, such as inbound logistics, operations, and sales, and secondary activities, such as human resource management, infrastructure and procurement, which support the primary activities.[34] Operations, reporting, and compliance aspects are integrated within all

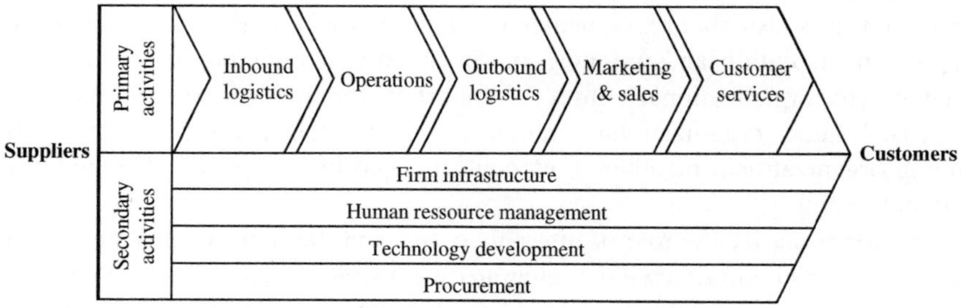

Fig. 2.2 The value chain of a manufacturing company.
Source: Adapted from Porter (1985, p. 46)

[31]Organizational governance roots in the separation of ownership from control. According to Berle and Means (1932, p. 6), this separation leads to a condition in which the interests of owner and managers "may, and often do, diverge, and where many of the checks which formerly [in the single entrepreneurship] operated to limit the use of power disappear". In general, the literature analyzes this separation with the agency-theory. The owner (principal) delegates 'control' to management (agent). This relationship between principal and agent is characterized through asymmetric information. Management, as organizational insider, has a better understanding and in-depth knowledge than the owners as organizational outsiders (Ruud 2003, p. 82).

[32]Because governance explicitly includes external parties such as shareholders and stakeholders but also mentions all means of attaining the organizational objectives (which represents internal control), the argumentation here is that governance is broader defined than internal control. Effective internal control can be understood as contributing to effective organizational governance.

[33]OECD (2004, p. 11).

[34]While the illustrated structure of the value chain of a manufacturing company represents only one possible example, each individual company has its own definition of the value chain. Internal control is pervasive throughout any organization's primary and secondary activities and is inherently affected by the way management runs the business (Pfaff and Ruud, 2007, p. 21; Ruud, 2003, p. 78).

these primary and secondary activities. Thus, according to the comprehensive view, internal control is not just part of finance and accounting, but of any other activity such as marketing and sales, logistics and technology development. The comprehensive view supports that internal control is not an exclusive function of board, executives, senior finance managers or internal and external auditors, but of all people in the organization.[35] Depending on the hierarchical level of the person and the size of the organization, the responsibility for internal control varies from function to function.[36] COSO (1992, p. 89) writes:

> [...] virtually all employees play some role in effecting control. They may produce information used in the internal control system – for example, inventory records, work-in-process data, sales or expenses reports – or take other actions needed to effect control. These actions may include performing reconciliations, following up on exception reports, performing physical inspections or investigating reasons for cost variances or other performance indicators. The care with which those activities are performed directly affects the effectiveness of the internal control system.

Internal control is more than fulfilling required manuals and forms. Equally as important, it is also about how people conduct internal control – how they design, implement, maintain and monitor control as part of their day-to-day activities. That is why organizational culture is important for internal control. As will be discussed later, organizational culture represents the common understanding among organizational members how controls need to be performed in an organizational setting.

To further clarify the role of internal control and the focus of this study, in the next section the definition will be integrated with strategic control and management control.[37] These research areas are closely related to internal control and their literatures will be partially included in the further course of the study.

2.1.2 Management Decision Processes

While internal control provides information quality for any decision maker in the organization, particularly influential for the achievement of the organizational objectives are management decision processes. Kinney (2000b, p. 83), envisioning himself as the CEO of a multinational corporation, asks:

> How would I know whether I was getting the right information for decision making, that my assets were being protected, and that my people were complying with laws, regulations, and company policy – all on a worldwide basis?

---

[35]CoCo (1995b, p. 6).

[36]CoCo (1995a, p. 7).

[37]Although internal control has a fundamental role for any business, in the literature relatively little attention is spent on integrating internal control with strategic control and management control (exceptions are Kinney 2000a; Merchant and Otley 2007; Simons 2000).

One important contribution to the solution to this question is internal control. Figure 2.3[38] illustrates the relationship between management decision processes and internal control.[39] As the figure demonstrates, internal control (illustrated in the center) has several inputs, such as information from transactions with customers, workers, and suppliers such as sales, payroll, and contracts (on the upper right), other events and conditions such as a new regulation or a natural catastrophe (at the lower right), other internal information (at the bottom) as well as information based on management decisions such as plans and authorizations (at the left).[40] Internal control prepares all this information for management decision processes and impacts the decisions made by management.[41] People's ability to fulfill their responsibility and make adequate decisions relies significantly on the quality of the information they receive.[42] In contrast, an organization can easily go in the wrong direction if the information people receive is incomplete, incorrect or manipulated.[43] Effective internal control provides people in the organization with appropriate, timely, accurate and accessible information.

Hence, information content is necessary, provided when required, includes the latest information available, and is correct and easily accessible by the appropriate

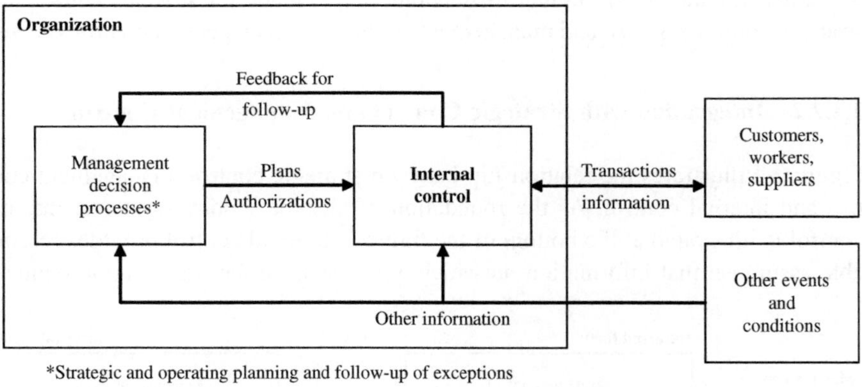

Fig. 2.3 Management decision processes and internal control.
Source: Adopted from Kinney (2000b, p. 85)

[38]Kinney's figure illustrates 'workers' outside the firm, which can be debated from COSO's perspective. In the COSO definition, 'personnel' are the one that effect internal control and are therefore part of the firm. Assuming that the term 'workers' represents the private person providing an economic exchange in form of workforce against payroll, this illustration sees workers outside the firm.

[39]CoCo (1995b, p. 11).

[40]Ulrich (2001, p. 250).

[41]Kinney (2000b, p. 85).

[42]COSO (1992, p. 6). Sunder (1997, p. 56) emphasizes that management depends on the information people share within the organization. It is the people's own decision which information they are willing to share and how accurately and truthfully they share it.

[43]Ulrich (2001, p. 249).

party and location.[44] Internal control contributes to decision-making by providing information for both the normal course of business as well as when there are operational issues, noncompliance with standards or other violations of policy and illegal actions.[45]

2.1.2.1 Control in General versus Control Systems

While control in general can mean anything from formal to informal control mechanisms, control systems stand usually for the "formal, information-based routines and procedures managers use to maintain or alter patterns in organizational activities".[46] Thus, when speaking of the internal control *system*, the formal mechanisms of checks and balances are understood. In contrast, when addressing internal control in general, formal and informal activities are included. For example, while an IT-based restriction of access to organizational assets is part of the internal control *system*, an informal discussion between a line manager and a hiring manager about the requirements for a job opening is part of internal control, but not part of the internal control system (as long as the discussion does not follow a prescribed formal procedure and will enter in a database). Similar distinctions can be made for strategic control and strategic control *systems*, and management control and management control *systems*.

2.1.2.2 Integration with Strategic Control and Management Control

Figure 2.4 illustrates the relationship between strategic control, management control and internal control. As the foundation of all other control systems, internal control is illustrated at the bottom of the figure.[47] Internal control provides reasonable assurance that information on which any system in the organization builds is

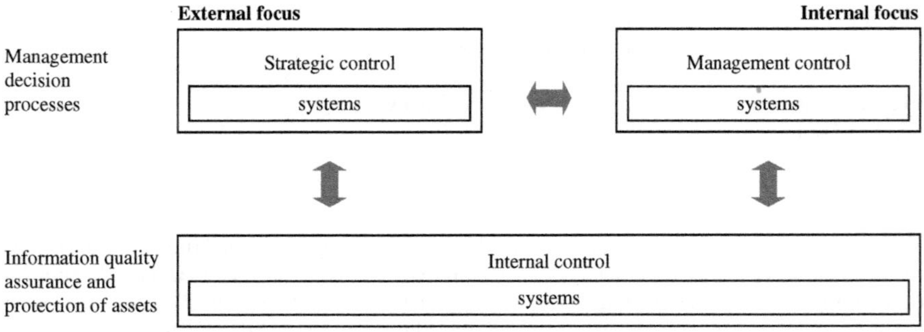

Fig. 2.4 Interrelation of strategic control, management control and internal control. *Source*: Adapted from Simons (1995, p. 128)

[44]COSO (1992, p. 62).

[45]COSO (1992, p. 87) and Kinney (2000b, p. 84).

[46]Simons (1995, p. 5).

[47]For example, Simons (2000).

reliable and that assets are being protected. The information quality provided by internal control enters into strategic and management control systems and builds the foundation for any formal and informal strategic and management control decision. As indicated with the gray arrows in Fig. 2.4, internal control, management control and strategic control interrelate.[48] Aspects of internal control are similarly discussed in strategic and management control, however, the focus differs. While internal control provides reasonable assurance for information quality and safeguarding assets, CoCo (1995b, p. 5) clarifies that internal control "cannot prevent the taking of strategic and operational decisions that are, in retrospect, incorrect". Whether management decides to act and what actions to take are outside of internal control.[49] Management decision-processes are part of strategic control and management control. Merchant and Van der Stede (2007, p. 7) explain that issues of strategic control:

> have a focus primarily *external* to the organization; they examine the industry and their organization's place in it. They think about how the organization, with its particular combination of strengths, weaknesses, opportunities, and limitations, can compete with other firms in its industry.[50]

Board and management decide on the mission, vision and value statements, as well as the overall objectives of the organization. Based on evaluations of the organization's strengths, weaknesses, opportunities and threats, board and management further decide on the overall strategy and performance goals to achieve the overall objectives.[51] In contrast to strategic control which is primarily concerned about strategic decisions, management control takes an *internal* focus. Of concern is primarily how organizational resources can be used so that people work toward organizational objectives. An often quoted definition is the one from Anthony (1965, p. 17), who defines management control as:

> the process by which managers ensure that resources are obtained and used effectively and efficiently in the accomplishment of the organization's objectives.[52]

Management uses tools including "short and long range plans, financial budgets, capital budgets, variance analyses and project reporting systems" in order to decide

---

[48]Similar to the internal control literature, the management control literature traditionally focused on accounting information and often separated from operational and strategic control. However, recent developments in the management control literature recognize that such a focus neglects impacts on management control from strategy and operations. Otley (1999, p. 364) remarks: "Although it may well have been sensible to concentrate initially on the core area of 'management control', it is now necessary to pay more attention to the neglected elements of strategy and operations".

[49]CoCo (1995b, p. 11). Internal control supports the achievement of organizational objectives. Therefore it is not an end in itself, but a means to an end (Pfaff and Ruud 2007, p. 22).

[50]Emphasis added.

[51]Ruud (2003, p. 75).

[52]An alternative definition provides Otley (1999, p. 364) who states that management control systems "provide information that is intended to be useful to managers in performing their jobs and to assist organizations in developing and maintaining viable patterns of behavior". This view from Otley on management control integrates internal control and gives little room for making a distinction between internal control and management control.

on objectives.[53] Management control is typically described as "a feedback process of planning, objective setting, monitoring, feedback and corrective action to ensure that outcomes are in accordance with plans".[54]

In summary, whether strategic control or management control,[55] both types of control rely fundamentally on control systems that are based on reliable information produced by effective internal control. Internal control provides decision makers in the organization with reliable information so they are able to choose among alternatives which are best for the achievement of organizational objectives.

2.1.3 *Internal Control Effectiveness*

The importance of internal control is most visible and prominent in cases when internal control is ineffective. How much do tools such as a Balanced Scorecard (BSC), Key Performance Indicators (KPI), and Customer Satisfaction Surveys help management in achieving the organizational objectives[56] if those tools are based on inaccurate or manipulated information? How much can external parties rely on financial reports for their investment decisions if these reports do not reflect the real economic conditions of the organization? What use do codes of business conduct have if organizational members confirm its content only as a formality to please regulatory requirements rather than actually act in consistency with these codes? These are questions that reflect the purpose of this study and ask what the role of organizational culture is for internal control. Before turning toward finding answers to these questions later in this study, this section discusses under what conditions internal control is effective and, if so, what benefits it provides.

2.1.3.1 When is Internal Control Effective?

Internal control is inherently complex and consists of many activities across, up and down, and inside and outside the organization. Defining control effectiveness provides the reference that organizations aspire to when they intend to achieve all the benefits of internal control. Contrary to the internal control process itself, which is a means to an end, effectiveness is a state or point in time.[57] Whether internal control is effective depends on a subjective judgment of how the

[53]Simons (1990, p. 135).

[54]Simons (1990, p. 130).

[55]Merchant and Van der Stede (2007, p. 7).

[56]See Kaplan and Norton (1992).

[57]COSO (1992, p. 20).

objective categories of internal control are implemented. Broadly defined internal control is effective, when board and management have reasonable assurance that:

- They know if and to what extent operational effectiveness and efficiency are achieved. While operational effectiveness focuses on output of operations, efficiency sets the priority on input, the use of resources and its costs. Aside from when organizations set different priorities on the balance between operational effectiveness and efficiency,[58] what is important is that management has a clear understanding to what extent they are attained. For instance, are streamlined and centralized processes implemented? Do the operational processes work in a cost-efficient manner?
- Published financial statements and internal reporting are prepared reliably.[59] Reliability requires that the measurement methods are carefully applied and that the displayed portrayal in reporting reflects the results correctly.[60] For example, do the numbers reflect the performance of the organization? Does internal reporting provide the right overview of inventory and assortment?
- Applicable laws, regulations, and internal rules are complied with.[61] Compliance is reached when records meet the external regulatory requirements such as production standards, accounting standards, tax requirements and further legal requirements, as well as internal policies.[62] Are the legal requirements of each country that the organization operates in being followed? Is the code of conduct implemented throughout the whole organization?

Merchant (1985, p. 10) writes that "good" internal control is said to be in place when "an informed person can be reasonably confident that no major unpleasant surprises will occur". Thus, the information provided by internal control supports people in optimizing the trade-off between risk and expected reward in decision-making. It helps people's decisions in addressing risks and taking appropriate actions[63] so that the remaining (uncontrolled) risks are deemed acceptable. CoCo (1995b, p. 2) explains that control includes the identification and mitigation of risks and includes not only known risks related to the achievement of a specific objective but also that the organization is able to address its opportunities. Knowing that risks are adequately managed and controls are installed, internal control provides confidence. Senior-level people feel more confident when signing off reports and employees in general are more confident in their judgments.[64] Moreover, effective internal control addresses the organization's risk of fraud. It safeguards assets from theft and prevents distorted results.[65] Effective internal control is important to the

[58]Ibid.

[59]Ibid.

[60]Kinney (2000a, p. 33, 62).

[61]See CoCo (1995b) and COSO (1992).

[62]Kinney (2000a, p. 33, 62).

[63]Kinney (2000b, p. 84).

[64]CoCo (1995b, p. 1). See also Ruud and Sommer (2006).

[65]CoCo (1995b, p. 2).

outside as well. The accounting and financial reporting system[66] represents a critical information source for external decision makers and is the main instrument for shareholders, as the owners of the organization, to have insight into the organization's earnings and financial conditions.[67] Effective internal control provides reliable information to external parties from investors to the public at large, and therefore builds confidence in the capital markets based on the information available.[68]

2.1.3.2 Internal Control and Performance

A key question discussed in the literature and in practice is whether internal control generates shareholder value.[69] Because internal control is inherent in the organization's activities and part of the essence of the business, its inherent nature in business activities already makes clear the direct link to performance. For example, when operations become more effective and efficient because management takes more emphasis on control design, it saves costs and brings about a positive impact on performance. When the organization's financial numbers are reliable and the organization complies with regulations, it is also less likely to be involved in costly lawsuits that negatively impact its reputation and performance. In contrast, there are many control aspects where the link to performance seems less clear. For instance, setting effective internal control equal to high formalization does not necessarily guarantee a positive impact on performance.[70] Instead it might bring an unnecessary cost burden. In general, management attention on internal control provides effectiveness and efficiency of operations, reliability of reporting and compliance with laws, regulations and internal policies.[71] As a consequence of this management attention on more effectiveness, internal control is likely to contribute to performance but is not a performance driver itself.[72]

In sum, the term effectiveness is understood as an overall term that stands for a well-functioning internal control including efficiency in operations, reliability in

---

[66]Information from financial reporting contains, for example, earning and financial condition measures, periodic disclosures of off-balance items, such as certain types of leases, and transactions with parties related to management or the organization itself (Kinney 2000a, p. 37).

[67]Kinney (2000a, p. 37).

[68]CoCo (1995b, p. 1). Reliability is understood as central aspect towards the outside. Other aspects, such as giving the organization direction and assurance, which is important for shareholders and other groups, are considered part of reliability here.

[69]These aspects are discussed in regard to Sarbanes-Oxley requirements (for example, Rittenberg and Miller 2005; Zang 2005), but also in regard to more general organizational design (for example, Burton et al. 2006; Simons 2005).

[70]See also the Sarbanes-Oxley debate: Ashbaugh-Skaife et al. (2007), Coates (2007), Doyle et al. (2007), Ge and McVay (2005), Leone (2007), Rittenberg and Miller (2005), Ruud and Pfister (2006), and Zang (2005).

[71]See Rittenberg and Miller (2005).

[72]See Simons (2005).

reporting, and compliance with rules.[73] If organizational culture contributes to internal control, it needs to support the achievements of these three objective categories. Defining effectiveness related to these three categories relies on a subjective judgment by senior-level people. How can senior-level people decide whether these objectives are achieved?

2.1.3.3 Inverse Relation to Control Deficiencies

Reasonable assurance is given when internal control is without any material weaknesses. This criterion is adapted from the Sarbanes-Oxley requirements, which address SEC listed companies. While the Sarbanes-Oxley requirements focus internal control over financial reporting and potential misstatements in reporting, this study applies them to the other objectives of internal control as well. Adapted from the SEC (2007) and PCAOB (2007), material weakness is then defined as a deficiency – or a combination of deficiencies – in internal control, such that there is a reasonable possibility that a material ineffectiveness and inefficiency in operations, a misstatement in reporting, or noncompliance with internal or external rules will not be prevented or detected on a timely basis.[74] PCAOB (2007) defines that a material weakness is the most severe type of control deficiencies. A control deficiency can be based either on the design of a control or its operation:

- A *deficiency in design* exists when (a) a control necessary to meet the control objective is missing or (b) an existing control is not properly designed so that, even if the control operates as designed, the control objective would not be met.[75]
- A *deficiency in operation* exists when a properly designed control does not operate as designed, or when the person performing the control does not possess the necessary authority or competence to perform the control effectively.[76]

This interpretation of control effectiveness means that it is inversely related to the amount of deficiencies that exist in the organization: The fewer deficiencies internal control has, the more effective it is. An ideal internal control would have no deficiencies and all control would be optimally designed and executed as intended. Taking this stand means that if organizational culture can contribute to control effectiveness, then it must reduce the likelihood of deficiencies in internal control.

---

[73]The term 'effective internal control' can also be used more specifically. For instance, it can stand for operations that are effective (but not necessarily efficient) or the term can be used to explain financial controls are reliable (e.g., in Sarbanes-Oxley context).

[74]This definition of material weaknesses in internal control is adapted from the definition of PCAOB Auditing Standard No. 5, which defines a material weakness as "a deficiency, or a combination of deficiencies, in internal control over financial reporting, such that there is a reasonable possibility that a material misstatement of the company's annual or interim financial statements will not be prevented or detected on a timely basis" (PCAOB 2007, p. 43).

[75]PCAOB (2007, p. 41; emphasis added).

[76]PCAOB (2007, p. 41; emphasis added).

Defining control effectiveness inversely related to the aggregated amount of control deficiencies leads to the question about the roots of control deficiencies.

2.1.4 Inherent Limitations

It is important to note that no matter how well internal control is designed it can only provide reasonable – not absolute – assurance. Two inherent limitations of internal control make it likely that the organization will not achieve its objectives. People in charge:

- Can make errors and omissions, or commit fraud
- Have to consider relative cost and benefit when designing and executing internal control

These two inherent limitations make it clear that even well-designed internal controls will retain some residual risks of the unexpected because outcome is not predictable.[77] Moreover, the limitations build a bridge to culture. For example, if people work lazy, inaccurate, or commit fraud is often founded in the culture. Likewise, whether management places value on detail-orientation and costly controls or takes a more pragmatic approach is similarly rooted in the culture of the organization.[78] Hence, the two inherent limitations of internal control are of importance for this study and are briefly introduced here.

2.1.4.1 Limitation 1: Errors, Omissions, and Fraud

In reality, people can be at fault in their judgment when making decisions and breakdowns can occur simply because of errors and mistakes. For instance, people must make decisions under business pressure, on time and with the information available at hand. These decisions can turn out to be incorrect at a later stage, and may need to be changed or corrected.[79] Risk assessments can be performed improperly by ignoring or misevaluating certain risks that affect the organization's ability to achieve its objectives. COSO (1992, p. 80) gives many more examples of what can go wrong even if controls are designed well:

> Personnel may misunderstand instructions. They may make judgment mistakes. Or they may commit errors due to carelessness, distraction or fatigue. An accounting department supervisor responsible for investigating exceptions might simply forget or fail to pursue the investigation far enough to be able to make appropriate corrections. Temporary personnel executing control duties for vacationing or sick employees might not perform correctly.

[77]COSO (1992, p. 15); Pfaff and Ruud (2007, p. 23).

[78]For example, CoCo (1995b, 2006b) and COSO (1992, 2004, 2006).

[79]COSO (1992, p. 80).

System changes may be implemented before personnel have been trained to react appropriately to signs of incorrect functioning.

Besides intended or unintended failures of personnel,[80] management can override controls and not follow policies and procedures for reasons of personal gain or to hide the real financial condition of the organization.[81] Besides individuals who cause control issues, two or more people can circumvent controls by collusion. An action can be perpetrated or concealed from detection through the collaboration of an employee responsible for an important control function and another employee, customer or supplier. Internal control contributes to minimize all of these human errors and failures but cannot warrant absolute assurance that these types of failures will not occur.[82] These examples illustrate the importance of management integrity, and of employees who work in the best interests of the organization, which are typical cultural aspects.

2.1.4.2 Limitation 2: Cost Benefit Trade-off

The second limitation relies on the inherent complexity of internal control, and the fact that it is not always directly observable and verifiable.[83] When designing control, management must consider the relative costs and benefits of specific controls.[84] Figure 2.5 illustrates that total costs rely on decision errors costs, asset loss, residual risks, and on the amount of resources spent for internal control.[85] The figure illustrates that optimal total costs are achieved when operating costs for internal control are balanced with decision error cost, asset loss, and residual risks. As the "quality optimum" indicates, when designing control, management is challenged to balance costs and quality.[86] The graph demonstrates that high formalization of internal control is cost-intensive, causes inflexibilities, and still incurs some residual risks (see right side of Fig. 2.2). Even within well-designed control

---

[80]CoCo (1995b, p. 3).

[81]COSO (1992, p. 80) describes many other reasons that cause top management or division managers to override controls. For example, they want "to increase reported revenue, to cover an unanticipated decrease in market share, to enhance reported earnings to meet unrealistic budgets, to boost the market value of the entity prior to a public offering sale, to meet sales or earnings projections to bolster bonus pay-outs tied to performance, to appear to cover violations of debt covenants or debt covenant agreements, or to hide lack of compliance with legal requirements. Override practices include deliberate misrepresentations to bankers, lawyers, accountants, and vendors, and intentionally issuing false documents such as purchase orders and sales invoices". Management override is a typical aspect which demonstrates the overlap between internal control and management control.

[82]See Pfaff and Ruud (2007).

[83]Kinney (2000b, p. 84).

[84]COSO (1992, p. 79).

[85]Kinney (2000a, p. 91).

[86]CoCo (1995b, p. 3, 20).

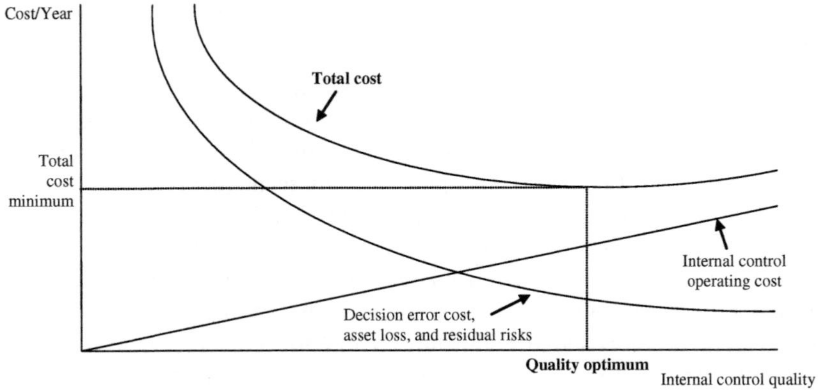

Fig. 2.5 Cost and benefit of internal control.
Source: Adapted from Kinney (2000a, p. 91)

systems, some residual risks will remain because the outcome is not predictable. The ability to invest in adequate internal control requires both financial resources and time, and varies depending on the organization's financial capacity.[87] For example, a poorly performing organization may simply be concerned with staying in business and therefore establish a "cost-savings" culture, which will not spend much on controls. Ge and McVay (2005, p. 151) explain: "poor performing firms may be undertaking actions, such as downsizing, which could create holes in their existing internal controls". On the other hand, an overemphasis on formal controls does not guarantee a much better control quality. This limitation brings into question how much formalism is needed for effective internal control, and also on what role organizational culture plays in these cost-benefit decisions.[88]

Errors, omissions and fraud, and cost-benefit trade-offs in control design and execution represent major reasons why internal control can only provide reasonable assurance, not absolute. Examples such as Lehman Brothers, Siemens, UBS, Enron and WorldCom demonstrate that the "cultural forces underneath" are part of control as well. In the management control literature, it is a well-accepted fact that management accounting and control systems need to be analyzed in the broader context.[89]

[87]Krishnan (2005, p. 652).

[88]Of particular importance for these cost-benefit discussions are mandatory regulatory requirements. Regulatory requirements for internal control (e.g., Sarbanes-Oxley Section 404) set minimum standards for how an organization must formalize its internal control and therefore impact the cost-benefit trade-off within organizations. The more these formal regulatory requirements are prescribed, the higher the minimum costs for internal control will be. As a consequence, regulation can have an important impact on internal control design and raise competitive disadvantages for organizations that would be able to design and executive effective controls also in a more informal manner than law requires.

[89]For example, Dent (1991) and Hopwood (1978, 1983).

Thus, to take an effective approach, control needs to be studied in its broad (informal and formal) context. A specific control might be a formal system in one organization, while in another company the same control might rely on less formalism.[90] Important is that the necessary controls are there (formally or informally) and that the whole control approach works effectively together. Culture makes it possible that the informal aspects (e.g., leadership, trust, values, and social norms) become part of the analysis. Taking this stance, culture provides the adequate foundation for analyzing internal control.

2.2 Organizational Culture

2.2.1 Definition

Many types of culture exist – national culture such as French culture, ethnic culture such as Islamic culture, regional culture such as Scandinavian culture, and more localized cultures such as the culture of a city, a specific neighborhood, or an institution.[91] Just as culture can refer to a nation or a region, it can also refer to an institution such as an organization.[92] Organization theory defines "organization" in two ways. In a general sense "organization" is understood as a task or coordination of activities,[93] while in a more specific way the term addresses the formal institution as a social entity. The literature describes these social entities as "large bureaucracies"[94] and "complex structures-in-motion".[95] This formal entity, which reflects the social structures established by organizational members, is the type of organization this study refers to.

Professionals and academics often talk about establishing the "right" culture – a culture that promotes "effectiveness", an "ethical culture", or a culture with the "right values". Organizational culture, then – assuming it is the right one – contributes to organizational performance because it is aligned with the organizational objectives and purpose.[96] For example, Microsoft emphasizes in its value statement a "passion for technology". Charles Schwab, a financial institution, sets "ethical financial services" and "earning customers' trust" as their priorities.[97]

[90]See Collier (2005) and Simons (2005).

[91]Keyton (2005, p. 18).

[92]Harris (1990, p. 741).

[93]See Mintzberg (1979) and Thompson (1967).

[94]Perrow (1986, p. 725, 1991).

[95]Clegg (1981, p. 545).

[96]For studies investigating culture and performance see Kotter and Heskett (1992), Siehl and Martin (1990), and Sørensen (2002).

[97]See www.microsoft.com and www.schwab.com.

These different cultural emphases make sense because the two organizations have different purposes and operate in different industries. Microsoft needs to have a culture in which people are passionate for technology in order to survive in a dynamic market, whereas Charles Schwab's success depends on people that enhance stability and the trust of its clients. Thus, not just any culture, but the "right" culture, supports the organizational objectives and purpose, and contributes to organizational performance.[98]

Before linking control and culture in the literature review in Chap. 3, this subchapter provides a holistic interpretation of organizational culture. Because culture is not always directly observable,[99] defining it is challenging. This challenge has led researchers to produce a variety of different interpretations. This subchapter will showcase the range of definitions, will develop a two-layered interpretation of culture in order to provide the setup for the further course of study, and will discuss discrepancies among approaches. This is necessary in order to understand the main part in which a framework is provided that captures how culture can be influenced so that controls are effective.[100]

2.2.1.1 Variety of Interpretations for Culture

Organizational culture has awakened the interest of many researchers from different areas, producing many ways of explaining the topic.[101] To name a few, Schein (2004) explains organizational culture through leadership; Deal and Kennedy (1982) focus on the amount of risk employed; and Harrison (1972) considers the extent of formalization and centralization within the organization. Besides these alternate ways of treating organizational culture, another discussion in the literature is the status organizational culture holds and how it relates to other organizational forms. For instance, Weik (2001, p. 354) writes that organizational culture and strategy partially overlap, while Hofstede et al. (1990, p. 286) gives culture a status similar to structure, strategy, and control.[102] This study adds to this discussion by linking internal control and organizational culture.

---

[98]Schein (2004, p. 7).

[99]See Keyton (2005).

[100]In order to meet the focus of this study, this subchapter focuses on defining organizational culture and does not discuss specific aspects such as the influence of leadership on culture or the relation between culture and climate.

[101]Hofstede et al. (1990, p. 286).

[102]If not more clearly specified, in the proceeding of this study, the terms 'culture', 'corporate culture' and 'organizational culture' are all used to explain the cultural phenomena related to an organization.

Table 2.1[103] provides a collection of interpretations which illustrate ways that culture is defined, interpreted and analyzed.[104] Due to the fact that culture is not entirely observable and describable,[105] the overview shows that many different interpretations have been developed. Each of these definitions referenced in the figure can be applied to culture. Synthesizing the various definitions from the figure, four characteristics of culture can be identified. Culture is:

- About shared understandings among group members
- About group member's interactions
- Implicit (and explicit)
- Is based on history and tradition.

Table 2.1 Categories used to explain culture

Definition	Description
Observed behavioral regularities when people interact	The language they use, the customs and traditions that evolve, and the rituals they employ in a wide variety of situations
Group norms	The implicit standards and values that evolve in working groups, such as the particular norm of "a fair day's work for a fair day's pay" that evolved among workers in the Bank Wiring Room in the Hawthorne studies
Espoused values	The articulated, publicly announced principles and values that the group claims to be trying to achieve, such as product quality or price leadership
Formal philosophy	The broad policies and ideological principles that guide a group's actions toward stockholders, employees, customers, and other stakeholders, such as the highly publicized "HP Way" of Hewlett-Packard
Rules of the game	The implicit, unwritten rules for getting along in the organization; "the ropes" that a newcomer must learn in order to become an accepted member; "the way we do things around here."
Embedded skills	The special competencies displayed by group members in accomplishing certain tasks, the ability to make certain things that gets passed on from generation to generation without necessarily being articulated in writing
Habits of thinking, mental models, and linguistic paradigms	The shared cognitive frames that guide the perceptions, thought, and language used by the members of a group and taught to new members in the early socialization process

[103] Schein's original figure was shortened. Also, authors that refer to the specific definitions were removed here.

[104] Although the focus here is on the organization, the concept of culture of any other instance is true for the specific culture of an organization as well. Therefore any definition of culture (whether referring to the organization or another reference) is included in this overview.

[105] See Keyton (2005).

First, culture is defined as "behavioral regularities", "ideological principles" or "the way we do things around here", which all reflect that culture is about shared understandings. Culture is about a shared understanding of the principles that are important for a group and the way actions should be performed. Thus, with regard to internal control, organizational culture stands for the common understandings within an organization how controls must be designed and executed. Second, culture is defined as "the way in which members of the organization interact with each other". Hence, culture has to do with group members' communications, which is another link to internal control.[106] Third, culture is "embedded" and "implicit", and relates to intangibles such as meanings, understandings and beliefs.[107] In the context of controls, this means that the existence of culture makes it possible to analyze social controls and its relation to explicit formal control mechanisms. Fourth, culture is based on history and tradition as it is "passed on from generation to generation" and reflects "the customs and traditions that evolve".[108] History links culture and control because both evolve over time. Together, these four aspects of culture offer criteria to be met when developing a holistic definition of culture.

2.2.1.2 Defining Organizational Culture

Combining the definitions from Schein (1990) and O'Reilly and Chatman (1996), in this study organizational culture is defined as a pattern of basic assumptions that a group has invented, discovered or developed in learning to cope with its problems of *external adaptation and internal integration*,[109] which is represented in a *system of shared values* defining what is important, *and norms*, defining appropriate attitudes and behaviors, that guide each individual's attitudes and behaviors.[110] This definition combines two common types of definitions on culture and emphasizes that an organization establishes its values and norms as a result of how the

---

[106]See Sect. 3.2.2.

[107]Alvesson (2002, p. 6).

[108]Bromann and Piwinger (1992) view culture in a timeframe and divide into what the cultural reality is, and what the desired status of the culture should be. They also argue that older organizations do not necessarily have "more culture". Often in young companies team spirit and entrepreneurial thinking can bring culture more clearly to the forefront than in an established company.

[109]Taking a dynamic view, Schein (1990, p. 111) defines organizational culture as "a pattern of basic assumptions that a group has invented, discovered or developed in learning to cope with its problems of *external adaptation* and *internal integration*, and that have worked well enough to be considered valid, and therefore, to be taught to new members as the correct way to perceive, think, and feel in relation to those problems".

[110]Taking a static view, O'Reilly and Chatman's (1996, p. 166) organizational culture is "a system of *shared values* defining what is important, and *norms*, defining appropriate attitudes and behaviors, that guide members' attitudes and behaviors."

organization has been reacting to important influences from the environment and incidents in the present and past.[111]

Figure 2.6 illustrates how the two views of culture interrelate.[112] The two arrows indicating external adaptation and internal integration illustrate how culture refers to the environment. Thus, starting with the environment, it is shown that culture externally adapts and internally integrates as a continuous and interrelated process.[113] Toward the outside, the organizational culture must adapt continuously to the external environment such as market, regulation and other factors that influence the organization. At the same time, the organizational culture needs to integrate internally and establish a common understanding of how things are going to be done in the culture. While these processes build the intermediate elements within the organization's environment, the common understanding of how to adapt and integrate is defined in the shared values and social norms among the organization's members. Representing the core and the more stable part, values and norms can be seen as the social and normative glue that holds an organization together.[114] Meeting the four requirements identified earlier in the chapter (shared understandings, interactions, implicitness, and history), the approach taken in this study

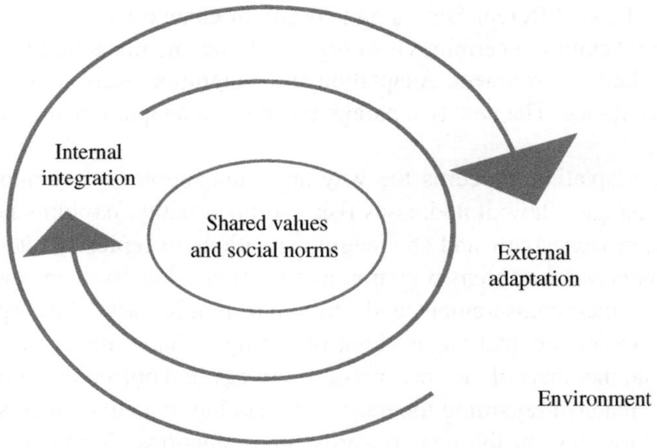

Fig. 2.6 Combined view

[111]Lim (1995, p. 17) and Schein (1990, p. 111).

[112]Traditionally, the concept of culture has been analyzed in anthropology. According to Kroeber and Kluckhohn (1952, p.181), culture "consists in patterned ways of thinking, feeling and reacting, acquired and transmitted mainly by symbols, constitute the distinctive achievements of human groups, including their embodiments in artifacts; the essential core of culture consists of traditional (i.e., *historically derived and selected*) ideas and especially their *attached values*" (emphasis added).

[113]Dent (1991, p. 709) writes that cultures "in organizations are not independent of their social context. They are interpenetrated by wider systems of thought, interacting with other organizations and social institutions, both importing and exporting values, beliefs and knowledge".

[114]See Collins and Porras (1996) and Tichy (1982).

represents a holistic definition of organizational culture. Following a two-layered definition of organizational culture, the next two sections discuss the components of the definition:

1. External adaptation and internal integration[115]
2. Shared values and social norms[116]

2.2.2 External Adaptation and Internal Integration

External adaptation and internal integration sees culture as the way an organization deals with its changing environment.[117] A culture can only be "effective" when it addresses its environment in a way that supports the organizational long-term performance. For instance, an international organization that operates in a short-lived and competitive market will need a culture that can deal with innovation and rapid change, while a small and locally operating organization in a more traditional industry might be more successful with a conservative culture that builds on stable products and customers. Hence, depending on the environmental characteristics, an organization faces different factors and speeds of change which it must adapt to. Organizational culture determines how organizational members build consensus on how to face their environment. Adaptation and integration occur in parallel and are of equal importance. The next two paragraphs discuss adaptation and integration in more detail.

External adaptation concerns the way an organization, as a group of people, deals with change – how it addresses risk and uncertainty, explores new possibilities, and approaches new and challenging situations. It represents *how* organizational members *reach consensus* on mission, strategy, objectives, means to achieve the objectives, their measurement, and corrections if necessary. Thus organizational culture (as external adaptation) is about obtaining a shared understanding among organizational members of the core mission, strategy and objectives. It is about how consensus is reached regarding the means of attaining objectives such as organizational structure, responsibilities, rewards, and sanctions. Moreover, consensus needs to be reached on the criteria to be applied in measuring how well the group is doing in fulfilling its objectives. Schein (2004, p. 88) writes: "This step [of external adaptation] also involves the cycle of obtaining information, getting that information to the right place within the organization, and digesting it so that appropriate corrective action can be taken".[118] Finally, consensus needs to be reached on the correction to be used if objectives are not being achieved. In contrast

[115] Schein (1990, p. 111).

[116] O'Reilly and Chatman (1996, p. 166).

[117] Schein (2004, p. 8).

[118] Schein's quote shows how close organizational culture and internal control are. The quote contains typical internal control matters such as discussed in the section on the benefits of internal control.

to internal control, which is about the means to achieve organizational objectives in general, external adaptation emphasizes *reaching consensus* about the means among group members.[119]

Although the two processes are discussed in sequential order here, internal integration occurs parallel to external adaptation.[120] Internal integration deals with how people form a group. Groups must develop clear assumptions about what is and what is not accepted in the culture. They also need to establish a common understanding of justice, regulation, norms and rules. To avoid false expectations, they need to find a common means of communicating and giving feedback. These integrative processes lead to solidarity among the group members.[121] Schein (2004, p. 133) describes that every group:

> must learn how to become a group. The process is not automatic; in fact it is complex and multifaceted. Humans, being what they are, must deal with a finite and describable set of issues in any new group situation. At the most basic level they must develop a common language and category system that clearly define what things mean. Formal languages do not specify with enough precision what work, teamwork, respect, quality, and so on mean. Groups must reach consensus on the boundaries of the group, who is in and who is not in. They must develop consensus on how to distribute influence and power so that aggression can be constructively channeled and formal status accurately determined.[122]

Internal integration means everything from defining what the group is and how the group works to coordinating activities so that specialized contributions complement each other and form the group as a whole.[123] Schein's quote demonstrates that internal integration is about how a group of people organizes itself, what social structures, hierarchies and relationships it creates, and also what behavior is accepted in the group and what is not. In addition, groups need to find explanations to deal with unpredictable and unexplainable events. In this sense, Schein (2004, p. 133) compares a group's culture as a functional equivalent to religion, mythology, and ideology, which are all used to explain the unexplainable.

While external adaptation concerns the external environment, members develop a common understanding of principles and behaviors inside the organization through internal integration.

In sum, organizational culture, as discussed in this section, deals with how organizational members reach consensus on adapting to the external environment and how the organization internally integrates. In contrast to the values and norms, which will be discussed shortly and take a more static view, the focus for adaptation and integration is dynamic – dealing with how people form a social system that has adequate internal stability to survive under changing conditions.

---

[119] Denison et al. (2006, p. 7).

[120] Schein (2004, p. 109).

[121] Meglino and Ravlin (1998, p. 357).

[122] Emphasis added.

[123] See Denison et al. (2006) and Meglino and Ravlin (1998, p. 7)

2.2.3 *Shared Values and Social Norms*

The core variables of culture are often described as shared values among members of a group.[124] In alignment with Schwartz and Bilsky (1990), Wiener (1988), O'Reilly and Chatman (1996), and Van Rekom et al. (2006) this study takes the position that values guide behavior.[125] Rokeach (1973, p. 5) defines a value as an "enduring belief that a specific mode of conduct or end-state of existence is personally or socially preferable to an opposite or converse mode of conduct or end-state of existence". This definition emphasizes that values can relate to both the action leading to an objective as well as the objective as end-state itself. The definition from Rokeach corresponds to Schwartz and Bilsky's observation (1987, p. 551) who find that most of the value definitions have in common that "values are concepts or beliefs, about desirable end states or behaviors, that transcend specific situations, guide selection or evaluation of behavior and events, and are ordered by relative importance". Thus, values are ordered in a value system, which reflects the relative priority of the importance of a value for a specific situation. Hence, what reflect the culture are the values that are instilled in people's day-to-day actions as a result of the underlying value system. Michela and Burke (2000, p. 229) explain that values are intertwined with norms:

> With values, the desired behavior is expected to follow if the predisposing values are instilled. With norms, getting the desired behaviors, by whatever means, creates conditions in which people infer they are the right ones or, at least, the socially approved ones (including when people are explicitly socialized to conform to the norms).

As this quote shows, while values lead to behavior when they are "instilled", social norms address what people in a group perceive as expected behavior (a conversion from "is" to "ought") and therefore sets expectations for behavioral standards in the group.[126] Values[127] are a fundamental concept (having a "transcendental quality"), and are deep-rooted and pervasive in nature.[128] In contrast, social norms are about social expectations.[129] These social expectations are based on underlying values. Therefore, as values interrelate with social norms, and the distinction between values and norms may be fluent, this study focuses primarily on values, but also

---

[124]Wiener (1988, p. 534).

[125]There are some scholars that deny this influence of values on behavior and say that values only rarely influence behavior (for example, Kristiansen and Hotte 1989; McClelland 1985).

[126]D'Andrade (1984, p. 229) and Michela and Burke (2000).

[127]Values must be distinguished from other concepts such as opinions and attitudes. A value is more general and less bound to any specific object as opposed to many attitudes and opinions, which are situation-bound. Therefore a value can underlie numerous opinions and attitudes (Akaah and Lund 1994, p. 418; England 1967, p. 54).

[128]Rokeach (1973, p. 17).

[129]O'Reilly et al. (1991, p. 492).

discusses them implicitly in their function as social norms.[130] Social norms represent what people within a group typically do, and shared understandings among the group members represent what people from the group are supposed to do.[131] Fehr and Fischbacher (2004, p. 63) interpret social norms as "normative standards of behavior that are enforced by informal social sanctions" and explain social norms as one of the distinguishing facets of human species. Thus, social norms define what people ought to do as part of a common understanding in the group.[132] In contrast to the value which is instilled, social norms reflect the social expectations of behavior in a group that is typically enforced by social sanctions.

In retrospect, two important points need to be mentioned here. First, to become a driver for organizational effectiveness, values, and norms need to support organizational goals and strategies.[133] Thus, the mere fact that shared values exist does not necessarily result in organizational success and task productivity. Values must enhance behavior that is appropriate for task performance and survival of the organization. Second, in the terminology of Schein's dynamic definition, values and norms must be adequate for both external adaptation and internal integration. Values for internal integration may be different from those values required for external adaptation. An organization can have high internal standards and apply these effectively. For adapting to the outside, however, those values could bring competitive disadvantage.[134] Consequently, values and norms need to be appropriate for the organization's objectives both within the organization and toward the outside.

2.2.4 Specifications

The broad definition of culture provides a holistic setup for analysis. As preparation for the further analysis in Part III, two important discrepancies are discussed in this section. First, the definition of organizational culture contains a dynamic and a static perspective, which offer different insights. Second, culture can be addressed from the perspective of different disciplines such as psychology, sociology or anthropology. Each produces different insights into the topic as well. Thus, including more than one viewpoint in this study is likely to bring different insights and as a consequence a more comprehensive view of culture. Because variations in viewpoints provide a breadth adequate to internal control, they are relevant for the premise of this study.

[130]In accounting and control research social norms are often discussed in regard to incentive systems (for example, Kunz and Pfaff 2002).

[131]Michela and Burke (2000, p. 229).

[132]See D'Andrade (1984).

[133]Wiener (1988, p. 536).

[134]Meglino and Ravlin (1998, p. 356).

2.2.4.1 Dynamic versus Static View

As the prior discussion on culture demonstrates, the conceptual spectrum of research on organizational culture can be interpreted as operating along a continuum, extending from dynamic to static approaches. On the one hand, culture is interpreted dynamically because it is seen as something "historically derived and selected". Culture is seen as a process, evolving with time, dynamic, and changing in nature.[135] On the other hand, research often interprets culture as more static, based on values and norms (or similar variables). Culture is then viewed as static, focusing on a specific point in time, relying on the idea that it is classifiable based on two or more variables such as a set of values and norms.[136] Because this static view looks at culture as a variable that can be distinguished through one or two variables, Alvesson (1989) uses the term "classification-oriented". In contrast, he uses "process-oriented" for the dynamic view because it portrays culture as a process that adapts to the environment and integrates internally. In this study, both views will be discussed similarly and referred to as the "dynamic" and the "static" views on culture. Table 2.2 gives a summary of the two views.

Schein (2001, p. xxiv) describes the fact that culture can be conceptualized dynamically as well as statically as a "chronic issue". Obviously, different interpretations can cause misunderstandings. They are not only different concepts but also imply different methods of dealing with culture.[137] Nevertheless, he concludes that both meanings of culture have utility for theory building. Social phenomena cannot really be understood "without understanding both the historical events and the cultural meanings attributed to those events".[138] Supporting Schein's argumentation, the variety of definitions on culture is seen as an opportunity to investigate different aspects of culture rather than as a conceptual dilemma. As will be discussed in more detail later, this study applies both the static and the dynamic view in order to produce a comprehensive understanding of culture.

Table 2.2 Dynamic versus static view on culture

Dynamic view	Static view
Based on adaptation and integration	Based on shared values and norms
Evolving and changing	Stable
Process-oriented	Classification-oriented

Source: Adapted from Schein (2004, pp. 12-13)

[135] Lim (1995, p. 17).

[136] See Hampdon-Turner (1990).

[137] While process-oriented approaches are often combined with theory-building and qualitative studies (see Alvesson 2002; Schein 2004), classification approaches often relate to quantitative studies in which culture is measured and related to specific organizational outcomes (see O'Reilly et al. 1991; Sarros et al. 2005; Sørensen 2002).

[138] Schein (2001, p. xxiv).

2.2.4.2 Organizational versus Individual Level

In the same way as the dynamic and static views reflect interests from varying origins, different disciplines also address culture in different ways and, as a result, produce different insights. This study divides these insights into two levels: the organizational (sociological) and personal (psychological) levels.[139] For instance, how culture impacts the actions of an individual can be investigated based on a psychological point of view. In contrast, how culture affects the interrelations of people in a group or an organization is a possible sociological study.

Keyton (2005, p. 18), taking a sociological stance, points out that through people's interactions, a unique culture in the form of a social structure is formed and is "continually reproduced by its members". Keyton explains culture as something that is produced through a group of people (e.g., an organization) and emphasizes that this group of people establishes autonomy based on social structures (e.g., a typical question of this type of research would be: what group dynamics take place in performing controls?). In contrast, Hofstede (2001, p. 9), defines culture as "the collective programming of the mind that distinguishes the members of one group or category of people from another". Hofstede considers what is going on within people and explains culture as something that "programs the mind". The last definition makes clear that organizational culture affects each individual participating in a cultural setting (e.g., what do people think when they perform controls?).

As these two examples demonstrate, different levels such as organization and individual turn out to deliver a different viewpoint and emphasis on culture, and also promise to bring different qualities to their results. As a consequence, any study of culture needs to clarify which level it addresses so that it can produce valuable results. This study considers on the organizational and individual level as well as on the dynamic and static view in order to link internal control and organizational culture more holistically.[140]

2.3 Summary

This chapter has discussed the basics of internal control and organizational culture to provide a common understanding of the two topics.

Internal control is a process, effected by all people within the organization, and designed to provide reasonable assurance for the achievement of the objectives in regard to effectiveness and efficiency of operations, reliability of internal and external reporting, and compliance with applicable laws, regulations and internal policies. Internal control primarily supports the achievement of these objectives by providing decision-makers with information quality and by the safeguarding of

[139]These are common differentiations in interdisciplinary research.

[140]See Chaps. 5–7.

organizational assets. Hence, internal control provides integrity for any control system within the organization. Internal control is effective if senior-level people have reasonable assurance that the three objective categories are achieved and that internal control is free of any material weakness. Because within any control design rests the risk of errors, omissions, and fraud, and relies always on a cost-benefit trade-off, internal control can only provide a reasonable assurance for the achievement of objectives, not absolute.

As with internal control, many interpretations for organizational culture have been developed. Extracting common patterns of definitions, culture is about shared understandings of a group's principles and actions, builds on members' interaction, and is implicit and historically derived. Based on these variations in interpretation, the study developed a two-layered definition of organizational culture. Organizational culture is defined as the way in which members of a group cope with external adaptation and internal integration, and how these processes of adaptation and integration are reflected in shared values and social norms. This definition is broad and covers a dynamic as well as a static view of culture. Moreover, this broad definition makes it possible that culture can be analyzed on a more organizational (sociological) level and on a more individual (psychological) level in the further course of study.

After having developed an understanding for internal control and organizational culture here, the next chapter proceeds with a literature review to examine how the two topics are related to each other in management accounting and control research.

Chapter 3
Literature Review

3.1 Linking Control and Culture

While internal control and organizational culture have been treated separately before, this chapter provides a literature review on the link between control and culture. Taking the perspective of accounting and control research, the literature review focuses on how the interrelations between control and culture have been conceptualized in research. Therefore, an emphasis on the literature review is given to existing control terminologies and control frameworks, including organizational culture.[1]

As illustrated in Fig. 3.1 the literature review is divided into three steps. The first step provides a literature review on research in internal control. As research on the comprehensive view of internal control[2] receives relatively little attention in research, the literature review presents and discusses three practice-oriented internal control frameworks. These frameworks provide a pragmatic overview of what internal control consists of and indicate links between control and culture. In addition, the first step discusses other internal control-related research and literature. The second step broadens the view to include the general area of management accounting and control research.[3] Three major control concepts from research are presented and discussed in regard to the objective of this study. These research-oriented control frameworks distinguish fundamental types of control mechanisms, which are relevant in organizational settings. They provide the basis for empirical studies, which will be also discussed in this section. Finally, the last step concludes with a presentation of issues from the literature to address in this study. These issues will be summarized in five theses which this study attempts to address in Parts

[1] This study treats the terms "control frameworks" and "control concepts" as synonyms.

[2] See Sect. 2.1.1.

[3] About the relation between internal control and other control areas in the management accounting and control area, see Sect. 2.1.2.

J. Pfister, *Managing Organizational Culture for Effective Internal Control*, Contributions to Management Science,
DOI: 10.1007/978-3-7908-2340-0_3,

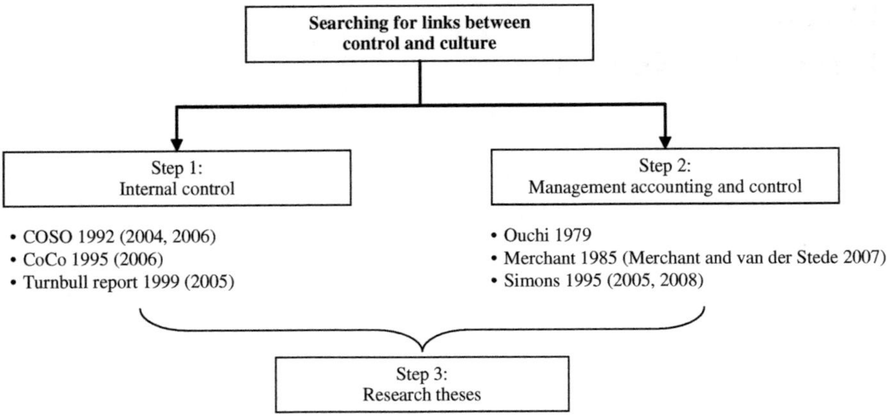

Fig. 3.1 Setup of the literature review

II–IV. For all discussed areas other frameworks exist, but these selected frameworks represent some of the most commonly accepted in their respective areas.[4]

3.2 Internal Control

3.2.1 Research Overview

Research in internal control can be classified into the focused and the comprehensive view of internal control such as defined in Sect. 2.1.1. The focused view of internal control, which typically focuses on accounting controls, is of particular interest in auditing research. Two examples of earlier studies are explained by Ashton (1974) and Mock and Turner (1981). Both are concerned with the auditors' judgment of internal control. Based on an experimental setup, these studies focus on auditors' judgment variations when being asked to perform the same experimental task. More recently, a plethora of studies has developed in the context of the US Sarbanes-Oxley Act of 2002.[5] Ashbaugh-Skaife et al. (2007) use internal control deficiency disclosures prior to mandated internal control audits, and find that firms disclosing internal control deficiencies have more complex operations, recent organizational changes, greater accounting risk, more auditor resignations, and have fewer resources available for internal control. In a concurrent study, Doyle

[4]For the importance of the selected internal control frameworks, see IFAC (2006). For the importance of the selected research frameworks, see Merchant and Otley (2007).

[5]As mentioned in Sect. 2.1.1, SOX brought mandatory rules for the disclosure of material weaknesses in internal control over financial reporting for companies listed on US stock exchanges.

et al. (2007) provide evidence that firms disclosing material weaknesses in internal control tend to be younger, smaller, financially weaker, more complex, growing rapidly, or undergoing restructuring. These studies provide important implications for the organizational characteristics which are associated with organizations that are more likely to have control deficiencies. While this stream of research emphasizes accounting and auditing aspects of internal control,[6] these studies offer limited attention to operations and compliance aspects as well as cultural aspects of internal control.

Merchant and Otley (2007) clarify that, particularly in the US, a common agreement in practice states that internal control should be viewed by the broad COSO definition. Research on the comprehensive view of internal control[7] has not been developed as much as the practical importance of the topic would indicate.[8] Only a few years ago, Kinney (2000b, p. 83) remarked that despite the fact that internal control affects "the welfare of management, corporate directors, shareholders, trading partners of an entity, auditors, and society at large", it is relatively unexplored.[9] In academia the comprehensive view of internal control gets the most attention in conceptual and practice-oriented publications, which rely on commonly accepted internal control frameworks. For example, Kinney (2000a) discusses the relationship between information quality assurance and internal control. Pfaff and Ruud (2007) provide guidance for companies in Switzerland to establish internal control in compliance with national regulations. Jenal (2006) conceptualizes an overall assurance concept in order to align different control functions and reduce duplications and control gaps. Biegelman and Bartow (2006) examine internal control in regard to fraud prevention and discuss from a practical orientation how executives can create a culture of compliance. These are all contributions to the literature, which are conceptual, based on case study research and/or existing literature and guidance.[10]

The literature review confirms the importance of practice-oriented internal control frameworks. Major internal control frameworks for overall internal control emerged in the 1990s with the framework from the Committee of Sponsoring Organizations of the Treadway Commission from the US (COSO) in 1992, the Guidance on Control framework from Canada (CoCo) in 1995, and the Turnbull guidance from the United Kingdom in 1998.[11] While there are other frameworks for

---

[6]See also Bryan and Lilien (2005), Ge and McVay (2005), Leone (2007) and Zang (2005).

[7]See Sect. 2.1.1.

[8]Maijoor (2000, p. 102). See also Jenal (2006, appendix). The comprehensive view of internal control was primarily promoted by practice-oriented internal control frameworks, which will be discussed later in this section.

[9]Kinney is a promoter of the comprehensive view of internal control as can be seen in his earlier publications (for example, Kinney et al. 1990).

[10]Textbooks in management control often mention the importance of effective internal control, however, relatively little space is given for explaining its role (for example, Anthony and Govindarajan 2006; Merchant and Van der Stede 2007; Simons 2000).

[11]IFAC (2006, p. 2).

internal control aspects,[12] COSO, CoCo and Turnbull represent major contributors to internal control guidance as can be seen that most other frameworks and guidance refer to these concepts.[13] While these practical concepts' primary purpose is to provide definition, criteria, and guidance to implement a systematic approach on internal control in organizations,[14] they also offer researchers the practical understanding and a common language for communication with professionals.

The following three sections discuss COSO, CoCo, and Turnbull, and analyze how these control concepts consider organizational culture. Although most of these frameworks have been complemented later,[15] for the sake of this study the focus is on the *original* internal control frameworks as they address the subject of this study.

3.2.2 COSO

The framework from the Committee of Sponsoring Organizations of the Treadway Commission (COSO 1992) is the most common internal control framework in practice.[16] According to COSO,[17] internal control is a process that provides reasonable assurance for the achievement of the following three objective categories:

- Effectiveness and efficiency of operations
- Reliability of financial reporting
- Compliance with applicable laws and regulations[18]

As illustrated in Fig. 3.2, COSO divides the internal control process into five interrelated components: control environment, risk assessment, control activities, information and communication, and monitoring. As shown on the left side of the figure, COSO illustrates the interrelations of the components as a pyramid. For example, while the control environment builds the broad foundation, monitoring is illustrated at the top of the pyramid as the supervising function of the internal control process. The COSO cube at the right side shows interrelations between the five components and the three objective categories, and exemplifies that they can be

---

[12] Various other frameworks, standards and guidance exist that relate to internal control such as the guideline on internal control and risk management from the Hong Kong Institute of Certified Public Accountants (HKICPA), the standards from The Institute of Internal Auditors (IIA), the EFQM-Model from the European Foundation for Quality Management, ISO 9000:2000 from the International Organization of Standardization, the IT-framework COBIT from the Information Systems Audit and Control Associations (ISACA) and the Framework for Internal Control in Banking Organisations from the Basle Committee on Banking Supervision.

[13] See also Sect. 2.1.1.

[14] Campbell (2003, p. 3).

[15] Complementary versions or alternative guidance will be mentioned in the footnotes in the respective sections.

[16] For example, Anderson et al. (2006), Kinney (2000a) and Ramos (2006).

[17] The COSO definition was introduced in Sect. 2.1.1.

[18] See also Sect. 2.1.1.

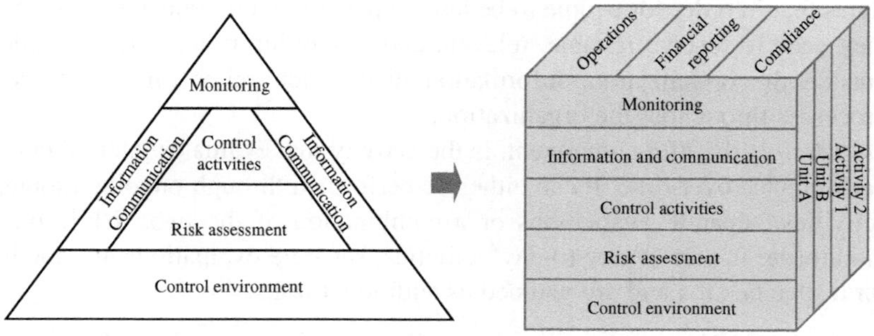

Fig. 3.2 The COSO framework.
Source: COSO (1992, p. 17, 19)

applied to any unit or activity of the organization.[19] For any organizational objective (top of the cube) and any organizational instance (right side of the cube), the five components (front of the cube) can be applied.

The following paragraphs briefly summarize the five components:

- The *control environment* builds the foundation for the entire internal control process. Influenced by management style and the manner in which the board fulfills its oversight duty, it is about how authority, responsibility, and discipline are assigned in daily business and how people are selected, organized and promoted. Having a pervasive impact on people's integrity, ethical values and competence, the control environment is typically associated with organizational culture.[20]
- *Risk assessment*, the second component, captures the risks from internal and external sources and forms the basis for an appropriate mitigation of risks that threaten the organization's ability to achieve its objectives. A precondition for risk assessment is objective setting, which must be integrated with the value chain and the various functions such as sales, production, marketing, and finance.[21]
- *Control activities*, the third component, are designed to address the identified risks and assure that risks are mitigated in a way that the organization achieves its objectives. Controls can be more proactive, such as directive and preventive controls, or more reactive, such as detective and corrective controls. They can be automatic such as an IT application, or they can be manual such as physical checks of inventory.[22]
- *Information and communication*, the fourth component, surround the other components of internal control and occur throughout the organization. COSO

[19]COSO (1992, p. 19).
[20]COSO (1992, pp. 19–29).
[21]COSO (1992, pp. 33–48).
[22]COSO (1992, pp. 59–68).

states that in order for people to be able to perform their control responsibilities they need to receive reliable, relevant and timely information from inside and outside the organization. Information distribution relies on communication processes throughout the organization.[23]

- *Monitoring*, the fifth component, is the activity that evaluates internal control's performance over time. It can either be performed through ongoing monitoring activities, separate evaluations or a combination of the two. While ongoing monitoring is part of day-to-day activities, separate evaluations are conducted for a specific area and are planned as additional tasks.[24]

These five COSO components apply to all types of organizations, from small to large entities, and from singular departments or business units within the organization as a whole.[25] The internal control process is integrated with the management process and is seen as a multidirectional iterative process in which almost any control component can and will influence another. When internal control is effective, it is an integral system that uses synergy and linkage among the control components to respond dynamically to changing environments.[26] COSO (1992, p. 16) reemphasizes that internal control relies significantly on how management runs the business. For example, a management group that sees internal control as an administrative burden will surely have different outcomes on internal control's quality than a management that integrates internal control within the business.[27]

Discussion: In general, the COSO framework provides a pragmatic and holistic approach, building a common terminology for internal control. The five components give an idea of what must be there so that internal control works properly. With regard to culture, the control environment represents many of the "soft" control factors, and links internal control with organizational culture. Hence, COSO strongly promotes the importance of cultural aspects for internal control. For example, it emphasizes the role of the tone at the top and leadership for internal control effectiveness, and makes aware that the absence of these aspects can lead to informal circumvention of formal control mechanisms by employees. Thus, the framework implicitly discusses that control and culture are interdependent and therefore supports the objective of this study. From a research perspective, the

[23] COSO (1992, pp. 49–58).

[24] COSO (1992, pp. 69–78).

[25] COSO (1992, p. 16).

[26] COSO (1992, p. 5).

[27] COSO (1992, p. 16). COSO released a framework on Enterprise Risk Management (COSO ERM) in 2004. The ERM framework does not supersede or otherwise amend the 1992 control framework. Rather, it offers alternative guidance that gives more weight to risk and strategy (see COSO 2004: enterprise risk management – integrated framework). To support companies in implementing the Sarbanes-Oxley requirements, in 2006 COSO published guidelines for smaller companies with respect to internal control over financial reporting (see COSO 2006: Internal Control over Financial Reporting – Guidance for Smaller Public Companies). COSO released an exposure draft for an additional guidance that focuses on monitoring (COSO 2008).

framework has also its limitations. The control environment gives the impression of containing many important elements of control (and culture) that do not fit in one of the other components, and as a result are collected in one component. COSO sets functions, beliefs, and other organizational activities next to each other without clearly separating their different levels and purposes. For example, integrity and ethical values, commitment to competence, and board of directors and audit committee are three separate elements of the control environment.[28] The criterion for this categorization seems intuitively unclear: while board of directors is a function, commitment to competence is a principle. For studying internal control and organizational culture in more depth, the framework contributes by supporting the importance of culture for control and providing a pragmatic checklist-like overview, but does not have a systematic approach to address the issue.

3.2.3 CoCo

The Canadian Institute of Chartered Accountants (CICA) issued a framework called Criteria on Control (CoCo 1995b). The CoCo framework builds on COSO, but takes a slightly broader approach. In contrast to COSO, CoCo adds internal elements and defines the three objective categories of internal control as following:

- Effectiveness and efficiency of operations
- Reliability of *internal* and *external* reporting
- Compliance with applicable laws and regulations and *internal policies*[29]

CoCo's broader approach is reflected in its terminology. Instead of using the term *internal control*, CoCo writes about the term *control* in general. The CoCo framework states that in any organization of people, the essence of control is based on four categories: purpose, commitment, capability, and monitoring and learning (see also Fig. 3.3). CoCo (1995b, p. 2) focuses on the smallest unit of the organization, the individual person.

A person performs a *task*, guided by an understanding of its *purpose* (the objective to be achieved) and supported by *capability* (information, resources, supplies and skills). The person will need a sense of *commitment* to perform the task well over time. The person will *monitor* his or her performance and the external environment to *learn* about how to do the task better and changes to be made. The same is true of any team or work group.[30]

Based on the four categories, CoCo articulates 20 criteria of control. The following briefly summarizes the four groups of criteria:

[28] Other elements of the control environment are management's philosophy and operating style, organizational structure, assignment of authority and responsibility, and human resource policies and practices (COSO 1992, pp. 19–29).

[29] CoCo (1995b, p. 2). Emphasis added.

[30] Emphasis added.

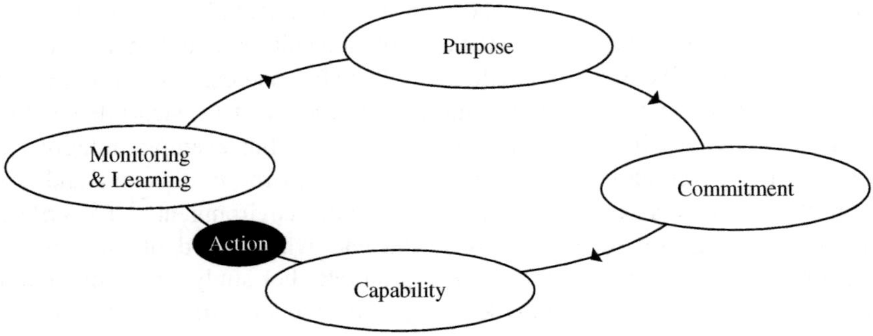

Fig. 3.3 The CoCo framework.
Source: CoCo (1995b)

- *Purpose criteria* provide a sense of the organization's direction. They address objectives, risks and opportunities, policies, planning and performance targets and indicators.[31]
- *Commitment criteria* provides a sense of the organization's identity and addresses ethical values, human resource policies, authority, responsibility, and accountability and mutual trust.[32]
- *Capability criteria* provide a sense of the organization's competence. They deal with knowledge, skills and tools, communication processes, information, co-ordination and control activities.[33]
- *Monitoring and learning criteria* provide a sense of the organization's evolution. They involve reviewing the internal and external environments, monitoring performance against targets, challenging assumptions, reassessing information needs and systems, establishing follow-up procedures and assessing the effectiveness of control.[34]

The CoCo framework provides a holistic perspective and can be useful in making decisions on the organization's designing, evaluating and reporting on control.[35] Compared to COSO, CoCo adds the perspective of the individual and makes clear that control is a continuous learning process. Although it provides important additions to the COSO framework from the US, the Canadian CoCo framework finds less attention in practice.[36]

[31] CoCo (1995b, p. 10).

[32] CoCo (1995b, p. 14).

[33] CoCo (1995b, p. 17).

[34] CoCo (1995b, p. 21).

[35] IFAC (2006, p. 5). CoCo (1995b) provides a comparison of COSO and CoCo (in Appendix 1).

[36] CoCo released in 2006 an updated version of the 1995 framework: Internal Control 2006: The next Generation of Certification Guidance for Management (see CoCo 2006a, b). It was the same as for COSO – additional guidance for smaller companies in internal control over financial reporting was developed (see CoCo 2007).

Discussion: The CoCo framework contributes to internal control concepts by adding internal elements to the aforementioned COSO framework. It also states that control "rests ultimately on the people assuming responsibility for their decisions and actions".[37] In contrast to COSO, which takes a view primarily at the organizational level, CoCo emphasizes the importance of each individual in performing control. The framework offers an alternative terminology, which seems intuitively more logical than the COSO approach. The criteria groups are closely related to each other and form a closed circle in which the individual and the organization can learn over time. Cultural aspects are particularly considered in the commitment criteria group. In this group of criteria, the importance that people work with ethical values and integrity is discussed. If people find organizational values acceptable they will be more likely to continue to encourage making improvement to the organization. In the same category it is discussed that people must have authority and bear responsibility for specific areas so they can be held accountable. CoCo highlights the need for open communication in order to establish trust between people. All these aspects concern interrelations between culture and control and vice versa. Likewise for COSO, CoCo does not provide an integrated and systematic approach on the interrelation between internal control and organizational culture. Nevertheless, CoCo offers important insights on cultural aspects, which are clearly distinctive from other frameworks.

3.2.4 Turnbull

The Turnbull guidance from the United Kingdom was released by the Institute of Chartered Accountants of England and Wales (ICAEW 1999). Turnbull takes the same objective categories as the aforementioned CoCo control framework. It promotes a principles-based guidance and, as such, is not as detailed as the aforementioned control frameworks. Turnbull differs from the COSO and CoCo framework as it is part of the Combined Code, which is a mandatory guidance for listed companies in the United Kingdom.[38] The guidance is based on a "comply or explain" clause. Such a clause requires companies to either follow the principles from Turnbull, otherwise they must explain why they do not. In alignment with COSO and CoCo, Turnbull sees control consisting of operational, financial and compliance aspects, and emphasizes that all people in an organization are responsible for internal control. Also, Turnbull promotes the importance of an embedded internal control within all business activities.[39] The Turnbull guidance builds strongly on COSO and CoCo and provides little additional insight.

[37] CoCo (1995b, p. 14).

[38] See ICAEW (1999). Based on a request of the London Stock Exchange, Turnbull was established to provide guidance for directors of listed companies.

[39] Turnbull was reviewed after the business scandals early in 2000, but only a few changes were made (IFAC 2006, p. 7).

Discussion: Turnbull offers little new insight for research on internal control and organizational culture. With regard to culture, Turnbull states that a company's system of internal control will reflect its control environment.[40] In the appendix, the guidance provides questions in order to assess the company's risk and control processes. One of them addresses organizational culture with the following question: "Does the company's culture, code of conduct, human resource policies and performance reward systems support the business objectives and risk management and internal control system?" This, however, is the only explicit link to organizational culture that the guidance offers. Therefore it does not provide any profound insights on the interrelation between control and culture.

3.2.5 Reflection

COSO, as the most prominent framework, takes the stance of an organizational setting as a whole and lists various functions, principles and aspects that should be established for an effective control environment. CoCo, the Canadian complement to COSO, takes the view of the individual and examines what must be there so the individual performs control effectively. Finally, Turnbull, the mandatory guidance from the United Kingdom, builds on COSO and CoCo and provides a principle-based approach. IFAC (2006) compares the three concepts and concludes that all three interpret internal control as a process that considers operational, financial and compliance risks. All three frameworks interpret control as an integral part of the organization.[41]

These concepts' primary purpose is to support practice by providing commonly accepted guidance. They define important elements of control including their interrelations[42] and improve the communication among involved parties in a pragmatic matter. They can build an evaluation tool for third parties,[43] offer a common language for reporting on internal control, and finally can set a quality signal to outsiders.[44] These practice-oriented concepts also provide a source for research. They provide an overview of internal control and what needs to be considered by researchers. All three frameworks consider the importance of organizational culture for internal control. For the purpose of the research objective of this study, these frameworks, provide limited input. As they are relatively pragmatic they give little systematic insight on how culture affects internal control, or how internal control can affect organizational culture. Instead these frameworks set

[40] ICAEW (1999, p. 7).

[41] IFAC (2006, p. 5).

[42] CoCo (1995b, p. 19).

[43] CoCo (1995b, p. 19).

[44] COSO (1992, p. 137).

partially different levels, functions and aspects equal to each other even though they are different in nature. Culture and control are linked in these control frameworks, but not in a systematic fashion.

In sum, the literature review on internal control demonstrates that in research surprisingly little attention is spent on (1) the comprehensive view of internal control[45] and (2) internal control-related ethical and behavioral issues in particular.[46] In fact, the comprehensive view of internal control is just barely becoming its own research discipline.[47] Therefore, the focus in the last three sections was on three practice-oriented internal control guidance in order to analyze how they relate internal control to organizational culture and vice versa. Because the internal control literature provides limited input on the interrelation between control and culture, the literature review continuous with a focus to the general management accounting and control area.

3.3 Management Accounting and Control

3.3.1 Research Overview

Because the comprehensive view of internal control is closely related to management control, and often interpreted as part of it, the following provides a brief overview of the consideration of (organizational) culture in management accounting and control research. In contrast to internal control, the broader management accounting and control area is a well established research discipline.

A large impact on management control research had the framework from Anthony (1965), who classified control into strategic planning, management control, and operational control. While Anthony provides a general framework for the field of management control, his approach gives relatively little attention to organizational culture. A major influence on research that considers organizational culture for control has the framework from Ouchi (1979). His framework, which will be discussed in more detail later in this section, builds on three control mechanisms: market, bureaucracy and clan. Representing organizational culture, the clan mechanism is based on socialization processes that eliminate goal incongruence among individuals.[48] Ouchi's study was one of the early approaches to conceptualize culture and control in one framework, and influenced many later concepts. One of the major terminologies in management control is the one from Merchant (1985) and more recently Merchant and van der Stede (2007), who further developed Ouchi's framework for the management control field. By re-labeling Ouchi's

---

[45] More attention is spent on the focused view of internal control.

[46] See Merchant and Van der Stede (2007).

[47] Maijoor (2000, p. 102).

[48] For more details see Sect. 3.3.2.

terminology into result controls, action controls, and personnel/cultural controls,[49] Merchant's terminology is based on the control objective.[50] A different, alternative framework offers Simons (1995), who is concerned with how strategy can be implemented in management control systems.[51] His distinction of control systems into belief systems, boundary systems, diagnostic control systems and interactive control systems considers cultural aspects as well.[52] The frameworks from Ouchi, Merchant and Simons are briefly discussed and related to this study here.

3.3.2 Ouchi

Most research on the role of culture and control "roots" or refers to the work of Ouchi (1979).[53] Ouchi is concerned with the design of control in order to achieve cooperation among individuals that share only partially congruent objectives. Three basic types of control mechanisms are distinguished: market, bureaucracy and clan.

- The *market mechanism* represents the mechanism that deals with how individual contributions can be precisely measured and rewarded. The market requires that all information is included in the price mechanisms (e.g., the contribution of each organizational member in an organizational setting can be measured exactly and rewarded).[54]
- The *bureaucratic mechanism* relies on a mixture of close evaluation of individuals' performance and reinforcing feelings of commitment to the organization by authority in hierarchies (e.g., commitment is achieved by both compliance mechanisms and by members' identification with the organization).[55]
- The *clan mechanism* is based on a selection of members and on socialization processes that eliminate goal incongruence among organizational members. The clan is based on informal channels and assures that the objectives of the individuals "substantially overlap" with the organizational objectives.[56]

---

[49] Another example of framework that roots in Ouchi's work is the one from Whitley (1992). Based on four characteristics that considerably differ among institutional contexts, he defines four distinct types of controls: bureaucratic, output, delegated and patriarchal.

[50] For more details see Sect. 3.3.2.

[51] See also Simons 2008.

[52] For more details see Sect. 3.3.3.

[53] For example, Abernethy and Brownell (1997), Birnberg and Snodgrass (1988), Collier (2005), Dent (1991), Lange (2008), Merchant and Van der Stede (2007).

[54] See Ouchi (1979).

[55] Ouchi (1979, p. 835).

[56] Ouchi (1979, pp. 836-837).

The market is an efficient mechanism because its only social requirement[57] is a norm of reciprocity.[58] Each individual is permitted to pursue non-organizational goals, but will then result in personal loss of reward. The bureaucracy requires a norm of reciprocity and also a legitimate authority, which has the power to evaluate performance and enhance feelings of commitment. Finally, the clan is based on not only a norm of reciprocity and legitimate authority, but also on shared values and beliefs. The clan therefore requires the highest social requirements. Ouchi clarifies that these three control mechanisms overlap in organizational settings and occur in various combinations, but for research it makes sense to analyze them as conceptually distinct.[59]

Discussion: Ouchi introduced culture in a research framework into the control literature. By defining the clan mechanism, Ouchi provides a basic classification for control that includes cultural/informal aspects. The clan is not relying on explicit prices or rules but rather on implicit social agreements based on values and beliefs. This terminology shows how closely related formal and informal control mechanisms are. Recognizing culture (the clan) as a control mechanism itself, Ouchi posits that culture has an impact on the control outcome, and also implicitly includes the other direction, how control influences culture, by stating that the clan has specific social requirements which need to be reached. Despite these innovations in the control literature, Ouchi's framework has its limitations. The terminology gives few systematic answers as to how much bureaucratic and market mechanisms rely on "culture" as well in order not to be informally undermined. Shared values and beliefs are only a social requirement for the clan mechanism. Referring to business and accounting scandals, it is questionable whether shared values and beliefs are not a requirement – at least for the bureaucratic form. While focusing on the distinction between different types of controls, Ouchi places little emphasis on how these controls interrelate. The interrelation of controls, however, is important in order to explain the effectiveness of a control system as a whole. As will be discussed later, Ouchi's frameworks found relatively weak empirical support. The way the clan is conceptualized in order to grasp culture seems to be difficult to prove in empirical research. A reason for this might be the combination of economic views (market, bureaucracy) with more social views (clan), which looks ad hoc constructed rather than being a consistent terminology.[60] Ouchi's contribution is to offer an early approach for culture and control. Seeing culture as a control

[57]Ouchi interprets social requirement as the minimum of agreement among people, which is necessary to employ a control.

[58]A norm of reciprocity "assures that, should one party in a market transaction attempt to cheat another, that the cheater, if discovered, will be punished by all members of the social system, not only by the victim and his or her partners" (Ouchi 1979, p. 838).

[59]Ouchi (1979, p. 834).

[60]Speklé (2001, p. 107) points out: "It is almost as if Ouchi suddenly shifts perspectives, adopting a fundamentally different view of the world. Implicitly, individuals in market and bureaucratic control archetypes are treated as "economic men" (or perhaps "administrative men"), whereas those in clan-like organizations are apparently held to be more aptly described as "social animals"".

mechanism itself, however, provides a limited perspective on the potential that organizational culture offers in explaining the interrelations of controls.

3.3.3 Merchant

Merchant (1985) and Merchant and Van der Stede (2007)[61] further developed Ouchi's terminology. Taking the management control perspective, the framework is concerned with how organizational members can be motivated to follow the organizational interests rather than others. The framework is based on the object of control.[62] By renaming Ouchi's classification, Merchant divides the types of control into action, result, and personnel/cultural controls:[63]

- *Result controls* define the outputs that are expected to employees. Often, the achievement of the results is reinforced by rewards. Result controls are adequate if performance is known and measurable, employees are able to influence outputs, and employees perceive managers' authority as legitimate.
- *Action controls* evaluate the means to the end and not the result in itself. Action controls prohibit undesirable behavior (behavioral constraints), derive desired employees' behavior from plans (pre-action review), and monitor behavior by direct observation or formal controls (action accountability).
- *Personnel/cultural controls* take into account recruitment, training, and the promotion of norms to reinforce employee self-control.[64] While personnel controls are primarily designed so that employees will design the desired tasks satisfactorily on their own, cultural controls shape organizational norms.[65]

Merchant and van der Stede discuss the advantages and disadvantages of the specific types of controls. They provide a better understanding of what it means to be able to measure outcomes and how specific outcomes should be judged. They also discuss both direct costs and indirect costs for specific types of control. Considering that all controls are behavioral controls, they discuss the concepts of tight and loose control to motivate people to work in the best interest of the organizational objectives.[66]

Discussion: Merchant contributes by re-labeling Ouchi's terminology and relating it to typical management control issues. The terminology is simple and relatively easily adaptable to different organizational settings. Distinguishing between

---

[61] Although the framework today relates to both Merchant and van der Stede, for reasons of simplicity the study will usually refer to Merchant who originally developed the framework.

[62] Merchant and Van der Stede (2007, p. 16).

[63] See also Merchant (1998) and Merchant and Van der Stede (2007).

[64] Merchant (1998, p. 121).

[65] Merchant and Van der Stede (2007, p. 76).

[66] Merchant and Van der Stede (2007, p. 225).

personnel/cultural controls (input), action controls (process), and result controls (output) provide a classification that is useful for research and practice. With regard to culture, Merchant's terminology includes culture as a separate type of control. Cultural controls "exist to shape organizational behavioral norms and to encourage employees to monitor and influence one another's behavior".[67] Culture is seen as an input control. Having organizational members that work with the same norms ensures that they work in best interests to the organization and that they will monitor one another. Therefore, an important contribution from Merchant (and van der Stede) is that they emphasize culture in the management control terminology. In the cultural controls the framework includes aspects of both – how culture influences control, and how cultural controls can be reached in order to establish social norms, which will impact people's behavior. When analyzing the framework from a cultural point of view, however, it has similar limitations as the framework from Ouchi. If conceptualizing culture as a control mechanism is ignored, the fact that culture is similarly reflected and influenced by action/result controls than by the so-called cultural controls. Therefore, important questions such as how different types of controls interrelate or how formal controls are informally undermined are only addressed in the terminology in a limited way. While Merchant's framework makes sense from a control-objective perspective, when observing from a cultural perspective the framework has its limitations.

3.3.4 Simons

Simons (1995) addresses how strategy can be implemented through formal control systems.[68] He builds his theory on the problems that stem from the tension between innovation and control, profitability and growth, between the goals of the organization (the manager) and those of the employees, and between the opportunity to create value in a market and the limited amount of time and attention available to managers. According to Simons, effective control systems rely on balancing these tensions.[69] Managers can use four types of control systems, which Simons calls four levers of control: belief systems, boundary systems, diagnostic control systems and interactive control systems.

---

[67] Merchant and Van der Stede (2007, p. 76).

[68] See also Simons (2008). Simons provides an alternative approach in 2005 in which he identifies four factors that impact design decisions: customer definition, critical performance variables, creative tension, and commitment to others. In this theory diagnostic control systems and interactive networks are included as well. For the purpose of this study, the 1995 categorization, which includes belief systems and boundary systems provide a closer relation to this study and are therefore discussed here.

[69] Simons (2000, p. 4).

- A *belief system*, as the first lever of control, represents a set of formal definitions on the organizational values, purpose and direction of the organization. These systems are communicated formally through documents such as mission and statements of purpose. For example, they address what level of performance is desired and how the organization wants to create relationships internally and externally. Belief systems are used to inspire and guide the search for new opportunities.[70]
- A *boundary system*, as the second lever of control, sets boundaries for the acceptable domain of activities for organizational members. In contrast to a belief system, a boundary system is used to set limits in the search for new opportunities. Based on the business risks, boundary systems set limits to both business conduct and strategy.[71]
- A *diagnostic control system*, as the third lever of control, is used to motivate, monitor, and reward the achievement of specified goals. Diagnostic controls are the formal systems that managers apply in order to monitor organizational outcomes and correct deviations from preset standards of performance. They are used to make sure that everything is on track and no surprises will occur.[72]
- An *interactive control system,* as the fourth lever of control, is used to stimulate organizational learning and the emergence of new ideas and strategies.[73] Managers involve themselves regularly and personally in the decision activities of subordinates.[74] By focusing on strategic uncertainties, these formal information systems provide a bottom-up process to identify opportunities and threats.[75]

These four levers of control can work simultaneously to balance the organizational tensions discussed above. Managers must understand how these four types of systems must be used and what purpose they serve.[76] For example, while belief systems and interactive control systems rely on the positive and inspirational forces, boundary systems and diagnostic control systems build constraints and ensure compliance.[77] Moreover, diagnostic control systems facilitate single loop learning, while interactive control systems enhance double loop learning. Single loop learning keeps a process within desired boundaries, while double loop learning questions the foundation on which strategies have been formulated.[78] These four levers from Simons' work of 1995 provide a fundamental categorization of

---

[70] Simons (1995, pp. 33-34).

[71] Simons (1995, pp. 39-40). Similar to belief systems, they are communicated through formal documents and must be reinforced continuously within the organization.

[72] They relate to "output control" or "result control" which was discussed by Ouchi and Merchant (Simons 1995, p. 62, 76).

[73] Simons (1995, p. 7).

[74] Simons (1995, p. 95).

[75] Simons (1995, p. 91).

[76] Simons (1995, pp. 4-5).

[77] Simons (1995, pp. 7-8).

[78] Simons (1995, p. 106).

organizational design that has since been discussed and replicated in management accounting and control research.[79]

Discussion: Simons captures the complexity of large organizations by focusing various tensions within organizations and how these tensions are reflected in formal control systems. In his approach, belief systems and boundary systems are closely related to organizational culture. Simons emphasizes the need to establish formal value charters that provide purpose to organizational members and define clear boundaries within which people can work relatively autonomically.[80] Simons also underlines the importance of explaining the interrelations of control systems: "The power of the control levers does not lie in how each is used alone but rather in how they complement each other when used together".[81] By that, he also clarifies that the tightness of controls will vary depending on the levels and functions within organizations. With regard to culture, formal and informal aspects are discussed, but the primary focus is always the formal systems. Thus, the fact that control can include both formal and informal aspects is considered, but finds mainly consideration in how the formal systems are used in the control terminology.[82] As the primary focus is strategy implementation, Simons gives little consideration to aspects such as tone at the top or leadership, which are important in regard to whether control systems are informally undermined. Similar to Ouchi and Merchant, culture is discussed as primarily associated within specific types of control systems (belief systems and boundary systems). The focus is on strategy implementation and how organizational members can be motivated to follow the organizational objectives. Organizational culture is there, but in the background.

3.3.5 Reflection

While traditionally the discussion on the connection between control and culture is widely emphasized by Ouchi's "clan mechanism", more recent approaches such as those from Simons (1995) attempt to include culture in a more integrated fashion. Thus the earlier research, primarily concerned with grasping culture in the context of control, was interested in classifying controls in a manner that included culture. More recent research recognizes the need for going deeper and developing a better understanding of the interrelations between culture and control.

[79] For example, Collier (2005) and Merchant and Otley (2007).

[80] See Simons (1995, 2005).

[81] Simons (1995, p. 153).

[82] The reason for this is that Simons researches large and multinational organizations, in which interactions need to be based on formal systems in order to reach organizational members.

Control frameworks are useful in investigating specific organizational settings, and the suitability of specific forms of controls. After Ouchi's publication came out, the study of the clan/social/cultural control mechanisms raised some problems for accounting and control researchers. In several cases, the focus of the studies got back to the more "technical" controls (e.g., action control, results controls). For example, Eisenhardt (1985) builds on Ouchi's framework and finds empirical evidence for the relationship between task programmability and the type of compensation package. Her findings suggest that more programmed tasks require behavior controls, while less programmed tasks require more elaborate information systems and result-based controls. Although she builds on Ouchi's framework, she basically focuses on outcome and behavior controls and only mentions the "social control" mechanism as important in case the other two mechanisms do not work. Similar difficulties can be found in the study of Govindarajan and Fisher (1990). Although they considered the clan mechanisms in their empirical data, respondents did not seem to use social controls. As a result, they added the clan to the class of behavioral control, and concluded that it seems like people need be controlled either by their output or their behavior. Abernethy and Brownell (1997) build on a prior study from Rockness and Shields (1984) and collect empirical evidence that non-accounting controls, especially personnel forms of control, contribute to control effectiveness, when task characteristics are unsuitable to accounting controls. Moreover, in a setting with low task analyzability and high number of exceptions, such as R&D, programmed controls (e.g., accounting, behavior controls) appear unsuitable. Thus, in these cases the clan mechanism needs to be in place.

A study that is more successful in capturing cultural forms of control is from Birnberg and Snodgass (1988). They take the stance of national culture[83] and compare how US and Japanese workers perceive management control systems. Providing empirical evidence for Ouchi's and Eisenhardt's theoretical conceptions, their findings support that the less bureaucratic management control system will be perceived equally explicitly by Japanese workers as the more bureaucratic system is by their US counterparts.[84] This is a result which they interpret as supportive of the argument that culture affects control.

While the studies discussed so far look at specific types of control and their suitability to an organizational setting, Dent (1991) provides a major contribution to the research of culture in a social and organizational context.[85] His longitudinal field study in a railway company investigates organizational change by focusing on how new accounting practices were influenced by the emergent organizational

[83]A wide range of studies on national culture in the context of control offers Hofstede (for example, Hofstede 2001).

[84]Birnberg and Snodgrass (1988, p. 461). Their results suggest that Japanese firms should save costs: "This should result in a significant cost saving to Japanese firms. Such a saving may be large enough to defray all, or at least a significant portion, of the cost of "lifetime employment" offered Japanese workers".

[85]The study on accounting in its social and organizational context is particularly encouraged by Hopwood (for example, Hopwood 1978, 1983).

culture. The contribution of Dent's study is the detailed description of the cultural context and the analysis of its impact on accounting practices. Whitley (1999, p. 516) broadened the scope to the institutional context and highlights the variability of these contexts across firms, sectors, and societies, and explains possible reasons for differences. Control systems are seen as closely linked to the "broader patterns of work organization and labor management strategies." A more recent example of this stream of field research offer Efferin and Hopper (2007) who explore the socio-cultural aspects of management control in a Chinesian-Indonesian manufacturing company. They investigate the interaction between Chinese businessmen's values with the workers' Javanese culture of pribumi values. Despite the Javanese cultural setting, they found that Chinese owners' preferences for control resided, among others, with behavioral controls, few rewards tied to results and the use of group rewards.

A different approach is offered in Mikes' (2008) action research.[86] Based on two in-depth case studies in the banking industry, she builds theory for the design of enterprise risk management. Her concept distinguishes four ideal risk management types that form the "risk management mix" in a given organizational setting. Mikes' research is one of the first attempts to build theory for enterprise risk management and links concepts from practice-oriented control frameworks (COSO ERM framework from 2004) with management accounting and control research.

In sum, these existing studies focus on culture as a contextual factor that influences specific control and accounting outcomes. However, they do not give much attention on the other direction, namely, how control influences culture. Also, they provide very limited empirical evidence for the role of culture in the context of control. After reviewing the internal control literature as well as the broader management accounting and control literature, Sect. 3.4 formulates research theses, which build the starting point for the theory-building process in Part II.

3.4 Research Theses

The first part of the literature review confirmed that research on the link between internal control and organizational culture is still at an early stage. While internal control itself is relatively unexplored in research, its link to organizational culture is primarily addressed in practice-oriented internal control frameworks. The second part of the literature review broadened the scope to the field of management accounting and control research. In this research area an established body of literature exists on the link between culture and control. However, culture still seems to be difficult to grasp in research. Based on the research objective of this study, several issues have been identified from the literature review that this study attempts to address. These issues will be summarized in five research theses.

---

[86] See also Mikes (2005a, b).

(a) *Culture as a dependent variable (instead as an independent variable)*

Research in the accounting and control area typically interprets culture as an independent variable. In a given contextual setting (which culture is defined as being part of), specific control outcomes are possible. Dent (1991, p. 706) provides a good illustration of this view:

> The operation of work technologies in organizations is not a purely technical-rational affair. Rather, it is embedded in a cultural system of ideas (beliefs, knowledges) and sentiments (values), in which actions and artifacts are vested with symbolic qualities of meaning.... *Inevitably, therefore, accounting is likely to be implicated in organization's cultural systems.*[87]

This view implies that the researcher tries to understand the cultural setting in order to interpret specific accounting and control outcomes. For example, while accounting systems typically are not that different from country to country in a multinational organization, the way they are used might differ significantly depending on the cultural background.[88] Thus, the researcher tries to understand the different cultural backgrounds[89], and examines how these different backgrounds lead to different ways of applications by control performers. Moreover, the researcher could look at under which circumstances organizational culture can make a synergistic element to the control system and facilitate its consistent operation.[90] The focus of this type of studies looks at how culture influences control.

In contrast to this traditional management accounting and control view, research from sociology and social psychology proposes that, to some extent, management and other influences can establish and change the organizational culture over time.[91] A view that offers an important implication because not only is accounting and control influenced by culture but, in turn, culture can be influenced by accounting and control practices. Taking the stance that culture can be the dependent variable addresses Bhimani's critique that studies on culture often ignore how and why cultures change.[92] Organizational culture can then be interpreted as a mediator between control mechanisms as inputs and control outcomes.[93] Based on this argumentation the following thesis is developed:

---

[87] Emphasis added.

[88] Dent (1991, p. 729).

[89] In this example the different cultural backgrounds mean the different nationalities operating in an organizational culture.

[90] See Ouchi (1979).

[91] For example, O'Reilly and Chatman (1996) and Wiener (1988).

[92] See Bhimani (1999).

[93] It is not uncommon to change the direction of cause and effect relationships in management accounting and control research. For example, Simons (1990, p. 127) exploring the relationship between strategy and control, argued that research followed the question of how strategy can be implemented in management control systems, but failed to address the importance of management control systems in the strategy implementation process.

Thesis 1: Cause and effect between culture and control go in both directions. In a setting that investigates control, culture can be seen as a mediator between specific controls that influence culture, and culture in turn influences specific control outcomes.

(b) *Culture as meaning (instead as a category)*

Major frameworks for management accounting and control consider culture explicitly or implicitly as one or two categories of control, standing next to other categories, which represent more technical/formal controls. An example is the terminology from Merchant and Van der Stede, who define personnel/cultural controls[94] as one category that stands next to action controls and result controls.[95] Their framework is based on the control objective: is the objective to control the input (personnel/cultural controls), process (action controls), or the outcome (result controls)? From a cultural point view, these frameworks create the impression that other than cultural control types, such as action controls and result controls, have nothing to do with culture. Culture seems to be collected in one type of control and can be controlled by one type of control mechanism, which can be distinguished from other forms of control.

This study takes a different stance. It is argued that culture relates equally to formal and informal aspects, and to input, process and outcome in an organization. Through the existence of culture the definition and consideration of social (informal) controls in an organizational setting is possible. Nevertheless, culture is developed and expressed through both the informal/social and the formal control aspects. In the terminology of Merchant and Van der Stede's framework this means that culture is equally formed by the amount, content and purpose of result and action controls such as the so-called personnel/*cultural* controls. The following thesis can be derived:

Thesis 2: A framework for control and culture needs to be based on the cultural meaning. Thus, a distinction into different types of controls needs to integrate the cultural meaning (influence) of each type of control.

(c) *The degree of perceived explicitness (instead of the degree of formalism)*

In their lead article in *Management Accounting Research*, Nixon and Burns (2005) summarize that management control in the twenty-first century needs to re-balance the optimal mix between formal and social controls. Scholars recognize an overemphasis on the technical (formal) control mechanisms relative to social (informal)

[94] As discussed previously, these personnel/cultural controls represent hiring procedures and socialization processes in order to enhance employee self-control and establish organizational norms.

[95] See Sect. 3.3.3.

control mechanisms.[96] Thus, management accounting and control research should include more of the informal aspects. Although these discussions of formal versus social controls support the investigation of culture, they can also be misleading. From a cultural point of view, Birnberg and Snodgas's study shows that culture may not be primarily a question of the degree of formalism that is important for the overall effectiveness of the control system, but more the degree of perceived explicitness. Hence, what is more important for the overall effectiveness of the control system is whether controls are perceived explicitly or not by organizational members. This perceived explicitness is understood in this study as how clearly people perceive what is expected from them. If there are controls that are perceived as being explicit and that are outside of the formal system, then the formal system may be undermined. Conversely, in a setting where informal controls fail, explicitness can be reinforced by institute formal controls. Birnberg and Snodgass (1988, p. 454) state: "Thus the degree of formality present in a system is not the same as the degree of perceived explicitness". This study argues that it is much more a question of the degree of perceived explicitness compared to the degree of formalism, which is important for the overall effectiveness of a control system. This perceived explicitness is understood here as being established by both explicit and implicit influences.[97]

Thesis 3: A study of culture and control needs not only to consider the degree of formalism, but also, and at least equally importantly, the degree of perceived explicitness.

(d) *Focus the process between culture and action (instead the topics themselves)*

Cultural mechanisms often work below the surface and are then only observable as a result rather than a process leading to a result.[98] There is little understanding of the link between cultural elements, such as values and beliefs on the one hand and action on the other hand.[99] In the context of national culture, Whitley (1999, p. 508) states that studies tend to see the relation between culture and control as something mechanical: "Unfortunately, many of these [studies] tend to posit a rather mechanical connection between dominant norms and values in a society and control practices, which ignores the processes by which the former impinge upon the latter". In order to understand how culture can be influenced by control, a profound

[96] In the literature, control mechanisms are often traced back to the distinction whether they are formal or informal/social. Both are control mechanisms, defined by Das and Teng (1998, p. 493) as "the organizational arrangements designed to determine and influence what organizational members will do". Some authors argue that administrative/formal controls are those that are intentionally derived, while social controls are those that "emerge" unintentionally through social interactions. Others argue that anything that has written evidence is seen as formal control, while all other activities are informal.

[97] This study will not measure any "perceived explicitness" but uses this construct during the theory-building process hypothetically.

[98] See Keyton (2005).

[99] See Meglino and Ravlin (1998), Whitley (1999).

understanding needs to be established on the link between culture and behavior. If this link can be understood, then control mechanisms can be used that attempt to achieve the optimal cultural conditions. In order to progress in this area, the management accounting and control literature needs to be connected more in-depth to literatures from other fields that provide more profound knowledge on cultural issues. For instance, control mechanisms are not only discussed in the management control literature,[100] but also in the literature of organizational behavior,[101] and in more specific literature such as the one on ethical behavior in organizations.[102]

Thesis 4: Culture has a transcendental quality to control behavior, and a terminology that integrates culture with controls needs to be based on profound interdisciplinary theoretical foundation.

(e) *Interrelations between controls (instead distinguishing between controls)*

As mentioned before, the focus in management accounting and control research is often about which control mechanism is predominant for a specific organizational setting. Researchers, however, identified the need to explore the relationships between the various types of controls. Abernethy and Brownell (1997, p. 246) remark that relatively little is known about the interrelations between controls even though in reality different types of controls occur simultaneously. They propose that "with a strengthened theoretical basis, research could begin to explore the implications of combinations of controls, studying their interactive effects on important organizational outcomes". An example of research on the interrelations between controls offers Simons. For instance, he clarifies that typically managers use only one control system interactively while others are used diagnostically.[103] This system should be used interactively, which addresses strategic uncertainties:

> If the organization has n control systems – planning systems, cost accounting systems, human resource systems, brand revenue systems, project monitoring systems, capital-acquisition systems, profit planning systems, and so forth – one of those systems will be used interactively and $(n-1)$ systems will be used diagnostically.[104]

Some control types work well in concert with each other, while others do not. While Simons strongly considers the interrelations between controls, in many other

[100] See Chenhall (2003).

[101] See O'Reilly and Chatman (1996).

[102] See Stansbury and Barry (2007) and Treviño et al. (2006).

[103] See Sect. 3.3.4.

[104] Simons (1995, pp. 102-103). From a strategic perspective, using control systems interactively provides learning and experimentation. If management uses too many systems interactively it risks "information overload, superficial analysis, a lack of perspective, and potential paralysis" because of limited energy and attention. Simons (1995, pp. 116-117) explains that in a crisis, managers temporarily use several or all systems interactively in order diagnose the problems and be able to survive.

studies the question why and how different types of control work together is weakly addressed in the control terminology.[105] To provide a better understanding of the interrelations among control types is important.[106]

Thesis 5: Interpreting controls through their cultural meaning provides explanations for the function of specific controls in an organizational setting and how various controls interrelate when applying them simultaneously.

These five theses provide a starting point for the own academic contribution in the next three parts. The five research theses are summarized in Table 3.1.

Based on these theses, Part II presents the own field visit study in which 31 senior-level people from 21 companies have contributed in order to provide an empirical grounding for internal control and organizational culture. Part III delves into the literature and combines insights from sociology, social psychology, and

Table 3.1 Overview of research theses

	Content	Description
Thesis 1	Culture as a dependent variable (instead as an independent variable)	Cause and effect between culture and control go in both directions. In a setting that investigates control, culture can be seen as a mediator between specific controls that influence culture, and culture in turn influences specific control outcomes
Thesis 2	Culture as meaning (instead as one type of control)	A framework for control and culture needs to be based on the cultural meaning. Thus, a distinction into different types of controls needs to integrate the cultural meaning (influence) of each type of control
Thesis 3	The degree of perceived explicitness (instead of the degree of formalism)	A study of culture and control needs not only to consider the degree of formalism, but also, and at least equally importantly, the degree of perceived explicitness
Thesis 4	Focus the process between culture and action (instead the topics themselves)	Culture has a transcendental quality to control behavior, and a terminology that integrates culture with controls needs to be based on profound interdisciplinary theoretical foundation
Thesis 5	Interrelations between controls (instead distinguishing between controls)	Interpreting controls through their cultural meaning provides explanations for the function of specific controls in an organizational setting and how various controls interrelate when applying them simultaneously

[105] See the discussions in Sect. 3.3.

[106] Lange (2008, p. 711).

research on organizational corruption in order to provide theoretical explanations for the observed data from the field. Part IV synthesizes the empirical and theoretical insights and presents the core result of the study: A new framework on control and culture which clearly distinguishes itself from existing research in management accounting and control and addresses the issues from literature such as discussed in this chapter.

Part II
Field study

Chapter 4
Drivers for Control Effectiveness

4.1 Purpose of Field Study

Internal control, as introduced in Sect. 2.1, represents the means to achieve organizational objectives. More specifically, if internal control is effective, it provides reasonable assurance for the achievement of effective and efficient operations, for reliable internal and external reporting, and for compliance with laws, regulations, and internal policies.[1] Also, it has been clarified that in order to achieve control effectiveness, the organization relies fundamentally on the people that perform control.[2] Therefore, organizational culture, as introduced in Sect. 2.2, is important for internal control. Organizational culture is about how consensus is reached among organizational members, and the underlying values and norms that guide people's behavior. Thus, Chap. 2 demonstrated the importance of internal control and organizational culture. Nevertheless, as the accounting and control literature review in Chap. 3 confirms, relatively limited clarity is given on what exactly senior-level people do to influence a culture for effective internal control. This lack of research on the influence of control on culture is also confirmed in practice. Ben Heinemann, a former General Counsel of General Electric, writes in the *Harvard Business Review* of April 2007 (103):

> The principles and practices top management follows to drive a performance-with-integrity culture deep into a company is ... not yet receiving appropriate discussion and debate within the senior ranks of the business community and within the burgeoning governance community of investors, analysts, academics, advocates, and interest groups.

The field study presented in this chapter addresses Heinemann's statement by providing a wide range of principles and practices senior-level people perceive as drivers to achieve internal control effectiveness. As discussed earlier, if internal control is effective, it will likely contribute to performance and also relies on people

[1] See Sect. 2.1.1.
[2] See Sect. 2.1.4.

J. Pfister, *Managing Organizational Culture for Effective Internal Control*,
Contributions to Management Science,
DOI: 10.1007/978-3-7908-2340-0_4,

that work in alignment with the organizational objectives.[3] Thus, if internal control is effective, a "performance-with-integrity culture" such as stated in Heinemann's quote can be reasonably achieved.

Keeping in mind the overall objective of building theory that explains how principles and practices affect organizational culture, and how culture in turn, affects control effectiveness, this field study provides an empirical grounding for the further theory-building process in Parts III and IV.[4] The field study has two primary interests:

1. *What principles and practices do senior-level people perceive as "drivers" for a culture that enhances internal control effectiveness?*
2. *Where do senior-level people typically expect the roots of control failures?*[5]

As illustrated in Fig. 4.1, these two questions provide a frame for the further theory-building process.[6] The first question addresses the left side of the figure and asks which principles and practices senior-level people perceive as drivers for control effectiveness. The second question addresses the right side of the figure, which indicates the degree of control effectiveness. As defined in Sect. 2.1.3, the degree of control effectiveness is inversely related to the amount and significance of control failures. Thus, the more attention is given to these roots of control failures, the more likely it is that internal control will be effective. The assumption here is that when knowing and addressing the roots of control failures, a higher degree of control effectiveness as an outcome can be achieved.

How does this field study setup build a foundation for further theory-building? In this study, organizational culture lies between the drivers (as input) and the degree of control effectiveness (as outcome). In other words, the drivers affect organiza-

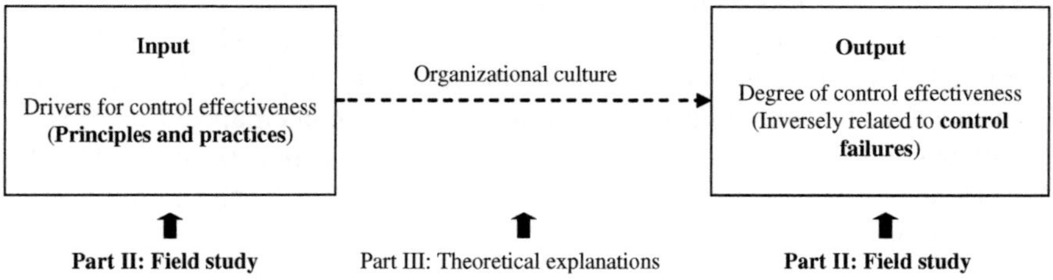

Fig. 4.1 Field study setup

---

[3] See Sect. 2.1.3.

[4] Although existing internal control frameworks address organizational culture, they do not provide a consistent approach to the principles and practices that senior-level people apply to develop a "culture" for effective controls.

[5] More details about the field study setup will be provided in Sect. 4.2. Examples of interview questions are provided in Appendix D.

[6] These two main questions are intentionally broad in order to gather a wide range of principles and practices and not limit the focus in advance. Otherwise, important issues would be excluded by the research setup.

tional culture, and in turn, organizational culture affects internal control effectiveness. As illustrated in Fig. 4.1, this link between culture and control is made via "organizational culture" which will be further investigated in Part III.

The purpose of the field study also needs clarification. First, as this study focuses on general principles and practices as input for further analysis, the purpose is not to evaluate specific cases, or to compare company cultures and control systems. Rather, the focus is on finding general insights across companies, industries and functions in order to generate a wide range of possible principles and practices that provide input for further theory-building. To what extent these principles and practices are relevant for each type of company is part of further research applying other methods (e.g., survey, case study).

Second, the field study builds on perceptions of senior-level people. The study therefore does not investigate whether professionals apply these principles and practice in practice. Asking about perceptions of ideal principles and practices supports the premise that people are more likely to speak freely. It also ensures that the answers given are underlined by a consistent purpose. For example, it is not of interest that this study gathers principles and practices that are applied in practice – senior-level people know they are not the "best" practices. Therefore, asking for "ideal" principles and practices ensures gathering answers with a consistent purpose.

These two aspects should be remembered throughout this chapter as they constitute an important part of the methods chosen. In the following sections, method, sample, proceeding, and analysis are discussed. This part will also further specify the interview questions.[7] Thereafter, the results from the field will be presented. Finally, at the end of the chapter is a discussion on strengths and limitations, the relation to practice-oriented frameworks such as COSO and CoCo[8] as well as how the field results provide input for further analysis.

4.2 Methods

4.2.1 Semi-Structured Interviews

A theory-building research design typically relies on qualitative research methods, even in the accounting and control field, for which only "numbers" count – traditionally and intuitively.[9] In alignment with the research purpose, the strength

[7] See Sect. 4.2.4.

[8] See Sect. 3.2.

[9] In fact, qualitative research in management control research is commonly accepted. See, for example, Ahrens and Chapman (2004), Collier (2005), Eisenhardt (1989), Mikes (2005b), and Simons (1995, 2005). Qualitative research differs from quantitative research in the sense that it is concerned primarily with words rather than numbers (Bryman and Bell 2003, p. 280).

of qualitative research is to gather information from a variety of perspectives.[10] The phenomena are complex, and studying senior-level people's principles and practices reveals a "symbolic and subjective component",[11] which can be captured by qualitative research. Semi-structured interviews, which are chosen as the research method for this study, are based on a set of subjects to be explored. They allow the researcher to ask follow-up questions during the interview, which generates more depth of the data gathered. Semi-structured interviews provide flexibility so new issues (that the researcher did not expect in advance) can be discussed during the interview. Such interviewing supports gathering insights that are rich in points.[12] Semi-structured guidance provides a certain interview direction, but the researcher can still follow another "surprising" path that can finally lead to "rich" insights and new theoretical patterns. Nevertheless, qualitative research for internal control and organizational culture is still underutilized.[13]

In contrast, a questionnaire or structured interview, as alternative methods, would focus the possible range of answers to the limited and specific questions defined in advance by the researcher. Questionnaires and structured interviews rely significantly on the researcher's background, his or her understanding of the topic, and the existing literature.[14] Thus, in a practical oriented setting which is relatively unexplored by prior literature,[15] questionnaires and structured interviews are more likely to be biased by the researcher's background and understanding of the topic than semi-structured interviews.

For exploring control and culture, semi-structured interviews are chosen to ensure the theory-building process builds on adequate practical input, and allows gathering data that is not expected in advance. Consequently, in alignment with the overall research objective and design, the stage of research and field study purpose, semi-structured interviews have been found as the optimal method.

4.2.2 Sample Choice

The sample of interviewees consists of 31 senior-level people from 21 medium to large-scale companies from the US and Switzerland, many of them well known and

[10] See also Treviño et al. (2003).

[11] See Conger (1998) and Treviño et al. (2003).

[12] See Alvesson and Skoldberg (2000), Jackall (1988), Mintzberg (1973), and Kunda (1992).

[13] See Sect. 3.2.

[14] See Bryman and Bell (2003).

[15] Such a practical-oriented setting matches the setup of this study.

operating internationally.[16] This section provides some basics on the sample choice and discusses:

- The challenge of accessing senior-level people
- The site selection and
- The email request

4.2.2.1 The Challenge of Accessing Senior-Level People

Accessing people at the senior level from major companies poses challenges. When approaching companies from the outside, they seem to be like fortresses. Barriers and other obstacles are installed in order to not be overwhelmed by requests from external parties such as business press, researchers and others. Hence, accessing senior-level people can be a frustrating and seemingly impossible task when trying to enter a company through its "public" doors.[17] In addition, people at the senior level have full schedules, multiple responsibilities with high priorities, and frequently are traveling.[18] Last but not least, from the perspective of senior-level people, time is money (also for a research interview). Therefore, it is, first, not self-evident to gain access to senior-level people; and second, it is challenging to convince them to participate in an interview. Despite these hurdles, to gain access to senior-level people, various institutions provided kind support. In Switzerland, the Institute for Accounting and Control at the University of Zurich has helped in addressing professionals through its social network. In the US, several centers from the Haas School of Business at the University of California at Berkeley have supported the project. In particular, the Haas Career Center, the Center for Financial Reporting and Management, and the Center for Responsible Business have all provided great assistance in contacting senior-level people.

4.2.2.2 Site Selection

As a result of the difficulty in accessing senior-level people, the site selection was not random. One basic rule defined beforehand was to gather as many different perspectives as possible. The goal was to gather a wide range of perspectives on practical insights in the area of internal control (which will be discussed Sect. 4.2.2.3). Another rule for the selection was to interview a maximum of three people from one company. In most of the companies there was one, in two companies two, and in four companies the maximum of three people were interviewed. Appropriate

---

[16] For an overview see Appendix B.

[17] These "public" doors primarily mean contact addresses on companies' homepages.

[18] Due to these facts, in one extreme case, the time between the initial request and conducting the actual interview was half a year.

to the field study's purpose, the people addressed were all at the senior level, and most of them worked in the areas of finance and internal auditing. Senior-level finance people have a profound knowledge and overview of all types of processes within the organization; therefore they have generally an understanding of the comprehensive view of internal control (including operations and compliance).[19] Likewise, internal auditors are concerned with aspects of strategy and risk management, operations, reporting, and compliance, and consequently have a comprehensive understanding of internal control. Also, they provide an outside perspective to line management as they (besides being managers themselves) are also evaluators of managers in the business line.[20] In sum, not only do senior finance and auditing people have a comprehensive perspective on internal control, they also have a particular interest in internal control as they represent top-level responsibilities.

4.2.2.3 E-Mail Request

Senior-level people have been contacted via email with a brief request that summarized the research project and purpose. The request mentioned that the project is about internal control and organizational culture. The initial request also stated that:

- Quotes are only used by confirmation from interviewees
- The study is not about comparing functions, companies, or industries
- Quotes from interviewees will be presented in a positive light

Senior-level people have been made aware that participating in an interview can be interesting and inspiring for them as well. Being interviewed provides an opportunity to reflect their work from a different viewpoint. These arguments brought positive willingness to participate in the project. Also, this setup ensured that senior-level people were willing to speak relatively freely about internal control matters. An important aspect in order to provide the researcher with practical insights that ensures the research is close enough to practice.

---

[19]As financial activities go up and down and cut across all levels and units of the organization, financial officers have a holistic insight into the processes of the organization. Financial managers are involved in setting plans and budgets, and track performance not only of finance, but also of operational and compliance aspects (COSO 1992, p. 6).

[20]Internal auditing usually indicates a department within an organization which provides independent, objective, assurance and consulting activities on behalf of the board (see Anderson 2003; FEE 2006, p. 6). COSO (1992, p. 84) states: "It should be recognized that the internal audit function does not – as some people believe – have primary responsibility for establishing or maintaining the internal control system. That, as noted, is the responsibility of the CEO, along with key managers with designated responsibilities (which may include the chief internal auditor)". The purpose of internal auditing is to add value by evaluating and improving effectiveness of risk management, control, and governance processes (see IIA 2005). Ruud (2003, p. 77) states that because of its organization-wide, in-depth knowledge, internal auditing today has advanced to become a major support function for management, audit committee, the board of directors, external auditors, and other key stakeholders.

4.2.3 *Sample Characteristics*

Interviewees come from different functions, levels and industries in order for the researcher to gather as many different perspectives as possible. As mentioned earlier, gathering different perspectives is strength of qualitative research.[21] Qualitative research requires that multiple perspectives must be systematically sought during the research inquiry.[22] Thus, collecting many perspectives ensures that the viewpoints reflect a broad collection of practical insights. Variations in perspectives were achieved using the following criteria, which are discussed below:

- Management levels and functions
- Company industries
- Company characteristics
- Company nationality

4.2.3.1 Management Levels and Functions

As illustrated in Table 4.1, interviewees are from different management levels. Among the participants are one chief executive officer,[23] five chief financial officers,[24] and two chairmen of the audit committee,[25] representing the top level.

Table 4.1 Functional breakdown of interviews carried out

Business and finance		
Chief Executive Officer	1	
Chief Financial Officer	5	
Senior Finance Manager (Controller, Accountant, Compliance Officer)	7	
Senior IT Assurance Manager	2	
Senior Communication Manager	1	16
Auditing		
Chairman of the Audit Committee	2	
Head Internal Auditing	6	
Senior Audit Manager	3	
Senior Audit Manager from Professional Service Firm	4	15
Total people interviewed		*31*

[21] See Treviño et al. (2003).

[22] See Strauss and Corbin (1994).

[23] The chief executive officer (CEO) has the ultimate responsibility for internal control and makes sure that all the components of internal control are in place (CoCo 1995a, p. 7; COSO 1992, p. 84).

[24] The chief financial officer (CFO) is a key player for internal control: "He or she provides valuable input and direction, and is positioned to focus on monitoring and following up on the actions decided" (COSO 1992, pp. 85–86).

[25] The board (or its equivalent) provides the organization's governance, guidance and oversight (COSO 1992, p. 86), and has an important stewardship function that impacts internal control (IIA 2005, p. 4).

Other interviewees report directly to executives, or are at some stage below. Hence, the interviewees include chief accountants, group controllers, general counsels, quality assurance managers, IT and compliance officers,[26] heads of internal auditing, and external auditors.[27] This variety among interviewees brought many variations in perspectives.

In addition, some interviewees primarily had an operations perspective, such as internal auditors and IT people, who are responsible for the operational area. Some interviewees had a particular interest in finance, while others worked in compliance functions. In addition, two interviewees had an external auditing perspective. All of them interpreted internal control according to the comprehensive view.[28] The majority of participants were male – in fact only three female participants are in the sample. Consequently, executive, senior, and upper middle management as well as varying interests in internal control supported gathering a variety of different insights.

4.2.3.2 Company Industries

Participating companies come from a wide range of industries such as chemical manufacturing, energy, investment services, major drugs retail, business services, computer peripherals and communications equipment.[29] A major industry factor with regard to internal control is the degree of regulation within an industry. For example, industries such as investment services and energy are tightly regulated and give companies relatively little freedom in designing internal control. In contrast, other industries such as technology and services are less regulated, which leads to more freedom in designing internal control. In this context, an empirical study from Ge and McVay (2005) shows that the technology industry has the highest occurrence of control deficiencies. In accordance with the research aim of finding the roots of control failures, a particular emphasis was placed on the technology industry.[30]

---

[26] Besides executives and financial managers, any manager owns controls in his or her area. COSO (1992, p. 6) remarks that every manager is a CEO at his own level: "In any event, in a cascading responsibility, a manager is effectively a chief executive of his or her sphere of responsibility".

[27] External auditing is defined as the accumulation and evaluation of evidence about the information to determine and report on the degree of correspondence between information and established criteria (see Arens et al. 2007). The auditors' findings address deficiencies in internal control and provide recommendations for their mitigation (COSO 1992, p. 90).

[28] See Sect. 2.1.1.

[29] For more details see Appendix B.

[30] The study includes eight technology-related companies, whereby three of them were founded within the last 10 years.

4.2.3.3 Company Characteristics

Companies involved also vary with regard to other characteristics such as age, size, growth rate, internationality, organization, and reputation. For instance, some companies have passed the start-up stage within the last ten years, while others were founded in the nineteenth century. Some companies are medium sized, while many others are large, well respected giants. The largest company involved is Hewlett Packard with group sales of USD million 104,286 and 172,000 employees in 2007, while the smallest company is Leadis with group sales of 39 million USD and 184 employees.[31] Some companies are fast growing, while others are more stable.[32] Some of the companies are international and operate in numerous countries, while a few companies are domestic. Moreover, companies range from "single cell" organizations to complex matrix organizations. In addition, as a result of discussions with experts in accounting and control, some of the companies have a reputation for engaging in leading-edge internal control, while others have not.

4.2.3.4 Company Nationalities

As companies from Switzerland and the US are in the same sample ensures having two types of mentalities involved. After the release of the US Sarbanes-Oxley Act in 2002, companies in the US got more attention on internal control. Likewise, in Switzerland, new regulatory requirements brought more awareness of internal control in companies.[33] Thus, although in both countries awareness of internal control was relatively high (which ensured that companies had an interest in participating in the project), having two nationalities from two continents provided a wider range of perspectives as well.

In sum, the sample across varying management functions and levels, industries, company characteristics and nationality was chosen in order to gather a variety of perspectives that allowed developing a holistic mapping of practical perspectives. The focus was to develop a collection of practical insights that is likely to be adaptable, to some extent, by most companies, even by varying degrees. Although the design was based on the limitation of semi-structured interviews to be conducted by one person,[34] the study sample was chosen to be as large as possible to observe patterns across firms. To ensure, as much as possible, "that the patterns adequately represent the observed world and are not merely a product of [the

[31] For more details see Appendix B.

[32] As the intention of the study is not to compare principles and practices, but to gather a variety of perspectives, for further information on the companies involved, the study refers to their internet sites.

[33] See Pfaff and Ruud (2007).

[34] Lillis (1999, p. 85).

researcher's] imagination",[35] many additional interviews have been conducted until the essence of new answers was largely predictable.[36] In comparison, the COSO project *team*, which developed the COSO framework, conducted 45 interviews as input to build its control framework. Of these 45 people, 32 represented professionals from companies or public accounting firms.[37] Having interviewed 31 senior-level people from 21 companies in this study seems to be a sufficiently large sample to be conducted by one person.

4.2.4 Interview Procedures

The interviews carried out had an average duration of 65 min. More than two-thirds of the interviews were conducted in person on site, while the other interviews were performed via conference call (see Table 4.2).[38] Interviews have been recorded and transcribed. With just a few exceptions[39] all 31 interviews were transcribed in their entirety.

The procedure for the interviews was standardized and included the steps illustrated in Table 4.3. These steps (as well as the number of pages of transcripts) give an idea that conducting interviews in the field is connected with comprehensive and time-consuming data collection and preparation. Also, although most of the data collected enters the data analysis, only a small amount of the data is

Table 4.2 Information on formal fieldwork activity

In person	21
Phone call	9
Via email	1
Transcribed	31
Number of pages (single-spaced)	Approx. 350 pages
Duration average (from 28 interviews[40])	1.05 h

[35]Ahrens and Dent (1998, p. 9).

[36]See also Mikes (2005b).

[37]The COSO (1992, p. 101) project team interviewed seven chief executive officers, 14 chief financial officers, two controllers, one internal auditor, eight legislators and regulators, eight senior executives of large, medium and small accounting and consulting firms, and five academics.

[38]In addition, the interview with Eric Schmidt, CEO from Google, was conducted via email. Due to time constraints, an interview date was not possible within the limited period of data gathering and stay of the researcher in the US. Participation via email was agreed on in order to conduct the interview within a reasonable time period. An additional supply of data constitutes documents such as annual reports, presentations and internal reports, which were provided by companies within the limitations of confidentiality.

[39]Four early interviews were transcribed only partially (as the content was not relevant to the study).

[40]In two cases the interviewees from the same company participated together in the interview.

Table 4.3 Steps taken for conducting interviews

Step 1	Sending request by e-mail
Step 2	Setting an appointment
Step 3	Sending interview guidance in advance
Step 4	Conducting and recording the interview (in person or via conference call)
Step 5	Transcribing interviews
Step 6	Analyzing transcripts
Step 7	Confirming quotes by interviewees

typically presented in the form of quotes in the final report.[41] Thus, these steps give an idea of the amount of time and data, which is behind a qualitative study such as this one.

The interviews took place over two time periods. The purpose and content of the interviews changed slightly between the preliminary interviews conducted in Switzerland, while subsequent interviews were performed in the US. The following paragraphs discuss the two rounds of interviews in more depth.

4.2.4.1 First Round of Interviews

In nine preliminary interviews, conducted with professionals in Switzerland between November 2005 and January 2006, the primary objective was to gain a practical understanding of internal control matters in companies. In addition, the aim was to discover what phenomena are of interest to professionals in order to further specify the research focus. The questions have been based on previous literature reviews. To ensure that the questions in the guidance were posed in a practical language, the guidance was reviewed with two professionals in advance. Before asking any questions, the interviewees were informed that the purpose of the interview was to collect preliminary practical insights into issues on internal control, and also that the research was at an early stage. These interviews resulted in several areas that, from the interviewees' perspectives, would be of interest to researchers. A few examples of the topics identified include:

- Variations among legal systems and their impact on specific internal control matters
- Connections between operations, reporting and compliance aspects of internal control
- Risk management from a control and auditing perspective versus traditional risk management in the banking industry
- Influence of the Sarbanes-Oxley Act on companies that are listed in the US

[41] For example, Ahrens and Chapman (2004) and Mikes (2005b).

These interviews also provided first insights into failures of control, and how they should be addressed. Moreover, the interviews resulted in the importance of studying organizational culture in the context of internal control. The interviewees repeatedly mentioned the relevance of organizational culture for internal control. At the same time, they stated that culture, as a "soft" factor, is difficult to grasp in practice. As a result the general research focus was narrowed to internal control and organizational culture.

4.2.4.2 Second Round of Interviews

The second round of interviews involved 22 people from US companies conducted from March to September 2007. In the second round of interviews, the research questions were designed in order to address the two main questions:

Question 1: What are principles and practices that senior-level people perceive as drivers for control effectiveness?

Question 2: In what areas do senior-level people typically expect the roots of control failures?

These questions were addressed by making the respondents aware that the research interest was about the relationship between internal control and organizational culture. Interviewees were also made aware that they should respond from their personal perception. The interview protocol was to first ask general questions about internal control such as roles and responsibilities, perceived key success factors, and roots of control failures (designed to generate spontaneous questions).[42] In addition, in order to give professionals some broad guidance, based on literature and first patterns identified in prior interviews, principles and practices were asked in order to address the categories of failures. This setup assured gathering principles and practices that were relevant for internal control effectiveness. Depending on the time available, and the interviewee's position and industry, guidance was slightly modified. For example, with people from the financial area, the Sarbanes-Oxley requirements were discussed. The Sarbanes-Oxley requirements provided professionals with a specific topic that brought up the discussion on the optimal degree of formalism and the role of organizational culture.[43] The combination of relatively open questions at the beginning of the interviews and more specific questions towards the end of the interview allowed the interviewer to record a broad range of data. In addition, by making progress and recognizing first patterns from prior interviews, possible plausibility of patterns were tested in later interviews. Particular attention was given to pose the questions in an open way that permitted people to

---

[42] See also Treviño et al. (2003).

[43] See also the list of more detailed interview questions in Appendix D. On conducting interviews see Bryman and Bell (2003).

speak freely. Moreover, from the researcher's perspective, the atmosphere during the interviewees was open and interviewees were quite willing to disagree.

4.2.5 Content Analysis

To discover the content of the field material, methods from Grounded Theory were applied in the analysis.[44] A basic method of grounded theory is the distinction into codes, concepts and categories. In a first step, the interview transcripts[45] were coded paragraph by paragraph, thereby capturing the key points of the data.[46] In a second step, codes with similar content were grouped into concepts. These concepts, which represent common themes, help in finding the major patterns in the underlying data. In a third step, these concepts have been grouped and regrouped into higher commonalities, which are named categories. The data analysis is presented in Appendix C.[47]

Based on the two research questions (see field study objective) and the applied grounded theory methods, the interview transcripts were analyzed based on the following steps:

1. Small talk and other parts of interviews that were not relevant for this study were extracted.

[44] Grounded theory was first developed by Glaser and Strauss (1967) in order to provide an inductive approach that can construct substantive and formal theory from observations. Although Glaser and Strauss developed the original theory together, the two authors parted later in different directions with different emphases. Strauss and Corbin (1994) further developed grounded theory for theory verification purposes. In contrast, Glaser (1992) argued that the original purpose of grounded theory was to discover theories from observations and therefore further developed theory-building approaches. As a consequence, grounded theory is not one specific approach. Instead researchers that have applied grounded theory produced a variety of applications and new forms of grounded theory. For example, the approaches focus on different levels of abstraction of the data (e.g., word-by-word, paragraphs, key issues), on different degrees of the coding (e.g., partial vs. full coding), and on theory-building vs. theory-verification. They also follow different opinions in how to include existing literature early in the research process, and differ in the way interviews are recorded and analyzed (transcripts, notes) (see, Dey 1999; Glaser 1992; Strauss and Corbin 1994). This study relates to Glaser's approach and uses grounded theory methods in order to build theory from data.

[45] Grounded theory does not necessarily require interview transcripts. For example, Glaser (1992) recommends that the researcher takes notes during the interview in order to extract the key points and develop codes.

[46] Strauss and Corbin (1994) recommended a micro-analysis of coding, which is about word-by-word and line-by-line studying. This detailed analysis, however, creates a mass of data and can easily lead to confusion because of a data overload (Glaser 1992, p. 40). In contrast to Strauss and Corbin, the approach taken in this study codified each paragraph.

[47] In Appendix C, codes are indicated as "observations" and concepts named as "topics".

2. The focus was first on building categories for roots of control failures. Building on prior research[48] and asking people openly where they typically expect to see the roots of control failures led to an overview of possible failures, which were, early in the research process, isolated from the interview transcripts. These codes and concepts were grouped and regrouped and led to broad categories of control failures which were examined and re-examined during the interview phase.
3. Similarly to the roots of control failures, the codes and concepts that address the drivers for control effectiveness were separated and grouped. These drivers were categorized based on the categories of control failures. Thus, each concept of drivers was sorted into a category. Many drivers were clearly sortable because they were discussed within the context of a specific category of control failures.
4. For each category, the five drivers that were mentioned most often and/or had some general importance were selected for presentation in the field study.[49] Drivers that were not mentioned multiple times were not considered to present in the main text. Appendix C provides an audit track of the entire analysis of control drivers.
5. From each transcript the relevant quotes were selected and reconfirmed by interviewees[50] to ensure that "the members of the social world being studied confirm that the findings reflect their views".[51] They also signed a form that gives the researcher permission to publish the quotes using the interviewee's and company name.

In sum, after careful patterning of the field material, five broad categories of control failures and 25 principles and practices that address these failures were discovered. While doing this analysis, the researcher was particularly careful to develop categories and drivers that had substantial empirical support.[52] Thus, the research aim was to investigate all data and not rely on only a few well-chosen examples.[53] This process of examining and re-examining the observed and gathered material

48 See Sect. 4.3.1.

49 After analyzing the empirical material, it was obvious that five drivers for each category, rather than four or ten, would provide an adequate overview of the field material. As Appendix C demonstrates, other drivers exist that are not part of the field study presentation.

50 With the exception of one interview partner who had time constraints, all participants have accepted their quotes.

51 Bryman and Bell (2003, p. 288).

52 Because grounded theory is primarily concerned about identifying categories (see Dey 1999), full coding is not necessarily required. The full coding of the interview transcripts, which this study performed, provides the opportunity to quantify the amount of statements (codes). Also full-coding provides more transparency of the study and offers the reader an audit track (see Appendix C). The full coding provided some sort of verification, which is helpful during the theory-building process. Nevertheless, the quantification in Appendix C does *not* indicate any verification in order generalize specific aspects of this study.

53 Silverman (2005, p. 211).

took place over the research and writing period. Within the boundaries of the sample, this iterative process supported moving systematically from field material to interpretation and explanation.[54]

4.3 Findings

4.3.1 Overview

As was discussed before, the analysis was based on the assumption that principles and practices discovered during the research process were sorted into categories of control failures they address. The following explains the presentation of the field material.

4.3.1.1 Categorization of Failures

Major existing schemes[55] for categorizing different types of control failures are based on the reason of the deficiency, the stage in process,[56] and the severity[57] of the control deficiency. This study builds on a *reason-based categorization* scheme of control failures. Categorization based on reason fits the purpose of the field study, as one focus is on finding the roots of control failures, which reflect reasons for control deficiencies.[58] An existing example for the reason-type of categorization is given by Ge and McVay (2005) who separate (financial) control deficiencies into staffing, complexity and general. Staffing, the first of the three categories, concerns inadequate personnel and resources that ultimately lead to untimely identification of control issues. The second category, complexity, relates to inconsistent applications of company policies across business units and to issues in interpreting complex

[54] Mikes (2005b, p. 6).

[55] Existing classification schemes for control deficiencies were mostly made according to disclosed deficiencies in internal control over financial reporting in the Sarbanes-Oxley context. Most often these disclosures refer to material weaknesses in internal control over financial reporting, which, per definition, is the most severe type of control deficiency.

[56] A classification scheme based on the *stage in process* can, for example, be based on failures of design and failures of operations such as those discussed in the context of control effectiveness in Sect. 2.1.3 (see also AICPA 2006, p. 432).

[57] A classification scheme based on the *severity* can, for example, be given by a separation into account-specific and entity-level deficiencies. Account specific issues relate to specific transaction-level processes or account balances, while entity-level weaknesses concern issues at the macro-level such as the control environment or the overall financial reporting process (Doyle et al. 2007, p. 25).

[58] Although many of the interviewees are in the financial area, internal control was discussed from a comprehensive perspective including operations, financial reporting, and compliance. As discussed in Chap. 2, financial managers as well as auditors have an in-depth insight into various aspects of internal control throughout the organization.

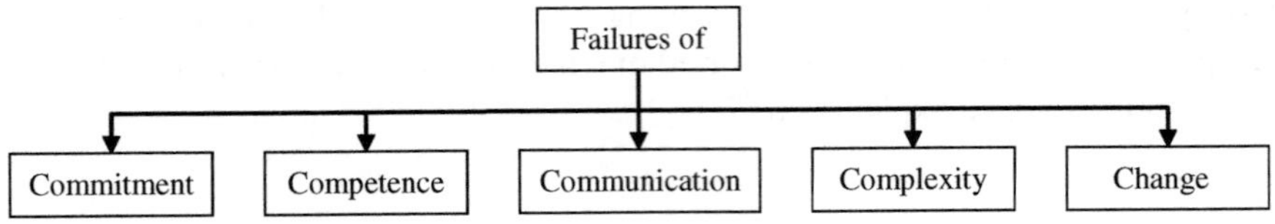

Fig. 4.2 Categories of control failures

accounting standards. Finally, the category "general" includes control weaknesses in contracting practices and poorly designed processes.[59] Combining the field data with the existing categorization from Ge and McVay, five aforementioned categories of control failures were identified. These categories are illustrated in Fig. 4.2.[60]

These categories partially reflect the findings from Ge and McVay, discussed above. While their "staffing" category is reflected in this study in "failures of commitment" and "failures of competence", their "complexity" and "general" categories here are part of "failures of complexity" and "failures of change". Taking the perspective of these prior studies on disclosed internal control deficiencies, a surprising result from the field is "failures of communication". Many interviewees emphasized a lack of or ineffective communication as a root of control failures. Because of its singular importance, in this study failures of communication are reflected in a separate category.

4.3.1.2 Categorization of Drivers

Within each of the five categories of failures, five drivers have been selected to address the failures.[61] Table 4.4 provides an overview of the results.[62] Based on the driver's potential influence on a specific categorization of failure, the category that seemed the best fit for a driver was chosen. Nevertheless, this categorization does not exclude that a driver (e.g., sorted into the category commitment) also mitigates potential failures from other roots of deficiencies (e.g., complexity category). In fact, these drivers interrelate with each other and often influence several areas.[63] The categorization provides a supportive tool in order to categorize the various principles and practices observed.

[59] Doyle et al. (2007, p. 25).

[60] In addition, knowledge from existing internal control frameworks provides support for these categories as well (for example, Sects. 3.2.2 and 3.2.3).

[61] To ensure confidentiality of the companies involved, the roots of control deficiencies are briefly summarized (not related to specific companies) at the beginning of the sections, while emphasis is given on the drivers for control effectiveness.

[62] Both the categories of failures as well as the drivers for control effectiveness were sorted based on logical sequence as chosen by the researcher. Therefore the order does not necessarily reflect importance and amount of statements by professionals.

[63] Likewise, one control issue might be based on several roots of control deficiencies (e.g., failures complexity and failures of change often go together).

Table 4.4 Overview of field study results[64]

Category of control failures	Driver for control effectiveness
1 Failures of commitment	1 Lead by example
	2 Ingrain sustainability
	3 Deal with reality
	4 Define process ownership
	5 Ensure accountability
2 Failures of competence	1 Select appropriate qualification
	2 Consider social skills
	3 Offer continuous training
	4 Make specialists available
	5 Establish an attractive work environment
3 Failures of communication	1 Set clear and continuous messages
	2 Promote effective communication
	3 Explain benefits
	4 Encourage constructive debate
	5 Announce actions
4 Failures of complexity	1 Keep a holistic view
	2 Focus on risks
	3 Measure processes
	4 Establish consistency
	5 Embed controls
5 Failures of change	1 Monitor continuously
	2 Capture change
	3 Standardize change
	4 Take appropriate time
	5 Enhance a positive attitude

In the following sections, each driver is illustrated based on two quotes from the field. In these quotes, the drivers are stated either explicitly or implicitly. While explicit means that a driver is clearly stated as contributing to control effectiveness by interviewees, other drivers have been identified by analyzing transcripts, and are expressed more implicitly. To clarify from which part of a quote a driver is interpreted, the relevant words are indicated in *italics*. Also, some quotes are stated in a positive way (practice x is necessary for control effectiveness), while others are described in an inverse matter (e.g., if practice x is lacking, control will not be effective).

Finally, although some aspects discussed in this chapter are common in the literature, in alignment with the research design of a theory-building process, the data presented reflects simple business reality. An empirical study to build theory such as this one, by definition, needs to be based purely on field input and not on academic theory.[65] In order to provide an overview of principles and practices the study does not indicate the degree of importance of each driver. First of all, such an

[64] These results will be referenced as *field study framework*.

[65] See Bryman and Bell (2003), DeVaus (2001) and Silverman (2005).

indication relies on the individual organizational case. Second, such additional information is part of future research based on other methods (e.g., survey).

4.3.2 Commitment

The first category of failures, failures of commitment, can be traced back to organizational members that do not follow organizational interests optimally. These control issues start with errors and omissions in day-to-day activities that happen because people do not make sufficient effort for their control responsibilities. In worst case scenarios, uncommitted people conduct fraud and steal from company assets or manipulate results for personal gain. Also, these deficiencies include behavior towards the outside of the organization. For instance, bribing can bring the organization short-term opportunities, but over the long term risks damaging its reputation. In sum, failures of commitment represent control issues caused by behavior that does not support the organization's long term performance.

To address failures of commitment, the following five drivers from the field are discussed below:

- Lead by example
- Ingrain sustainability
- Deal with reality
- Define process ownership
- Ensure accountability

1-1 *Lead by example*

Leading by example builds commitment to the organization if followers identify with their leaders. Because every employee in a leadership function (e.g., country manager, general manager, team leader, group responsible) sets an example for his/her subordinates, leading by example is true for everybody fulfilling a leadership function. Of particular importance is leading by example from board and executives in order to set a clear tone at the top.

Statements:

Erwin Heri, Chairman of the Audit Committee, Ciba Specialty Chemicals

Finally, leading and having a company in control is all about ethics. The living of ethical standards and *leading by example*.

Eric Schmidt, Chairman and Chief Executive Officer, Google

The key success factors to control effectiveness *are leaders that lead by example* and sensible internal systems that demonstrate trust and empower individuals.

Heri states the importance of ethics for internal control, and makes clear that these values need to be lived and taught by example. Likewise, Eric Schmidt remarks that leading by example is a key factor to achieve effective internal control. Using the visibility of their behavior to clarify what behavior is accepted and what is not, leaders can demonstrate to their followers how control needs to be performed and that it needs to be taken seriously.

1-2 *Ingrain sustainability*

Ingraining sustainability supports taking a long-term perspective when designing and executing controls. Senior-level people see it as important to encourage organizational members to think sustainably in order to build commitment to the organization's long-term interests.

Statements:

Jennifer Ceran, Vice President and Treasurer, eBay
Each of my direct reports is responsible for *building long-term systems and processes* within their organization.

Mark Fuchs, Vice President of Finance and Chief Accountant, Google
We are on a steep-growth trajectory. We have a go-go-go culture. At the heart of our DNA, people don't want to be encumbered by process.. . . It all comes down to a cost benefit analysis and we have to make those calls. *Believe me; we are never, ultimately, going to go to the extreme to sacrifice [control effectiveness].*

Ceran speaks about the "building of long-term systems and solutions", and Fuchs clarifies that in his company they are never "going to go to the extreme to sacrifice" control effectiveness. In order to support the organization's long-term performance, often short-term opportunities need to be sacrificed, which is challenging. Senior-level people are convinced that in the long run, short-term thinking makes systems ineffective and illegal, or unethical actions that have been done to gain short-term opportunities (e.g., getting benefits through bribes) will come to light.

1-3 *Deal with reality*

Dealing with reality means that senior-level people take action as soon as control issues arise. Whether control issues relate to people, structure, systems, or any other root deficiency, being disciplined in taking immediate action assures that issues stay small. If issues are addressed immediately, people will be committed to the organization's interests.

Statements:

Hans Ploos van Amstel, Chief Financial Officer, Levi Strauss & Co.
We do not wait until the flames come to the seventh floor [at Levi-Plaza] to put out the fire. When there is a small fire, we go very early. And some people might say too early. But I think that's good. *Do something immediately. You* [*want to*] *make sure things always stay small.*

Geoff Ribar, Chief Financial Officer, Sirf Technology
One of [our values] is *deal with reality*. Again, I think no process is perfect to catch all problems. If you have a problem, highlight it to the audit committee, highlight it to the auditors. *Deal with it.*

As Ploos van Amstel states, immediately doing something assures that issues always stay small. Dealing with reality is required from both senior-level people as well as their employees. Business pace and multiple responsibilities make it likely that internal control issues become a relatively low priority for organizational members. As a consequence, important control issues are put off and not addressed in a timely manner. Therefore, Ribar says: "Deal with it".

1-4 *Define process ownership*

To ensure people at all levels of the organization have an interest in assuring that controls are effective, senior-level people cascade ownership down to lower hierarchical levels in the organization.

Statements:

Phil Grybas, Chief Financial Officer, SureWest
For each key control within the company that has been identified, we have *a name associated* with that control. And if something goes wrong with that control, that person is very aware that it's his/her responsibility and he/she is in the line for that control.

Mark Tellini, Senior VP and Deputy General Counsel, Charles Schwab Corp.
Ownership is a key factor [*for control effectiveness*]. The first, most important step is to confirm who is responsible for a data point; that individual will then have a vested interest in the effectiveness of the controls.

Defining process ownership down in the organization shapes member commitment by making them feel they are an integral part of the organization. As the example from Grybas and Tellini demonstrate, people will have a "vested interest" in controls if their respective names are associated with a specific control. Whether general managers, business leaders, or supply chain leaders being the owners of controls, they are more likely to implement, maintain, execute and modify controls if necessary.

1-5 *Ensure accountability*

Accountability is another factor that enhances people's commitment. When people are not only the owner of controls but also know that they are being held accountable for their performance, they are more likely to work committedly.

Statements:

Gus Shea, Senior Audit Manager, Intel
If people are doing something willfully wrong versus just neglectful. [If] Neglectful, you are likely *to get a warning*, and you need to do your job right. If it looks like you did it on purpose, *then you should be out of here.*

Marilee Byers, Director of Financial Compliance, Microsoft
Not only are [people] accountable, but they are rewarded when they spend time and effort on internal controls. *So I think that's been a key success factor, in the personal accountability* for strong compliance, along with strong tone from the top and a very engaged Audit Committee.

Ensuring accountability means that people are rewarded and sanctioned depending on whether their actions are appropriate or inappropriate. As Byers states, ensuring accountability stands for enforcing sanctions, but also rewarding people when they properly follow organizational interests. Ensuring accountability is a principle that enforces people's commitment to the organization.

Leading by example, ingraining sustainability, dealing with reality, defining process ownership, and ensuring accountability have been identified as five major drivers to address potential failures of commitment. Not only do people need to work committed, but also work competently. This is discussed in Sect. 4.3.3.

4.3.3 Competence

Failures of competence address any issue caused by inadequate skills, training, or experience. Also, people can lack critical thinking such that they are not able to detect and correct errors in a timely manner. In these conditions, a "check the box" mentality can be created, which leads to control failures because people do not understand the entire process. Failures of competence can also mean that people lack the social skills that fit with the organizational environment. Incompetence can have its roots in inadequate hiring policies, a lack of training, or even a lack of available expertise.

To address failures of competence, the following five drivers have been chosen. These are also discussed below:

- Select appropriate qualifications
- Consider social skills
- Offer continuous training
- Make specialists available
- Establish an attractive work environment

2-1 *Select appropriate qualification*

Selecting appropriate qualifications ensures that people with adequate skills come into the organization so that controls are performed competently. Having people with the right education and experience assures that they are able to understand how internal control works, what quality standards control needs to achieve and where it needs to be modified.

Statements:

Timothy van Oppen, Partner, Deloitte
The only way to address complex accounting standards is to *hire smart and qualified people* and motivate them to do it right.

Gus Shea, Senior Audit Manager, Intel
The people – *getting the right people [is a key success factor for internal control]*. They don't have to have the right training you want, but if you get smart people that can understand where the business risks are, then they are also able to put the right controls in place.

Both van Oppen and Shea state that getting "smart" and the "right" people is crucial for control effectiveness. Defining what standards and skills are required for a specific position and hiring people that fulfill those requirements ensures the appropriate qualifications. Based on the required competence level, hiring procedures can be more or less formalized (e.g., simple interview vs. multi-step interview process with checklists).

2-2 *Consider social skills*

Besides hiring the right expertise and experience, interviewees reemphasize that social skills are important for control as well. Hence, considering social skills ensures that people coming into the organization bring both technical but also social competence to perform internal control effectively within the group.
Fuchs states that people need to fit into the culture. He asks: "Do they have a moral compass?" Thus, social competence is an important driver for control effectiveness

Statements:

Mark Fuchs, Vice President of Finance and Chief Accountant, Google
[When you grow that fast] it is *more difficult to maintain the culture*. This is one of the reasons the hiring committee spends so much time in hiring, looking over each hiring packet. It just shows a tremendous emphasis on hiring the right people. It's not just the pedigree, but what is the feedback, and *would they fit in with the culture* (confident and down-to-earth) at Google. Do they have a moral compass?

Erwin Heri, Chairman of the Audit Committee, Ciba Specialty Chemicals
To find the right people you need a reasonable selection process.... *But looking into an individual's eyes is at least as important as formal selection procedures.*

because it affects whether a person fits within the culture or not, and as a consequence how people perform controls as part of the group. Likewise Heri says "looking into an individual's eyes" is at least equally important to any formal hiring mechanism.

2-3 *Offer continuous training*

Offering continuous training is important for control effectiveness because it ensures that people have the appropriate expertise, and are up-to-date with most recent standards and rules as well as technical opportunities.

Statements:

Robert Pashley, Director of Enterprise Financial Reporting, Hewlett Packard
We also have a *top down education* process on standards of business conduct, to ensure consistent compliance with rules. We force everyone in the company to make it a priority and to take *online education* at least once per year.

Michael Garber, Director of Assurance Management, Motorola
It really comes down to *a lot of training*... People go through a series of formal classes and informal coaching.

Pashley and Garber's quotes demonstrate that training is an important factor to ensure that both organizational members are up-to-date with most recent rules and techniques, but also that they are aware of the standards of business conduct. Also, training is a way to promote the organizational values to employees. For example, if organizations clarify in their training program that controls are a necessary part for the organization, people are made aware for the importance of control.

2-4 *Make specialists available*

Making sure that specialists are available to organizational members assures that complex issues are addressed with the appropriate competence. Regardless of whether specialists are made available from inside or outside the organization, their availability ensures that failures caused by a lack of competence can be minimized.

Statements:

Rod Winters, General Auditor, Microsoft
For revenue recognition there are specific revenue recognition rules for software. The way we deal with that is we have *specialists* that have competency in the requirements of those rules. The complexity itself is an additional risk factor. You build a process; you build an organization capable of managing that complexity.

Maxwell Downing, Shared Services Controller, Intel
In those [complex] scenarios, we address those complications by getting those *experts* involved and providing the right technically correct answers to those particular situations.

Winters and Downing state that certain control scenarios are too complex even for competent and trained people. In these scenarios (for instance, in accounting; dealing with acquisitions, taxes, or revenues), policy experts can give employees the right and technically correct answers. In this sense, making specialists available is a driver that relates to failures of competence.

2-5 *Establish an attractive work environment*

Having an attractive work environment ensures that the organization has a large pool of potential employees. In this way the organization can choose the appropriate people for each level of competence required for each organizational function.

Statements:

Phil Grybas, Chief Financial Officer, SureWest
Therefore, you *have to create an environment that is very conducive to the employee's line of thinking.* ... You have to make sure that your salary system is attractive, fair and appropriate; you have to make sure that you talk the talk in terms of the work-life balance; for instance, you have to be [a] little bit more flexible in terms of dress code; you have to look at some of the benefit programs, [which] obviously is very important [and] flexible working hours.

> **Geoff Ribar, Chief Financial Officer, Sirf Technology**
> The key thing is the people that execute those [controls] and keeping those people as intact as possible. Unfortunately, the demand for those folks who can do this has gone up immensely. *It's getting good people, keeping them on board and keeping them enthusiastic and motivated. That will help you more than anything else.*

Grybas points to the need to distinguish an organization from its competitors. For example, to draw people an organization can offer an attractive salary and compensation plan, a good work-life balance, a degree of freedom in dress code, and flexible working hours. As Ribar states, an attractive work environment includes "keeping [the employees] on board and keeping them enthusiastic and motivated". An attractive work environment therefore is a key driver for competence.

Selecting appropriate qualifications, considering social skills, offering continuous training, making specialists available, and establishing an attractive work environment are five drivers that can be applied to address failures of competence. While failures of commitment and failures of competence concern the capability of each individual, Sect. 4.3.4 looks at communication, which addresses the interactions within the group.

4.3.4 Communication

Inadequate communication is another major root of control deficiency. Failures of communication can raise unclear expectations among organizational members and cause misunderstandings about the benefits of particular activities. Deficiencies can also be raised because the environment does not allow people to speak up if control issues arise. Failures of communication relate to all other failure categories because any requirement and changes that are not communicated appropriately are likely to lead to control failures.

To avoid control deficiencies that are caused by communication, the following five key drivers are defined:

- Set clear and continuous messages
- Promote effective communication
- Explain benefits
- Encourage constructive debate
- Announce actions

3-1 *Set strong and continuous messages*

The driver "set strong and continuous messages" is closely related to leading by example introduced earlier. This driver here supports a tone at top from executives and senior-level people that makes clear to everyone in the organization what is accepted and what is not.

Statements:

Jaap van Oerle, Deputy Head Internal Audit, Novartis
The CEO sets the tone at the top. *What he says and does drives behaviors of others.* He displays leadership that shapes a culture of values and behaviors, and that is what people are looking for.

John Allen, Chief Financial Officer, Leadis
I need to know that there is *a culture, a climate here that is conducive to strong internal control.* And I am part of building, establishing and maintaining that culture among employees... In particular at the executive level to make sure that *we set very strong messages there.* And that is expected to be percolating down throughout the organization.

Van Oerle remarks the importance of the tone at the top. If, starting with the CEO, "doing the right thing" in internal control is promoted through strong and continuous messages, people are aware that controls are important and need to be in place. Allen reemphasizes that these clear and strong messages support that the expected behavior is received at all levels in the organization.

3-2 *Promote effective communication*

Promoting effective communication means that the appropriate amount of communication among departments, teams and people flows on a regular basis. Effective communication ensures that synergies and gaps in internal control are managed and that people have the appropriate information to design and execute control.

Statements:

Ryan Dick, Director of Internal Auditing, Advanced Micro Devices (AMD)
An area [of roots in control effectiveness] would be *failure to communicate effectively in expectations.* Well-intentioned individuals do not understand and execute the wrong thing and be control deficient.

Lisa Lee, Director of Internal Auditing, Google
You have to make sure you are *communicating effectively*; otherwise I think some of the responsibilities overlap.

Dick points out the importance of communicating "effectively" so that people know what is expected. In this sense, effective communication requires information flow through the right people. Moreover, it needs to be clarified to organizational members what is required and how controls need to be performed. Lee states that, for example, if responsibilities for internal control are not clearly communicated, people start working parallel on the same internal control issues without using synergies.

3-3 *Explain benefits*

Explaining the benefits goes beyond promoting effective communication. People not only need to know what is expected from them for control, but also why there is a need to perform control activities.

Statements:

Jeffrey Beckman, Director of Worldwide Communication, Levi Strauss & Co.
From the very start Hans [CFO] and his group did a very clear setting of the tone at the top. ... that the messaging has been up to the forces around the world. *We are doing this because it's right for the business and that there is a direct benefit.*

Lisa Lee, Director of Internal Auditing, Google
If you have embedded the processes, the documentation and *if people are aware of why they are doing these controls*, I think the controls will continue to be performed. ... You can continuously talk about Sarbanes-Oxley, but if you don't relate it back to why it is important to them, they are going to forget.

Beckman offers this example: "We are doing this because... there is a direct benefit". If people learn why there is a need to perform seemingly "bureaucratic" control activities, then they can see a benefit behind the procedures. Lee states that people need to know why they need to perform specific controls, then they are more likely to perform them well. For instance, knowing that the business will run better and that the activities are connected to a benefit raises an interest in internal control throughout the organization.

3-4 *Encourage constructive debate*

Encouraging constructive debate ensures that necessary communication flows. Senior-level people are willing to let organizational members speak up if they identify control issues. A constructive debate is part of a management philosophy that takes employees' concerns and opinions seriously.

Statements:

Steven Barlow, Head Internal Auditing, Novartis
The objective is to *have a culture where you're not going to be penalized* when you identify issues and concerns.

Hans Ploos van Amstel, Chief Financial Officer, Levi Strauss & Co.
There needs to be a culture *where people just can speak their minds*. And this is also our management philosophy.

As Barlow says, it is about a culture where you are "not going to be penalized when you identify issues and concerns". Constructive debate helps identifying control issues in a timely manner because thoughts from more people at lower levels are involved. If managers do not listen to their employees, the risk of ineffective and inefficient controls as well as financial misstatements increases. A constructive debate that takes place at all levels of the organization therefore is a major driver to avoid control failures.

3-5 *Announce actions*

Actions taken by senior-level people need to be communicated broadly throughout the organization. Regardless of whether the actions are solutions for control issues, rewards for good control performance or sanctions for inappropriate behavior, organizational members need be informed.

Statements:

Wieland Noetzold, Quality Assurance Manager, Novartis
One way of addressing misconduct is making selected cases proactively known to the employees, e.g., in the Intranet, and explaining the way they were dealt with. This demonstrates how serious management is in dealing with breaches of the company's rules.... It is crucial that top management consistently conveys the message "*We really mean it when we talk about a Code of Conduct, we really implement it, and do not just use it to promote our company to journalists, etc*.

Mark Fuchs, Vice President of Finance and Chief Accountant, Google
As I said earlier, the tone at the top and *making sure everyone understands that we won't tolerate someone not doing the right thing*. That is just not acceptable. That is a significant criterion for success with internal controls.

Communicating sanctions such as illustrated by Noetzold and Fuchs helps avoiding inappropriate behavior in the future. In this sense, announcing actions is closely related to accountability, as was discussed earlier. In the case of a control issue, announcing actions provides people with information about what happened, how it was fixed, and whether it was just an incident or whether this can happen further.

Setting clear and continuous messages, promoting effective communication, explaining benefits, encouraging constructive debate and announcing actions are five major drivers to address failures of communication. Another category of failures at the level of the group is complexity, which is discussed in Sect. 4.3.5.

4.3.5 *Complexity*

Complexity in structures, systems, regulations, and tasks can make internal control so complicated that individuals and groups are not able to design and execute controls properly. These failures often relate to a lack of an overall control concept in which risks are addressed and how controls relate to one another is clearly defined. In addition, these failures can originate from inconsistencies in policies and procedures, from controls that are not embedded into structures and responsibilities, and from inadequate measuring of significant controls. Another aspect could be that people are not given appropriate tools (e.g., reviews, reconciliations, control self-assessments) that support them in fulfilling their tasks in an effective matter.

To address failures of complexity, many solutions can be found. Five key drivers that cover most of these solutions have been identified and are presented below:

- Keep a holistic view
- Focus on risks
- Measure processes
- Establish consistency
- Embed controls

4-1 *Keep a holistic view*

Whether focusing operations, finance, compliance, auditing or any other function, keeping a holistic view identifies the links between the control aspects and provides an understanding of their influence on each other. Therefore, keeping a holistic view ensures senior-level people keep the overview and can avoid failures of complexity.

Statements:

Steven Barlow, Head Internal Auditing, Novartis
Trying to take a holistic view, as much as possible for corporate governance, risk management ... or policies and procedures is the appropriate approach.

Alvin Lee, Project Manager Quality Business Systems, Genentech
In order for a control to be effective, everyone who is affected by, is measuring the control, or is enforcing the control must have a common understanding of the control. This common understanding starts with a clear understanding of one's own job well as well the job roles of those that are impacted by their work and the job roles that impact your own work. *Having this level of understanding and transparency is crucial to having successful systems of internal control.*

Keeping a holistic view ensures that the people involved understand the whole picture. Keeping a holistic view is about how control aspects such as various functions, information flows, and policies and procedures come together as outcomes such as reports and decisions.

4-2 *Focus on risks*

Another step in addressing complexity is to select the more important aspects compared to the less relevant. Risk assessments provide the right scope so that the emphasis is placed on key control issues and thereby reduces complexity.

Statements:

Hans-Ulrich Pfyffer, Head Risk Management Advisory, KPMG Switzerland
It is less about the question of defining control, and much more about how to control a company: *what are my key indicators*, what is my leadership concept, etc... For large organizations this is more about using COSO to implement some structure so that the *most important risks* are covered.

Maxwell Downing, Shared Services Controller, Intel
At Intel, we have requirements that every account is reconciled, and we triage the accounts *based on risk*. All high risk accounts are reconciled every month, all medium risk are reconciled every month, and low risk are cycled through. The ones that seem to be the most problematic for us, is making sure the reconciliation quality is at the right level.

As the examples from Pfyffer and Downing show, risk is considered in various control areas. Focusing on risks assures that procedures are designed for the key risk areas. When risks are properly categorized, senior-level people can optimally allocate their attention. Thus, taking a risk-based approach supports reduction of complexity in internal control and helps avoiding failures of complexity.

4-3 *Measure processes*

If control processes are measured, the performance can be evaluated, corrected and improved, and the responsible people can be held accountable. Measuring processes leads to management reports and augments management attention. As a result, these processes are more likely to be performed effectively and failures of complexity can be reduced because people place emphasis on the most significant control processes.

Statements:

Michael Garber, Director of Assurance Management, Motorola
What we look at is if we can manage the level of knowing what we are doing. So, a lot of it is *defining* it all. You write it down, tell people what to do, what is the operating definition of how you do it and then you come back and *measure* what's done. That generally *works in any kind of a process area.*

Robert Pashley, Director of Enterprise Financial Reporting, Hewlett Packard
Another driver for control effectiveness is providing the right level of management attention and supervision. What is effectively measured and reported to and by management is generally achieved. Therefore you need to provide an oversight to show that it has been looked at, and it has been performed and the results have been achieved. What's measured, get's done, this is key at HP. *When we measure something, it gets usually done very well.*

Pashley states "when we measure something, it usually gets done well". He clarifies that if processes are measured, it ensures adequate management attention and the likelihood that controls are performed properly increases. Garber adds that measuring helps in "knowing what we are doing". Measuring processes starts with defining what is required, how controls need to be performed, and finally how the process can be measured in metrics.

4-4 *Build consistency*

Building consistency means standardizing (and automating) controls in order to reduce complexity. As a result, internal control can be simplified, information is consistent, and the organization becomes more productive.

Statements:

Jennifer Ceran, Vice President and Treasurer, eBay
You need to make sure that in the processes that the treasury group owns there are adequate resources to manage the process. That you are *building automation*, leveraging systems and technology ... Eventually systems can be a way to enhance controls.

Hans Ploos van Amstel, Chief Financial Officer, Levi Strauss & Co.
We documented all the controls. *I believe there is value in documentation.* I don't think all companies saw the value of doing so. We saw the value in documentation because we could *simplify the controls.* We could standardize them, and make the organization more productive. We asked, "How can we drive more simplification in the organization? How can we optimize the controls, simplify and redefine them?" You measure the books and they are getting thinner every year.

Ceran speaks about "building automation" and Ploos van Amstel talks about the value of documentation in order to simplify controls. Both examples stand for building consistency, which is identified as a factor to address complexity. Building consistency is a balancing act between standardizing and considering local rules in exception policies. Some companies reinforce centralized databases to capture information, report on it and track progress in a consistent way.

4-5 *Embed controls*

If controls are embedded in the structure and responsibilities, failures of complexity can also be reduced. That is because control responsibilities are then part of day-to-day job activities and not something extra to do at the end of the day.

Statements:

Ryan Dick, Director of Internal Auditing, Advanced Micro Devices (AMD)
[Internal control] is part of a person's responsibilities. It is part of their process, their day to day job activities. It is not something extra you do at the end of the day. Instead, it is part of your daily job expectation.

Marilee Byers, Director of Financial Compliance, Microsoft
Part of that commitment is decentralizing and embedding compliance requirements and the structure throughout the organization. It's not just the job of a centralized team. *It's the job of many people around the world.*

Dick sees a lack of embedding control as "the number one reason there are deficiencies". Byers talks about embedding compliance requirements and says "it's the job of a lot of people around the world". Embedding controls needs to go beyond one's own controls. For instance, if some changes in operations affect financial reporting reliability, people from operations should inform people from finance: "Does this affect your work?" Thus, controls are embedded in the structure if people care about them in day-to-day activities.

Keeping a holistic view, focusing on risks, measuring processes, building consistency and embedding controls are five major drivers that have been identified to address failures of complexity. Failures of complexity are closely related to failures of change, which are discussed in Sect. 4.3.6.

4.3.6 Change

Failures of change usually happens if inappropriate attention is given to identifying and addressing issues arising from change. Failures can exist because the organization lacks appropriate processes that assure changes are tracked and mitigated in a systematic matter. Failures of change can also be caused by new people coming into the organization, by implementing new systems and structures, integrating a merger or an acquisition, or by a new regulation that is not understood in all its complexities. In addition, people can oppose necessary changes, which can lead to control issues as well.

Similar to the other categories of failures, the following five drivers have been identified to address failures of change:

- Monitor continuously
- Capture change
- Standardize change
- Take appropriate time
- Enhance a positive attitude

5-1 *Monitor continuously*

Monitoring continuously assures that changes are identified and mitigated at the appropriate time. While changes can bring both opportunities and risks, what is important is that senior-level people are open and aware of coming changes.

Mark Fuchs, Vice President of Finance and Chief Accountant, Google
There is no finish line. We will never say we have the optimal organizational structure and optimal controls in place. It will be constantly evolving. We went through a big restructure last year. We are still playing around with it. It takes up a ton of time. I wish I had the elixir to make the perfect structure. *It will always be a process, a journey.*

Hans Ploos van Amstel, Chief Financial Officer, Levi Strauss & Co.
Never get complaisant. I think you need to have a healthy paranoia. There is a good culture in a company where it is okay to ask questions.

As Fuchs and Ploos van Amstel say "there is no finish line" and "never get complaisant". Businesses continuously change and as a result internal control must change as well. Therefore, senior-level people reemphasize how important it is to be aware that internal control never stops changing. Being aware of this constant dynamics assures management attention so that change is effectively managed by senior-level people.

5-2 *Capture change*

Closely related to continuous monitoring is capturing change. While the prior driver addresses management awareness for continuous change, capturing change concerns processes that ensure that changes are identified.

Statements:

Eric Schmidt, Chairman and Chief Executive Officer, Google
In light of our rapid growth as a company and organization, *we are constantly and rigorously evaluating the strength of our existing structures, processes, and management instruments.*

Marilee Byers, Director of Financial Compliance, Microsoft
We have a number of ways of *identifying control changes*, primarily through our 302 quarterly survey process, which is quite extensive. We have 300 or so people around the company who fill out quarterly surveys for changes that are coming up on the horizon in our company, such as new applications coming on line.

Capturing change starts by identifying likely and desirable changes that are coming up. These foreseen changes can be aggregated in a tool (e.g., an enterprise risk management) in order to design change around key change initiatives. Byers' example illustrates that there is a need to establish policies and procedures, which capture changes throughout the organization. If the next changes that influence internal control are captured early enough, control processes can be built around the changes in a timely manner.

5-3 *Standardize change*

Another way to address change is to standardize it as much as possible. People need to understand the standard process and, in case somebody wants to make changes, they need to follow a prescribed path. Thus, changes in the processes must have controls around how that process is changed.

Statements:

Adel Amin, Group Controller, Advanced Micro Devices (AMD)
For an *acquisition* we have different committees; one responsible for finance, one for operations, and another for the legal side aspect of the acquisition.

Additionally, we had other committees who managed the visibility study upfront prior to the announcement of the acquisition in the news. All of these committees are synchronized. Our *internal control group is synchronized with all of them* to make sure that internal controls are adapted in a timely manner and sufficient internal controls were imbedded in the process to bring another company into our existing environment.

Rik Thorbecke, VP of Internal Auditing/ERM, Levi Strauss & Co.
That is part of a different initiative. We are rolling out our SAP globally. So we are trying to standardize as much as is possible. We standardize processes globally. *If you make a change, you change it once around the world.*

Standardize change is about encouraging organizational members to make changes in a similar way as much as possible. Therefore it is the senior-level people's task to promote these standardized processes for change. Thorbecke refers to an enterprise resource planning software and says "if you make a change you change it once around the world". If change is standardized, people (and systems) perform similar changes throughout the organization and failures of change are less likely to happen.

5-4 *Take appropriate time*

To avoid surprises after embedding new systems and structures into the organization, appropriate attention should be taken to test the planned changes in advance. Therefore taking the time to implement changes is another drives for addressing change.

Statements:

Robert Pashley, Director of Enterprise Financial Reporting, Hewlett Packard
Most of the acquisitions at HP are relatively small. What we typically do is: Analyze the acquired companies processes, analyze their control structures, and identifying how we then transform those flows of into our own environment and then we start implementing our own control structures in there place to enable efficiency and consistency in the processes. We have a separate group that looks at acquired company processes and controls and test as needed. *In this way we have a controlled transfer over an integration timeline.*

Phil Grybas, Chief Financial Officer, SureWest
My basic rule is that it has to be done in the *appropriate time, we cannot accelerate the implementation of an IT-system because*, in my career, I have seen too many disasters whereby something has been rushed [and] not given adequate thought... and you pay the price two or three years down the road. ... I mean the system that is implemented too fast will work, but it does not work as efficiently as it possibly could.

Pashley's example demonstrates that implementing changes (e.g., new systems, acquisitions) requires adequate testing and time. Looking back on his career, Grybas explains that he has "seen too many disasters whereby something has been rushed [and] not given adequate thought". For changes such as new systems and structures, senior-level people interviewed say that taking appropriate time is important. Often, time pressure makes people in charge make decisions about implementations too early. Consequently, appropriate time makes sure possible scenarios are tested, and actions are prepared for potential issues after implementation.

5-5 *Enhance a positive attitude*

Enhancing a positive attitude toward changes within the organization can help build the ability to manage change adequately. If people see change as a good thing, less resistance will raise against necessary changes.

Statements:

Jennifer Ceran, Vice President and Treasurer, eBay
We typically, on an annual basis, review our processes and systems with senior people. It's kind of our roadmap for where we are going. *And we see change as a good thing.*

Rod Winters, General Auditor, Microsoft
We have an organization at Microsoft that *embraces change*; *we are agile instead of rigid.* And so we have subject matter experts that are monitoring their particular business area, identifying likely or desirable points of change. It's part of the overall enterprise risk management system, while recognizing that change can bring opportunity or risk, but processes and people are in place that can react to it.

Senior-level people state that changes are not always welcomed by organizational members. Therefore, if potential opposition by organizational members is addressed and people are open for changes, an opportunity is given to improve the organization. In this sense Ceran states "we see change as a good thing". Winter's statement similarly indicates an organization that promotes addressing change. Having a positive attitude towards change among organizational members improves identifying, analyzing, and escalating necessary changes and finally leads to improvements in internal control.

Monitoring continuously, capturing change, standardizing change, taking appropriate time and enhancing a positive attitude towards change are five drivers that can help avoiding failures of change. Changes can impact all the other categories of failures and consequently are similarly the end of this overview as well as a starting point of any new failure that arises in any of the five categories.

4.4 Discussion and Evaluation

4.4.1 *Input for further Theory-Building*

The field study findings provide a broad overview of principles and practices that managers apply to drive control effectiveness. This section will discuss how these results are used for further theory-building, will relate the *field study framework* to practice-oriented internal control frameworks, and will evaluate the strengths and limitations of the field study.

The key motivation for the field study was to provide an empirical grounding to observe the relationship between internal control and organizational culture. The field study provides this empirical grounding based on semi-structured interviews with 31 people from 21 companies. As illustrated in Fig. 4.3, examining and re-examining the field data resulted in five categories for control failures: commitment, competence, communication, complexity, and change, and 25 drivers for control effectiveness. These "drivers" present a wide range of formal and informal control mechanisms including more unintentional influences (e.g., leadership behavior) to address the typical roots of control failures.

Referring back to the overall question of this study, which is how managers can establish a culture for effective controls, the field study provides drivers for control effectiveness, which now need to be analyzed in regard to organizational culture. Culture as a mediator, which is influenced by principles and practices and in turn, which influences control effectiveness as an outcome, is the subject of Part III and IV (see Fig. 4.3). For example: How do these drivers influence organizational culture? How does organizational culture influence control effectiveness? What implications can be derived for board, management, and auditors? While Part III implicitly incorporates the field data and offers theoretical explanations for the role of culture, Part IV synthesizes these field results with the theories in order to explain how the drivers need to be mixed. Consequently, the field study has achieved its purpose by providing an empirical grounding for the further theory-building process.

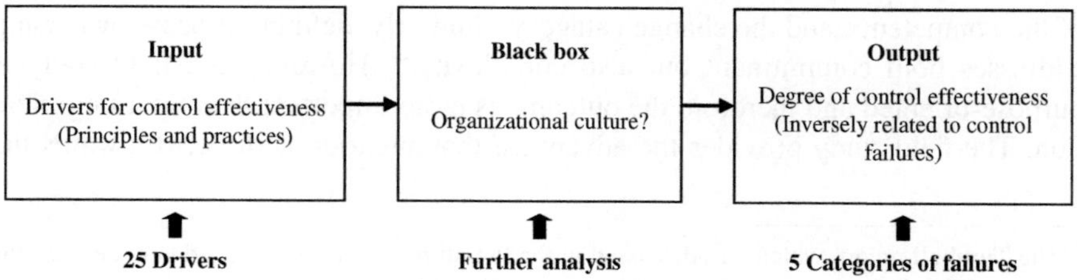

Fig. 4.3 Further analysis

4.4.2 Distinction from COSO and CoCo

The findings from the field do not only provide input for further theory-building, but also give insights for practice. The interviewed senior-level people accentuated how challenging it is to implement these drivers in daily business. Often, time constraints, business pressure, profit opportunities, as well as work overload can make the application of these drivers difficult. As a consequence, a list of these drivers for control effectiveness and typical areas of control failures can help senior-level people in identifying what they must address to assure that internal control works properly. Also, such an overview supports internal and external auditors and other parties in evaluating the control environment.

In general, the field study results reconfirm the content of the existing COSO and CoCo frameworks. However, the findings from the field have also some important distinctions from these well-established frameworks, which will be discussed in this section.[66] As shown in Table 4.5, the *field study framework* differs from COSO and CoCo in its objective.

While the other two frameworks seek to provide comprehensive internal control guidance, the *field study framework* offers an overview of principles and practices in order to mitigate typical roots of control failures. The three frameworks also differ with regard to their categorizations. While the *field study framework* divides categories according to distinctive types of control failures, the other frameworks' categories are more artificial.[67] COSO divides internal control into five loosely coupled components, while CoCo presents four groups of criteria, which seem similarly devised. A major difference is also the purpose of the three frameworks. While COSO and CoCo attempt to provide comprehensive guidance as benchmarks for internal control, the *field study framework* offers a complementary tool to other frameworks. The *field study framework* does not provide comprehensive guidance, but directs attention towards the mitigation of typical control failures. As can be seen in the table, while COSO primarily addresses culture in the control environment and CoCo emphasizes culture in the commitment criteria, the *field study framework* captures culture in a more implicit way. Culture is not seen as part of one category, but rather culture is addressed by all drivers.

A limitation of the *field study framework* lies in the ambiguity of the categorization. For example, providing experts for acquisitions is a driver which could be part of the competence and the change category. Similarly, defining process ownership addresses both commitment but also complexity.[68] However, the field study is purpose-oriented and therefore the outcome is more important than the categorization. The field study provides the advantage that attention is directed towards the

[66]The Turnbull report, which was discussed in the literature review, is excluded here because the content of Turnbull is mostly integrated in the COSO and CoCo frameworks.

[67]See discussion in Sects. 3.2.2 and 3.2.3.

[68]For the evaluation of advantages and disadvantages of COSO and CoCo, see Chap. 3.

Table 4.5 Distinction from COSO and CoCo

	Field study framework	COSO	CoCo
Objective	Provides an overview of drivers for control effectiveness in order to address five broad categories of control failures	Provides comprehensive guidance on internal control based on five components	Provides comprehensive guidance on control based on 20 criteria for control
Classification (e.g., category, components, criteria)	– Failures of commitment – Failures of competence – Failures of communication – Failures of complexity – Failures of change	– Control environment – Risk assessment – Control activities – Information/ communication – Monitoring	– Commitment – Purpose – Capability – Monitoring and learning
Classification criteria	Typical roots of control failures	Constructed (components for internal control)	Individual's needs to perform control
Purpose	Complementary tool to other frameworks/ input for further theory-building	Benchmark	Benchmark/ Complementary to COSO
Consideration of culture	Implicitly included (drivers identified in the context of control and culture)	Control environment	Commitment criteria
Major advantage	Directs attention towards mitigation of typical roots of control failures	Provides a comprehensive concept on internal control	Provides alternative concept to COSO by focusing on the individual
Major disadvantage	Categorization of drivers into categories of failures is partially ambivalent	Concept sets functions from different levels equal to each other (inconsistent)	Less comprehensive than COSO

typical roots of control failures, and therefore the field study framework can support professionals as a tool.

4.4.3 *Strengths and Limitations*

In evaluating the research method applied here against the purpose of the field study design, strengths and limitations can both be identified. Accessing senior-level people from many renowned companies is challenging, but this study was able to interview 31 senior-level people, most of them with top-level control responsibilities at major US and Swiss companies. Compared to other studies that interview a large number of people within a few companies to conduct in-depth case studies,[69] accessing senior-level people from a larger number of companies requires additional effort to gain access to additional companies. Thus, the number of top-level interviewees from several major companies conducted by one researcher seems to be of sufficient size.

Similar to the study of Treviño et al. (2003), this study brings a broader and deeper understanding of practice than would have otherwise been possible applying survey methods or other techniques. As is typical for qualitative research, anecdotal quotes are rich in points. Interviews give the researcher an in-depth understanding of the practical issues and the social context. Providing an innovative perspective to existing studies in organizational design, this study demonstrates how managers describe what they perceive. Thus, the field results not only offer a framework for classifying control failures and drivers for control effectiveness, but the research method provides an innovative viewpoint for internal control research.

As in any quantitative as well as qualitative study, there are also limitations in study design that the reader must be aware of to interpret the results in an adequate light. As described earlier, the difficulty of accessing senior-level people brought a sample that is not random. Other interviewees (or if another researcher with another background had conducted the study) might have resulted in working with different drivers. The majority of people interviewed were from the finance and auditing area, and many of them were particularly interested in discussing Sarbanes-Oxley requirements as part of the interview. Therefore, although the results are based on a comprehensive perspective of internal control,[70] they have an emphasis on financial controls. Interviewing more people with responsibilities other than finance therefore might bring different results. Also, the study focused primarily on globally operating companies. Thus, results from a sample with smaller companies might give a different outcome. In addition, as discussed at the beginning of the chapter, although the sample includes companies from many industries, emphasis is placed on technology companies. Conducting a study with an emphasis on another industry, for example one that is more regulated, might give slightly different results as well. Also, the people interviewed are from Swiss and US (most of them Silicon Valley) companies with a majority from the latter. The insights therefore give a Western, mostly US perspective. The inclusion of interviewees from more countries around the world, and particularly from Asian countries, would likely bring significantly different insights and results.

Consequently, other principles and practices that are not discussed in this study might be important as well. This study therefore provides a selection of drivers that

[69] For example, Ahrens and Chapman (2004) and Mikes (2005b).

[70] See Sect. 2.1.1.

are likely to be important for many companies and businesses. In alignment with the purpose of qualitative research,[71] however, the study does not claim any universal generalization.[72] Providing a collection of practical insights is the purpose of this study to provide input for the theory-building analysis as well as for further research that aims to confirm the generalization of this field results. Thus, the study achieved its purpose because "It is the intention of theory-building studies to inform future research which may be conducted in more controlled settings".[73] Even if operating in less controlled settings, qualitative research needs to meet commonly accepted research standards.

As with quantitative research, qualitative research needs to be evaluated against established criteria. Otherwise qualitative research lays itself open to criticism (particularly from quantitative researchers) as being "merely subjective assertion supported by unscientific method".[74] Established criteria for evaluating the research offers the opportunity to highlight the study's strengths and limitations, therefore the researcher can claim critical thoughtfulness in the approach taken. As illustrated in Chap. 1, in the discussion about theory-building and theory-testing research, qualitative research and quantitative research have different purposes. As a result, they also need to meet different evaluation criteria. Being explicit about these criteria provides the reader with a better transparency of the research, and allows judging the work on its own terms.[75] Likewise to quantitative research, which often evaluates research on common criteria such as internal and external validity,[76] reliability,[77] and objectivity,[78] Lincoln and Guba (1985) provide well-established criteria for qualitative research based on credibility, transferability,

[71] For example, Silverman (2005).

[72] Qualitative research does not aspire to extrapolate statistically findings from a specified sample to the wider population. Instead, qualitative research is concerned about the transferability of meaning or relevance to other contexts and situations (see in more detail Bailey 2007; Bryman and Bell 2003).

[73] Lillis (1999, p. 97).

[74] Ballinger (2006, p. 235).

[75] See Bryman and Bell (2003).

[76] Reliability refers to the consistency of the means of data collection. By definition, qualitative research does not attempt to be consistent or to gain consistent results. Rather it researches situations at a specific time and location, which are never exactly replicable.

[77] Validity refers to the extent to which research measures what it intended to measure. This criterion is based on the assumption that there exists one objective truth to be measured. As discussed in Chap. 1, when taking a constructivist stance, there is not one objective truth. Instead, qualitative research, by definition, requires subjective interpretations (e.g., by interviewee and/or researcher).

[78] Objectivity refers to the extent of objectivity given by the research. This criterion is based on quantitative measures that are relatively value-free, and therefore objective. However, it is also questioned by many researchers, who address the true objectivity of statistical measures and, indeed, the possibility of ever attaining pure objectivity at all.

Table 4.6 Evaluation criteria and methods to ensure quality[79]

Quantitative research	Qualitative research	Methods used to ensure quality
Internal validity	Credibility	Data confirmation by interviewees; Prolonged engagement in the field
External validity	Transferability	Description of setting; Transparency of interviewee's name and company
Reliability	Dependability	Documentation of data, methods and decisions
Objectivity	Confirmability	Presenting much data; Self-critical discussion of strength and weaknesses

dependability, and confirmability. Table 4.6 shows how these criteria relate to the one from quantitative research.

(a) *Credibility*. Credibility refers to the extent to which the findings make sense. Typically, the credibility criterion is met by participants' check of interview transcripts, prolonged engagement in the field and triangulation of data.[80] In this study, the data presented have been confirmed by interviewees. Thus, the interviewees had the opportunity to agree and disagree with data used. Also, having two relatively long periods of interviewing ensured a prolonged engagement in the field, which provides the opportunity to examine and re-examine the data and its interpretation repeatedly.[81]
(b) *Transferability*. Transferability requires the researcher to provide a detailed description of the setting in which the study was performed. The purpose here is to provide adequate information so that the applicability of the results to other contexts can be judged by the reader.[82] The beginning of this chapter provides an in-depth explanation about the setting for the study. Also, the quotes declare participants' name and company, which provides the reader with information on the applicability of the results for other settings.
(c) *Dependability*. Dependability requires the researcher to provide an audit trail (documentation of data, methods, and decisions about the research). Dependability provides transparency of the research. Showing the findings assures that they could be repeated by another researcher doing a similar study.[83] The first part of the field study explains in detail the sample selection, the procedure of the interviews, as well as the analysis and patterning of the data in order to give the reader a comprehensive overview of the approach. In addition, the appendix provides a comprehensive overview of the field study data and analysis.
(d) *Confirmability*. Confirmability stands for the degree of neutrality of the study. Confirmability represents the extent to which a study is shaped by

[79] Adapted from Lincoln and Guba (1985).

[80] See Bryman and Bell (2003).

[81] In addition, the applicability of the results to existing theories from other fields provides another way to test the credibility of the data, which will be conducted in Part III and Part IV.

[82] See Bryman and Bell (2003).

[83] See Bryman and Bell (2003).

the respondents, and not by the researchers' bias, motivation and interest.[84] In Sect. 4.4.3 strengths and weaknesses of the study were openly discussed in order to provide a self-critically reflexive analysis of the study. In addition, presenting much of the data (as was done in this chapter and in the appendix) ensures that the reader is sufficiently close to the field material and has the opportunity to imagine alternative interpretations.[85]

To conclude this evaluation, another important criterion discussed in qualitative research is trustworthiness, which is achieved when a researcher can convince the audience (and him/herself) that the study is worth paying attention to.[86] With the discussion on the four criteria referenced above, the study attempts to provide trustworthiness to the reader as the study has evaluated itself against commonly accepted evaluation criteria. Moreover, the discussion has provided the reader with a critical evaluation on the study, which provides the reader with adequate information to evaluate the study him- or herself.

4.5 Summary

This chapter has presented the results from the field study, focusing on two major questions. On the one hand, the focus was on finding where professionals typically expect the roots of control failures. On the other hand, principles and practices (drivers) that senior-level people perceive as contributors to control effectiveness (addressing the roots of failures) were searched. Field study purpose, sample, procedures, and content analysis were described in order to give the reader a thorough understanding of the research. The interviewee sample consisted of senior-level people (executives, senior finance and audit people) from medium- to large-sized companies in Switzerland and the US, most of which are renowned and operate internationally. Despite the limitations and difficulty of accessing senior-level people, a multi-perspective sample was achieved (e.g., variety of management functions and levels, company industry and other characteristics). This sample provided a general map of practical insights. The resulting *field study framework* consists of five categories of control failures (commitment, competence, communication, complexity, and change) and 25 drivers for control effectiveness (e.g., leading by example, measure processes, and capture change). The results contribute to both practice and research by providing a framework tool for professionals and a collection of categorized drivers for further theory building.

---

[84] See Bryman and Bell (2003).

[85] This statement represents strength of qualitative research. For other strengths of field research, see Bruns and Kaplan (1987).

[86] See Bryman and Bell (2003).

Part III
Theoretical explanations

Chapter 5
Capturing Culture

5.1 Purpose of the Theoretical Explanations

Part II has provided an overview of the drivers for control effectiveness. These drivers, representing principles and practices that senior-level people apply to establish a culture for effective controls, were presented as a collection of best practices and were organized according to typical categories of control failures. However, it was not yet clear how these drivers interrelate, nor how they need to be mixed in order to establish a culture where controls are effective. In this part, the course of study goes one step deeper in order to explain the role of organizational culture in the context of internal control. Understanding the role of culture for control is important for deriving implications about how an adequate culture can be built, and only once a theoretical basis has been established in this part, can the study go on in Part IV to define how the drivers should be mixed so that managers can establish a culture for effective controls.

As illustrated in Fig. 5.1, this study interprets organizational culture as the processes that take place, between the drivers for control effectiveness and the outcome of control effectiveness. The study argues (and will need to prove) that the drivers that senior-level people apply[1] have an impact on culture, and that culture in turn has an impact on how control is performed by organizational members. Organizational culture is indicated as a black box because the processes that work between input and outcome are often invisible and difficult to grasp. Three questions, which are indicated in the figure above, are therefore central to the analysis in Part III:

1. How can cultural aspects that are important for internal control be explained theoretically?
2. How does culture influence the outcome of control effectiveness?
3. How do the drivers for control effectiveness influence organizational culture?

---

[1] The choice of driver itself reflects the culture, which will be discussed in Chap. 8.

J. Pfister, *Managing Organizational Culture for Effective Internal Control*, Contributions to Management Science,
DOI: 10.1007/978-3-7908-2340-0_5, © Springer Physica-Verlag Berlin Heidelberg 2009

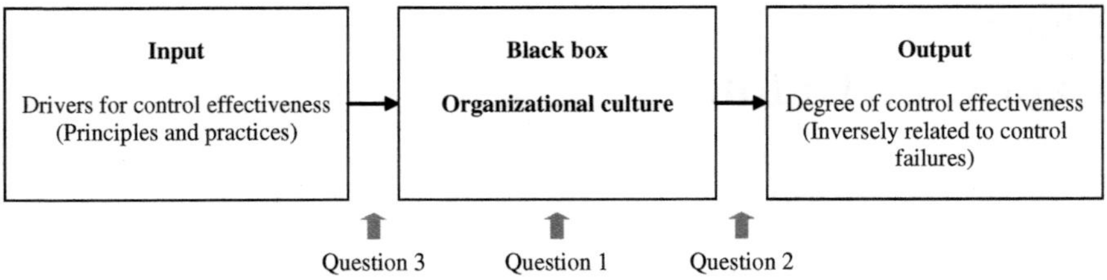

Fig. 5.1 Culture as a black box

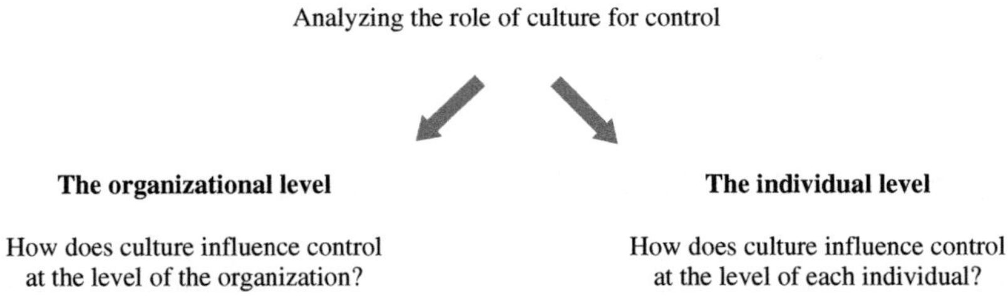

Fig. 5.2 Organizational versus individual level

The first question asks for theoretical patterns that explain culture in the context of internal control. Developing theoretical patterns that explain parts of the black box is a precondition for analyzing the role of culture for control. Based on the theory developed from answering the first question, the second question then addresses under what conditions culture can positively impact control effectiveness. Thus, this second question examines criteria for a culture that supports effective control behavior. Finally, the third question goes back and investigates how the drivers for control effectiveness can influence organizational culture so that the culture positively impacts control effectiveness. So this last question prepares for Part IV, which discusses how the drivers can be mixed so they will most likely enhance a culture for effective controls.

Part III attempts to investigate culture at two different levels (see Fig. 5.2). First, the interest is on how culture affects the control behavior of the organization as a whole (or any group within the organization). Culture at the organizational level influences what control behavior is commonly accepted among organizational members. Examining culture at the organizational level leads to criteria that a culture must reach in order to continuously learn and avoid that ineffective behavior[2] becomes normal in the culture. Second, the focus is on how culture affects each

[2]Ineffective behavior is understood here to be any behavior that does not support control effectiveness (e.g., unreliable, corrupt, inefficient behavior).

individual in performing control. At the individual level, the interest is primarily in how culture affects the behavior of an individual. For example: why an individual might follow the behavior of the organizational culture rather than his or her personal interest in case they are distinct. By examining what criteria need to be in place for a culture that supports effective internal control behavior at the organizational as well as the individual level, a holistic examination of culture will be gained.

This chapter proceeds with a discussion on how culture can be captured throughout the remainder of this study. It looks at whether culture should be interpreted as a variable or as a metaphor. The chapter also briefly introduces and explains the choice of the two theories – the theory of social systems and the value theory – which will be used to examine the organizational and individual levels in Chaps. 6 and 7.[3]

5.2 Theory-Building versus Theory-Testing

5.2.1 Culture as a Black Box

Culture is shown as a "black box" in Fig. 5.1 above because the difficulty of explaining culture lies in that many cultural aspects are invisible. Culture as a concept is an abstraction – only its behavioral and attitudinal consequences are concrete.[4] In other words, what is visible is the behavior as an outcome of organizational culture, but not the underlying factors that lead to that behavior. Schein (2004, p. 8) writes that, in this sense,

> culture is to a group what personality or character is to an individual. We can see the behavior that results, but often we cannot see the forces underneath that cause certain kinds of behavior. Yet, just as our personality and character guide and constrain our behavior, so culture guides and constrains the behavior of members of a group.

This part shows that the invisible cultural "forces underneath" can be described and observed. Even though it is challenging to explain cultural processes, existing theories from sociology and social psychology provide explanations for the role of culture for control. These theories are important for deriving implications for management practices. Only if the impact of culture on control can be explained, then the drivers for control effectiveness[5] can be reevaluated in

---

[3] The setup of Part III is based on the assumption that – with the exception of organizational founders – individuals usually enter an existing organization and culture. As a consequence, in this study it makes sense to first discuss culture at the organizational level and then discuss it at the individual level.

[4] Schein (2004, p. 8).

[5] See Chap. 4.

order to examine how they can contribute to establishing a culture for effective internal control.

5.2.2 *Variable versus Metaphor*

Section 5.2.1 clarified that many cultural aspects are difficult to grasp as they seem to be invisible. How much of this "invisibility" can be captured in a study is relevant when setting organizational culture in relation to another topic such as internal control. A typical distinction of capturing culture is to either interpret culture as a variable vs. interpreting it as a metaphor. The two interpretations (and how they refer to this study) are briefly discussed below.

5.2.2.1 Culture as a Variable (Theory-Testing[6])

The traditional way of approaching culture in research is to view it as a variable. Studies interpret social reality with a functional view and try to improve models of the organization by defining socio-cultural subsystems with traditionally recognized variables. As a result, organizational culture becomes measurable based on criteria that are selected as a proxy for culture. Such an approach has the advantage that culture can be measured and operationalized. However, it also has the disadvantage that, when measuring culture as a variable, research needs to rely on existing frameworks. With regard to theory-building, such an approach is suboptimal because these existing variables of culture may be inadequate in the context of internal control and this study. Thus, when interpreting culture based on existing literature, the chosen variables are likely to present a misleading emphasis. Culture as a variable is therefore seen as inadequate for theory-building.

5.2.2.2 Culture as a Metaphor (Theory-Building[7])

In contrast, by interpreting culture as a root-metaphor,[8] research attempts to grasp the topic in a more interpretive and holistic way. Organizations (including internal control) become the culture itself which, according to Alvesson, shapes the basis for

[6]See discussion in Sect. 1.3.

[7]See discussion in Sect. 1.3.

[8]With a metaphor in general an object is perceived and understood from the viewpoint of another object. Alvesson clarifies: "A metaphor is created when a term (sometimes referred to as 'modifier') is transferred from one system or level of meaning to another (the principle subject), thereby illuminating central aspects of the latter and shadowing others". For example, when interpreting the COSO pyramid (illustrated in Sect. 3.2.2), internal control itself is the principle subject, the "original" pyramid is the modifier and the metaphor is interpreting internal control as a pyramid (adapted from Alvesson, 2002, p. 17).

exploring new theories and paradigms.[9] This approach allows more of the invisible elements of culture to be captured because the research perspective is not limited to a given set of variables. With the metaphor approach, culture is no longer measurable and translatable into numbers.[10] However, the culture-as-a-root metaphor implies that everything that goes on in an organization is perceived and interpreted through cultural images. This interpretation of culture underlines the pervasive role of culture for control. Almost in all organizational aspects – such as structures, strategies, rules, process flows, communication and monitoring activities – culture can be discovered.[11] Instead of interpreting organizational culture as part of internal control, approaches from the root-metaphor-view stress the idea that internal control is organizational culture itself, or can be viewed as if it is culture.[12] Thus, thinking and interpreting with the culture-as-a-root metaphor encourages a critical view of established ideas and consequently provides inspiration for new ideas and concepts.[13]

5.2.2.3 Application in this Study

Interpreting culture as a root-metaphor allows for emphasis on organizational culture as an integral part of internal control. Therefore, Part III interprets culture as a metaphor. Applying the metaphor view in this part of the study has three benefits. Control frameworks generally describe organizational culture as being inherent for internal control. Whether formal principles, rules or procedures, if these formal control mechanisms are ingrained in the culture of an organization they will be effective.[14] The metaphor view contends that culture is a pervasive part of internal control in control frameworks (see Table 5.1).[15]

Secondly, as discussed above, taking the metaphor view enhances theory-building more than with culture as a variable because it allows exploring new concepts, ideas and patterns more easily, which have importance for internal control. Thirdly, these new theoretical patterns that can be developed with a metaphor view provide input for developing new variables that can measure culture. Hence, exploring culture with the metaphor view generates criteria for developing variables that can be measured.

---

[9] Alvesson (2002, p. 24).

[10] Insights that are developed through the metaphor view can lead to new variables, which can be measured.

[11] Alvesson (2002, pp. 25-26). In contrast to other metaphors, which are more focused, culture as a "root"-metaphor means that everything about internal control can be reflected through cultural meaning. The terminus "root" therefore stands for the transcendental quality of this type of metaphor. Whenever the following text refers to metaphor, this broad and pervasive 'root' metaphor-type is to be understood.

[12] Alvesson (2002, p. 25).

[13] Alvesson (2002, p. 38).

[14] Mintz (2005, p. 584).

[15] See Sect. 3.2.

Table 5.1 Culture as a variable versus a metaphor

Chapter 6	Chapter 7	Chapter 8
Culture as a root-metaphor	*Culture as a root-metaphor* (also discussing culture as a variable in the form of values)	*Culture as variables* (defined in framework)

Based on this argument, Chaps. 6 and 7 build on the metaphor view to identify criteria that can be used in Chap. 8, which finally offers suggestions for how cultural aspects in relation to internal control can be measured and operationalized.

5.3 Choice of Theories

5.3.1 Selected Theories

To provide theoretical explanations for the organizational and individual levels of organizational culture, the study adapts two existing theories from sociology and social psychology to organizational culture. These theories support explaining control behavior and generating implications for establishing a culture for effective internal control. Applying these theories means that their theoretical concepts are applied to cultural phenomena. Table 5.2 provides an overview of the approach taken in Part III.

As can be seen in the table, in Chap. 6, control behavior at the organizational level is studied by building on the theory of social systems. This theory provides the basis for analyzing culture as external adaptation and internal integration. In Chap. 7 culture at the level of each individual is examined. Chapter 7 builds on value theories and is linked to the definition of culture as shared values and norms of organizational members. Together, the two theories cover a holistic perspective of organizational culture such as defined in Sect. 2.2.1, where organizational culture was described as the process of external adaptation and internal integration, reflected in shared values and social norms. This setup is covered by the two theories. The following two paragraphs briefly discuss why the theory of social systems and the value theories were chosen for this analysis.[16]

5.3.2 Explanations

The general systems theory is an instrumental approach and is applied in numerous sciences such as biology, physics, psychology or sociology. The general systems

[16]The two theories will be complemented by literature from organizational corruption (for a literature review see Ashforth and Anand, 2003) and ethical behavior in organizations (for a literature review see Treviño et al. 2006).

Table 5.2 Setup of theories in Part III

	Chapter 6	Chapter 7
Level of analysis	Organizational level	Individual level
Object of investigation	Control behavior of the organization (e.g. team, group, department)	Control behavior of the individual
Definition of culture	External adaptation and internal integration	Shared values of organizational members
Theory	Theory of social systems	Value theories

theory is a meta theory in which scientific problems lose their discipline identity and are reduced to what they are – one scientific perspective of real phenomena among others.[17] The theory of social systems relates to and is based on the general systems theory, but specialized to fit sociological aspects.[18] The theory of social systems provides a theoretical basis for explaining how a group of people establishes social structures, and how these structures relate to their environment. The theory of social systems is useful for analyzing organizational culture at the organizational level because: One, the theory of social systems explains social phenomena developed by a group of people (e.g., organizational members). Moreover, the theory demonstrates how cultural dynamics are created and give culture its own identity and autonomy as represented in the social system of the organization. Therefore, this theory captures cultural mechanisms at the organizational level precisely. Two, the theory of social systems matches the setup of culture that was developed in Sect. 2.2 as it directly explains how culture (as the social system) adapts externally and integrates internally. Hence, the theory of social systems and the literature on organizational culture match and complement each other. Interpreting culture as the social system of the organization therefore provides the desired theoretical insight for control behavior at the organizational level.[19]

Values can be studied at various levels such as personal, organizational or cultural values. They appear in all sciences that are concerned with human behavior such as sociology, anthropology, psychology, political science, education, business, economics and history.[20] Rokeach and Ball-Rokeach write that values are "among the very few social and psychological concepts that have been successfully employed across all social sciences disciplines".[21] Values have become a central part in all of the social sciences and play a key role in the understanding of business phenomena.[22] Similar to the theory of social systems, value theories have been

---

[17] See Ulrich (2001).

[18] The approach taken of the theory of social systems is based on Luhmann and Willke (for example, Luhmann 1984; Willke 2001), and is partially complemented by other approaches.

[19] The match of the theory to the analysis of control and culture will be discussed in more depth in Sect. 6.1.

[20] Williams (1968, p. 286).

[21] Rokeach and Ball-Rokeach (1989, p. 775).

[22] Agle and Caldwell (1999, pp. 326-327).

chosen for two major reasons. First, values explain human behavior and serve as a means to capture the influence of culture on the behavior of an individual. More specifically, "values" is a concept that can explain discrepancies between personal and organizational interests and provide an alternative to common economic theory.[23] While economic theory typically addresses human behavior by assuming various archetypes (e.g., opportunistic, altruistic), applying the value theories can capture more variety and allows interpreting human beings in a more differentiated way.[24] Thus, the value theories fit the personal level because they can explain psychological aspects that affect each individual that is part of the culture. Second, the value theories match the definition of culture developed in Chap. 3.[25]

5.4 Summary

Part III provides explanations[26] for the role of organizational culture as mediator between the drivers of control effectiveness and control outcomes in the two subsequent chapters. Thus, Part III attempts to explain how culture is influenced by the drivers for control effectiveness and, in turn, how culture influences control effectiveness. In order to study the role of culture the study distinguishes between organizational and individual levels in the next two chapters. The chapter also explained that in Part III, culture is interpreted as a metaphor in order to generate new theoretical insights, while in Part IV the discussion will come back to how culture can be operationalized and measured in relation to internal control.

---

[23]For example, agency theory (see Jensen and Meckling 1976; Ross 1973).

[24]This setup is based on the assumption that the predominance of economic theory in order to analyze human nature and its interactions can be suboptimal. A theoretical abstraction into simple archetypes such as done in economic theory can possibly be misleading as important facets of social reality are not captured (for more in-depth argumentation, see also Osterloh and Frost 2007).

[25]The match of the theory to the analysis of control and culture will be discussed in more depth in Chap. 7.

[26]Chapters 6 and 7 provide theoretical 'explanations' and therefore do not provide complete theories, which cover all aspects. Instead these theories provide patterns that are useful for further theory-building.

Chapter 6
The Organizational Level

6.1 Setup

Culture differs from organization to organization, department to department, and workgroup to workgroup.[1] Culture influences what behavior is commonly accepted in the organization, and consequently builds a context for how controls are performed by organizational members. This chapter examines how social structures in the organization (whether workgroup, department, or organization) impact control behavior (see Fig. 6.1).

For example, how can it be explained that in one culture it is common to perform controls accurately and in detail, while in another culture it is common to perform controls more pragmatically and less precisely? How can it be explained that in one culture bribery and short-term thinking is normal, while in another not? This chapter provides theoretical patterns in order to analyze how culture relates to its environment, and how specific control behavior becomes part of the culture. Moreover, under what conditions specific control behavior stays outside the culture and under what conditions specific control behavior can transfer into the culture is analyzed. This analysis is important in order to understand how the drivers for control effectiveness identified in the field study[2] influence organizational culture. Moreover, the analysis is necessary to understand how managers can apply the drivers to establish common behavior in the culture that enhances effective controls. As introduced earlier, to analyze the organizational level, this chapter applies the theory of social systems to organizational culture. Adapting the theory of social

[1] In this chapter organizational level represents any organizational collective such as a work group, department, or organization. The study claims that in any of these organizational instances some common values can be identified, which define a cultural instance (for example, Chatman and Jehn 1994, p. 524).

[2] See Chap. 4.

J. Pfister, *Managing Organizational Culture for Effective Internal Control*, Contributions to Management Science,
DOI: 10.1007/978-3-7908-2340-0_6,

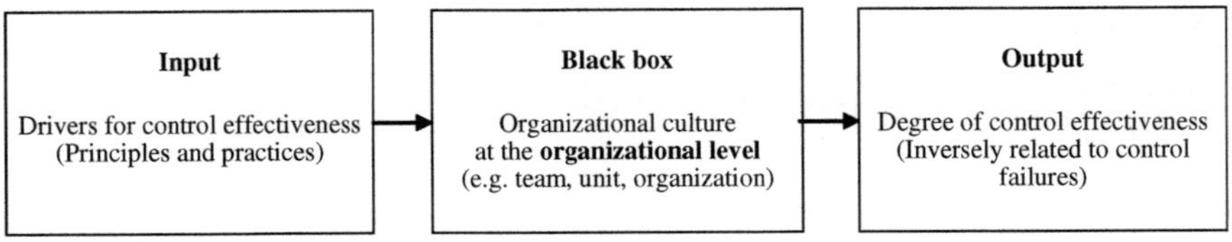

Fig. 6.1 Examining culture at the organizational level

systems means that culture is set equal to the social system of the organization.[3] From a systems-theory perspective, organizational culture can be understood as a purposeful social system, one that consists of networks of communication that define the culture's identity and boundaries, and influences the way the culture changes.[4] Social systems constitute their own meaning and purpose, establish structures and processes, and develop their own histories. Social systems also adapt to their external environment and integrate internally.[5] These basics of social systems offer several parallels to the literature on organizational culture, which will be discussed throughout this chapter. The social system can explain how culture at the organizational level:

- Builds on communication
- Is constituted based on purpose and purpose boundaries
- Adapts externally and integrates internally[6]

The following sections explain these basics of the theory of social systems and build the link to organizational culture at the organizational level. Based on this setup, the second part of the chapter examines how transfer between culture and environment can take place. This is important for analyzing how managers can influence culture so the culture supports effective control behavior.

[3] As explained in Chap. 5, the theory of social systems matches the setup of organizational culture from Sect. 2.2 and provides theoretical patterns that explain social structures at the organizational level. The two terms social system and organizational culture are used interchangeably throughout this chapter. The theory of social systems matches for the analysis of culture because culture at the organizational level and the social system of the organization address and explain the same social phenomena. Moreover, the two literatures substitute and complement each other.

[4] See Luhmann (1986), Willke (2004, p. 15). More abstractly, Maturana defines these social systems as "unities, as networks of productions of components, that recursively, through their interactions, generate and realize the network that produces them and constitute, in the space in which they exist, the boundaries of the network as components that participate in the realization of the network" (Maturana 1981, p. 21).

[5] For example, Luhmann (1984, 1986), Ulrich (1969, 2001, p. 373), and Willke (2005).

[6] See also the definition of culture in Sect. 2.2.1.

6.2 Culture as the Social System

6.2.1 Elements

The central elements of culture (as the social system) are the communicative interactions between people within the culture. Keyton (2005, p. 3) explains that "communication is the complex and continuous process through which organizational members create, maintain, and change the organization". She (2005, p. 74) continues:

> Organizational cultures are symbolic performances, as organizational members are simultaneously responding to and creating a social and symbolic reality from which the organizational culture emerges. Thus, organizational culture is communicatively constructed. It is both the process of interacting and the product of those interactions.

Communication is not only central to organizational culture, but actually represents the basic element of the social system. In fact, the key to understanding the theory of social systems is to see that the elements of the system are defined as communicative interactions and not as the people themselves.[7] In the typical organization, people have a life outside of the organization,[8] and therefore an interpretation of human beings themselves as elements would produce an incorrect basis for analysis. Because the organizational role has only an indirect relation with the personal motives of the individual who fills the role,[9] as Luhmann (1986, p. 177) states, communication is the only "serious" candidate for the position of the elementary unit of the social system.[10]

For example, Levi Strauss & Co., one of the world's leading branded-apparel companies, in 2007 hired more than 11,500 employees in 35 countries, selling its products in more than 60,000 retail locations in more than 110 countries, and has a long history, as it was founded in 1853 by Bavarian immigrant Levi Strauss.[11] Every minute, there are countless communicative interactions between people associated with Levi Strauss going on around the world. The Chief Financial

[7] For example, Luhmann (1984), and Willke (2001).

[8] Sunder (1997, p. 17).

[9] Simon (1964, p. 1). This does not mean that employees do not influence the social system. This influence, however, is part of the internal environment of the social system, which will be discussed in Sect. 6.1.3.

[10] In this study, communication interactions as basic elements of the social system are defined broadly and include communication and action. This is important because some theorists argue that a social system's element is action, not communication (see, for example, Habermas 1981; Parsons 1937, 1951). The term communication therefore integrates action as "non-verbal" communication. Consequently, human beings, when awake and interactive, cannot "not" communicate because even if they consciously refuse to communicate explicitly, they communicate more clearly in an implicit way (see in more detail Willke 2004, p. 48-49).

[11] Source: Levi Strauss & Co. (2008).

Officer and his finance staff in San Francisco have a meeting, two employees in Singapore correspond via email, a sales person in Brazil prepares the display window to attract customers, or a general manager in Switzerland signs a contract for a new location. All these (verbal and non-verbal) communicative interactions constitute the social system of Levi Strauss & Co. Even when an employee leaves the company, the communicative interactions he or she was involved in during his or her tenure will stay as part of Levi Strauss & Co. Thus the communication "belongs" to the social system, while the person itself is outside the organization. The Levi Strauss example is just one that shows that organizational culture interpreted as a social system naturally consists of communicative interactions as basic elements.

Defining communication as the basic element for organizational culture also builds the link to internal control.[12] In control frameworks communication is seen as essential for internal control.[13] In addition, inadequate communication was identified as a typical root of control failures in Part II.[14] Hence, communication as a basic element of culture not only links culture with the social system, but also sets the link to internal control.

6.2.2 *Boundaries*

Based on the theory of social systems, communication is now the basic element from which culture at the organizational level is constructed. Another way to analyze culture is to define the boundary between the inside and the outside of the culture. In other words, how can the boundary of culture be defined? Willke (2001, p. 12) states that the modern system theory is a system-environment theory, which builds on the relationship between the system and its environment.[15] Thus, a clear understanding of the environment is a precondition for the analysis of the internal structure of the social system.[16] When looking at the organization as a

---

[12]See Sect. 3.2.2.

[13]For example, COSO (1992).

[14]See Sect. 4.3.4.

[15]Since an analysis of organizational culture must emphasize the social aspects of control, other theories that deal with environment are less broadly focused and not appropriate for the purpose here. For instance, in accounting the contingency theory attempts to match management accounting systems (MAS) to its environment (For example, Chenhall 2003; Hartmann 2005; Hopwood 1983; Otley 1980). Although the contingency theory and the theory of social systems are closely related, the approach of the theory of social systems takes a stronger emphasis on social aspects. Thus, appropriate to the topic of organizational culture, the approach of the theory of social systems is more fitting as an analyzing tool than, for instance, the contingency theory that focuses on MAS.

[16]Gomez (1988, p. 391).

social system, however, it must be considered that many boundaries are not directly observable.[17] For instance, are the communicative interactions of an employee in his or her private life also part of the culture of the organization? For the analysis of a culture and its environment to be pertinent, clear answers to this type of questions are necessary in order to define the boundary. According to Luhmann (1984, p. 266), the differentiation between the system and environment is not determinable until there are what are called purpose boundaries. Translating these insights to organizational culture, the purpose of organizational culture can be found within the mission, vision and value statements of the organization, and can range from overall organizational goals to small and specific objectives at every organizational level.[18] For instance, if an accountant uses a company car to drive to another location,[19] the event can be placed within the culture or outside it. More specifically, if he or she uses the car for a meeting at another company site, it is obviously related to the purpose of the organization because the objective is to participate in an organizational meeting. On the other hand, if he or she uses the car without the company's permission to help a private friend move, the instance generally lie outside the culture because, although he or she uses the company car, the purpose of the "car drive" is private in nature. However, and this is important for the further analysis, if it is common practice in the organization that company cars are used privately and everyone knows that it is done this way, the car drive is within the organizational culture and becomes part of the culture's purpose. In this case, the culture does not set clear purpose boundaries which makes it clear to organizational members that using the company car for private use is unacceptable. Thus, in this latter case, the organizational culture contains private car drives as part of the purpose.[20]

In sum, purpose defines what is inside and what is outside the culture, and this purpose must be clearly defined by leaders.[21] Leaders set the tone at the top and can establish purpose through communicating the values of the culture and through sanctioning people that do not act in conformity with those values.[22] Purpose boundaries directly relate to internal control because leadership and tone at the top are typical aspects of the control environment.[23] Hence, likewise to communication in Sect. 6.2.1, purpose boundaries provide another link between the social system, organizational culture and internal control.

---

[17] Luhmann (1986, p. 174) explains that social systems ("autopoietic systems") cannot exist on their own, rather they must exist within an environment. However, he clarifies: "But there is no input and no output of unity".

[18] See Ruud (2003).

[19] The car drive is interpreted as non-verbal communication.

[20] Purpose is also discussed in the CoCo framework (see Sect. 3.2.3).

[21] See also Simons (1995, 2005).

[22] Chatman and Jehn (1994, p. 524).

[23] See COSO (1992).

6.2.3 Environment

A third link between organizational culture and internal control is vital to the analysis of culture, which is to know what the environment of culture consists of. Figure 6.2 illustrates that the environment of the social system can be divided into an internal and an external environment.[24] The external environment, associated with the external relations of the organization, consists of shareholders,[25] stakeholders and other external parties. The external environment is driven by factors such as local laws and regulations, technology, and cultural traits and practices of the markets the organization operates in. As introduced in Sect. 2.2, the organizational members need to reach consensus on how they adapt to this external environment.

In contrast, the internal environment, associated with the employees of the organization, defines the relation between the organization as a social system and the organizational members with their individual attributes.[26] People bring unique backgrounds and have different priorities and needs, which is why they do not always understand, communicate or perform consistently.[27] This distinction between an external and an internal environment is derived from defining communication as basic elements of the social system. Because communication is the basic element, people themselves represent the internal environment of the social system. As such, the distinction between an external and an internal environment offers a

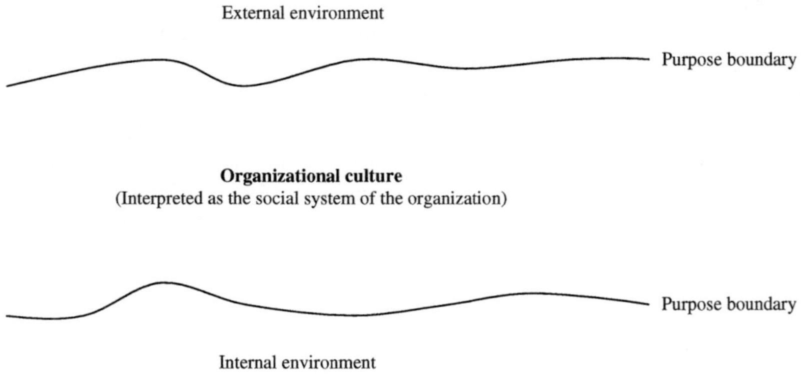

Fig. 6.2 Internal and external environment

[24] Adapted from Kiefel (2003, p. 80).

[25] Although shareholders are formally the owners of the organization, from a management perspective they are classified as outsiders because of their lack of knowledge about the organization and its future capabilities (Kiefel and Wille 2002, p. 10).

[26] Simon (1964, p. 1).

[27] See Chatman (1991).

basic categorization for the analysis of environment, and also provides a foundation for analyzing external adaptation and internal integration.

6.2.3.1 External Adaptation

External adaptation deals with how the social system responds to impulses from its external environment.[28] As illustrated in Fig. 6.3, these external impulses consist of influences from external parties as well as the underlying regulatory, technological, cultural and other environments the organization must deal with. As introduced in Sect. 2.2, consensus needs to be reached in the culture on how to adapt to these external impulses. This adaptation process is about reaching consensus in the culture about mission, goals, and the way those goals are achieved, measured and corrected to meet the requirements of the external environment.[29] The greater the number of business areas and locations that the organization operates in, the higher and more varied the complexity is which a culture must adapt to. These complexities and dynamics of the external environment lead to varying and changing expectations from external groups, and bring both risks and opportunities that the organizational culture must deal with.[30] Organizational culture determines how the organization responds to these complexities from the external environment[31] and how the social system establishes a common understanding on how to succeed in that environment.[32]

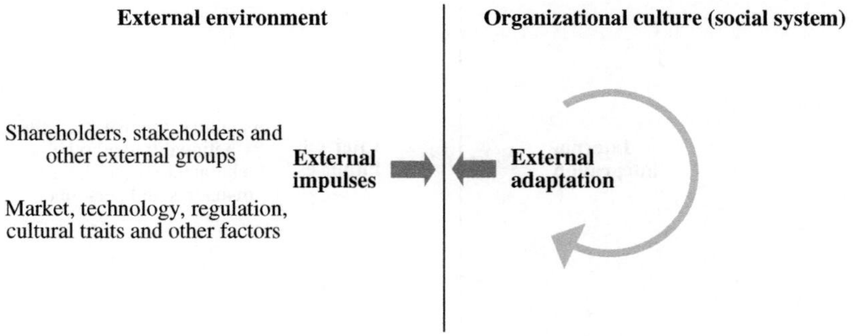

Fig. 6.3 External adaptation

[28]See Schein (2004). See also Sect. 6.1.3.

[29]Because of the need to actively and dynamically adapt to the complexity and changes of the external environment, the description of these external impulses shows that an organization has only relative autonomy (see Willke 2001).

[30]For example, Kinney (2000b).

[31]Mintz (2005, p. 593) states the need to tailor corporate governance systems to varying legal, economic and cultural circumstances. The roots of these differences from country to country are deep and related to the underlying variations in laws, financial markets and cultural aspects.

[32]Ulrich (2001, p. 351).

6.2.3.2 Internal Integration

In contrast to external adaptation, internal integration deals with how the culture responds to impulses from its internal environment.[33] As Fig. 6.4 shows, these internal impulses include influences on the social system from the personal characteristics of the organization's members. In their communication, people incorporate a personal style that reflects their values, habits and personalities.[34] Thus, people's backgrounds influence how they fulfill their organizational functions as part of the organizational culture.[35] For instance, a permissive personality behaves differently than an authoritarian type, a detail-oriented personality differently than a pragmatic one, a helpful personality differently than a selfish one, and an American personality differently than a German one.[36] Although all of them might be able to fulfill the same organizational role, they differ in personal aspects such as style, motivation, teamwork,[37] and how they contribute to organizational culture.

Internal integration deals with how the social system subsequently develops a collective identity, which becomes the organizational culture.[38] Internal integration influences day-to-day relationships, the way people communicate, and how power and status are allocated.[39] The social system's members must, for example, communicate the same "language" not only in terms of linguistics, but also in the sense of the underlying cultural mindset.[40] In other words, internal integration is about

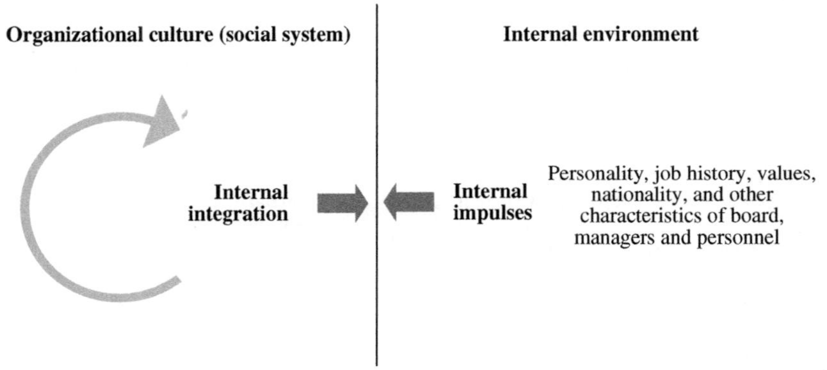

Fig. 6.4 Internal integration

[33] Schein (2004, p. 109). See also Sect. 6.1.3.

[34] For example, Chatman (1991), Keyton (2005), Sunder (1997) and Wiener (1988).

[35] Simon (1964, p. 14).

[36] Sunder (1997, p. 17).

[37] Schein (2004, p. 109).

[38] Schein (2004, p. 109).

[39] See O'Reilly and Chatman (1996).

[40] Gannon (2000, p. 7).

how the group develops a common and often invisible understanding of internal structures and behaviors of the organizational culture.[41]

In sum, this subchapter has introduced organizational culture at the organizational level using the theory of social systems as an analysis tool. The importance of communication, purpose boundaries as well as the environment has been underlined. Most importantly, the chapter has provided a foundation for analyzing how the culture adapts externally and integrates internally. As a consequence, the theory provides a tool to analyze transfer between culture and environment. This transfer will be examined in Sect. 6.3 to see how effective control behavior can be emphasized in the culture while keeping ineffective behavior outside.

6.3 Transfer between Culture and Environment

6.3.1 Defining the Transfer

As demonstrated in the prior subchapter, the social system can provide a foundation for analyzing how culture adapts externally and integrates internally. These processes of adaptation and integration define what behavior is commonly accepted among organizational members for dealing with the external and internal environment. What is particularly important for internal control and has not yet been answered in this chapter so far is how behavior from the external and internal environment transfers into the culture, and vice versa. For example, under the assumption that bribes are a commonly accepted practice in one country the organization operates in, how could bribery as part of the external environment suddenly become part of the culture?[42] That is, how can bribery transfer from the external environment into the culture? Another example, which is illustrated in Fig. 6.5, is when a few employees – assuming they are leaders with a significant influence on culture – create a culture that supports conducting illegal behavior? How does illegal behavior transfer from the internal environment into the culture? Culture determines how it generally is dealt with such questions. The example of bribery as part of the external environment and the example of employees that are likely to act illegally are illustrated in Fig. 6.5. These two examples stand for any behavior that relates to internal control.

The literature on organizational corruption describes in detail how corrupt practices such as the two examples become embedded into structures and processes. Referring to corrupt behavior, Ashforth and Anand (2003) explain that leaders are

---

[41] See Schein (1990), Schein (2004, p. 111). These aspects of internal integration have also been discussed in the context of organizational culture in Sect. 2.2.

[42] Questions concerning the relationship between the external environment and organizational cultures is typically studied in the research field of corporate social responsibility (for example, Scherer (2003), Scherer et al. (2006)).

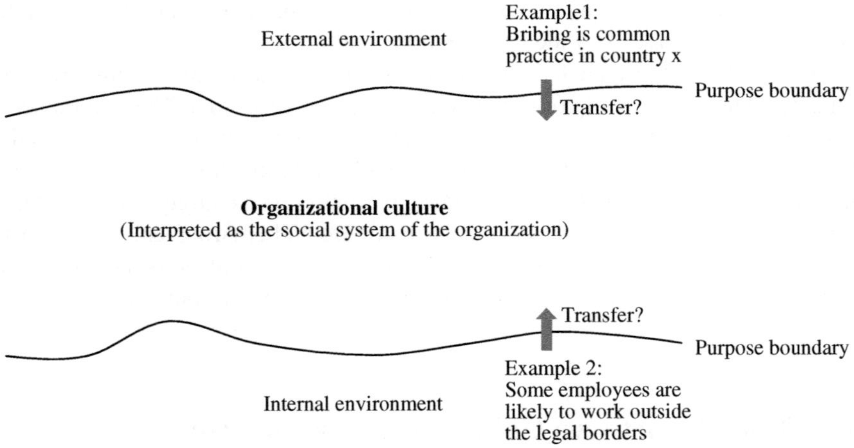

Fig. 6.5 Transfer from environment into culture

key to what becomes part of the culture because they shape the climate that encourages an initial corrupt decision or act, which later can become an embedded and routinized part of the culture.[43] Leadership plays a key role in routinizing any type of behavior that relates to internal control.[44] The further analysis in this chapter particularly looks at how leaders can influence what behavior becomes part of the culture and what does not.

As introduced earlier in this chapter, according to the systems theory the boundary between environment and system is constituted by purpose.[45] Purpose stands for what people typically assume to be common practice in the culture. Hence, the transfer from environment into the culture happens through purpose boundaries that change over time. Ones part of the environment has become accepted inside the culture it will be part of the purpose of the culture. This study divides these purpose boundaries into:

[43] In the literature on normalization of corrupt behavior, three pillars are proposed that explain normalizing corrupt behavior: institutionalization, rationalization and socialization. Institutionalization, which is closely related to this chapter here, is the process by which corrupt behavior becomes routinized (often with unconscious thought). Rationalization is the process by which individuals legitimate their behavior in their own eyes. Socialization is the process by which newcomers are taught to perform and accept corrupt behaviors (Ashforth and Anand 2003, p. 3–5).

[44] Adapted from COSO (1992).

[45] For example, Willke (2001, 2005). Also, Weik (2001) uses "sense-making" in a similar context and Simons (1995) uses "belief systems" and "boundary systems" that relate the concept of purpose boundaries as discussed in this chapter.

- Closed boundaries
- Open boundaries

The two types of boundaries can be interpreted like doors of a house. When the house is closed, it will not be entered, but when it is open it can be entered. Likewise, a closed boundary rejects behavior from the environment to come inside the culture, while an open boundary makes the culture open for specific behavioral patterns. While these two types of boundaries are discussed in the following two sections, the third section concludes and explains how the two types of boundaries relate to each other.

6.3.2 Closed Boundaries

Closed purpose boundaries clearly define that specific behavior is not accepted in the culture, and environment cannot easily become part of the culture. In the examples above, this means that if leaders in the organization clearly define that bribery and illegal behavior is outside the culture, unacceptable, and will be sanctioned, leaders establish a closed purpose boundary. Organizational members (when fulfilling their organizational function) will know that this type of behavior is outside of the culture (see Fig. 6.6). In order to be effective, these purpose boundaries need to be strong. Only if they are reemphasized and clear to organizational members will the environmental influences stay outside and not become part of the culture. Conversely, if these purpose boundaries are not strongly reemphasized or only pro-forma reemphasized by leaders then it is likely that these practices

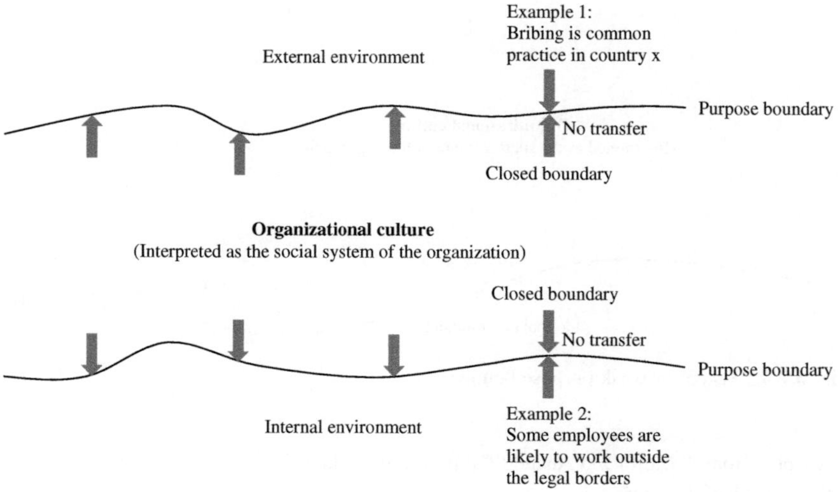

Fig. 6.6 Closed purpose boundaries

will enter the organizational culture.[46] Figure 6.7 demonstrates an example of a culture with weak closed purpose boundaries, in which illegal behavior and bribery are transferred and become part of the culture.

Therefore, in order to keep ineffective behavior outside the culture, leaders must establish closed purpose boundaries. For example, if leaders make it clear that any type of ineffective behavior (e.g., untimely or inaccurate reporting practices, bribing) will not be accepted in the culture, then closed purpose boundaries can help maintain a culture for effective internal control.

Closed boundaries, however, have also some fundamental disadvantages. Often, cultures that are corrupt are based on a strong culture established by corrupt leaders.[47] In these cultures corrupt behavior can become *normalized*. Organizational members know that they need to perform corrupt activities because it is the expected behavior in the culture and unconformity will not be rewarded but sanctioned by social norms. Leaders are able to close the culture so that internal and external opposition cannot oppose against corrupt behavior. Selection and socialization processes can assure that new members are predisposed to the culture or can be socialized to corrupt behavior.[48] This assures hardly any chance for opposition. Ashforth and Anand (2003, p. 3) address the question of "how a person who is a loving parent, thoughtful neighbor and devout churchgoer is able to engage in workplace corruption". One answer is having strong closed purpose boundaries. Because leaders set strong closed boundaries, the line between the social system and its external and internal environment is clearly drawn and hardly any transfer can take place. In the terminology of Ashforth and Anand (2003, p. 36-37): "... a clear line [between system and environment] helps individuals and groups to

Fig. 6.7 Inexistent or weak purpose boundaries

[46] Adapted from Ashforth and Anand (2003). See also Chap. 7.

[47] See Anand et al. (2005).

[48] See Ashforth and Anand (2003).

cognitively segment their micro and macro worlds, allowing them to blithely do what they might loudly renounce in other contexts".[49]

Thus, when the culture is closed, a culture can establish its own dynamics and separate and estrange from its environment. The corrupt culture does not support that people speak up when they are personally against corrupt behavior. The corrupt culture does not encourage constructive debate in which the purpose of the culture is continuously evaluated by its organizational members. If the purpose boundary between culture and its environment is closed, the culture (and particularly its leaders) has no need to justify its values and common practices towards its environment.[50] As illustrated in Fig. 6.8, in this case no transfer between culture and environment takes place. Hence, if a few leaders are able to establish a strong culture that is closed to its environment, then the opinion and consideration of the internal environment (employees) and the external environments (e.g., law, cultural traits, market conditions) have hardly any influence on the culture.[51] Consequently,

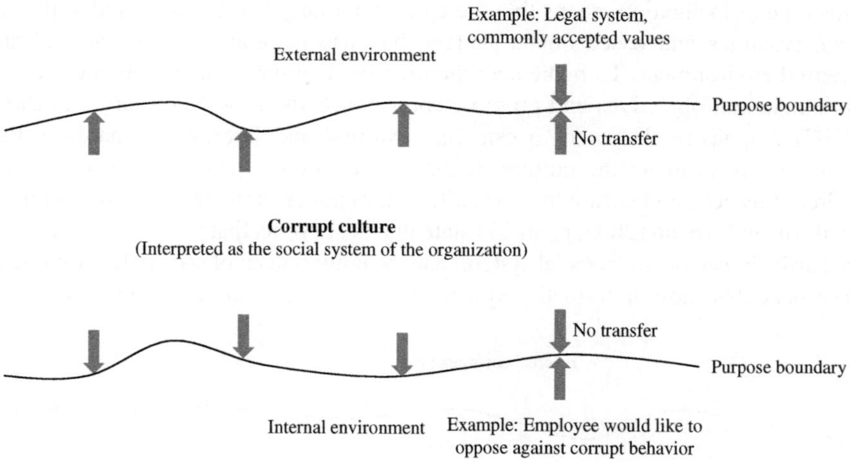

Fig. 6.8 Negative effects of closed purpose boundaries

[49]The "macro world" can be interpreted as the internal environment represented by organizational members, while the "micro world" can be seen as the organizational members fulfilling their organizational function as part of the social system.

[50]For more depth see Ashforth and Anand (2003).

[51]Another example would be if leaders aspire to establish the most powerful organization in their market and to achieve this objective they close all boundaries to the external environment. In the case of Enron and WorldCom such behavior led to illegal reporting practices, which were far away from what is accepted in the culture's legal external environment. Another example is the Swiss bank UBS, in which the leaders aspired to become a leading investment bank. Although this is a legitimate goal, the way senior-level people attempted to achieve this performance objective resulted in aggressive investment strategies in the US subprime market. The bank ignored its competitors which sold the investments in this market earlier on. UBS got huge losses from the investments. Thus, to achieve its investment goal, the bank ignored its external environment (competitors and other developments in the market) and invested "blindly" in these positions.

a culture that sets strong closed purpose boundaries can develop its own dynamics and rules that are far from what the average employee might see as his or her personal values.[52]

6.3.3 *Open Boundaries*

In alignment with Scherer and Palazzo (2007, p. 1114), a culture should not suppress "dissenting voices".[53] Instead, this study posits that culture needs to provide boundaries of the social system, in which democratic processes and consideration of different opinions can take place. Therefore, there is a need for open purpose boundaries. Open purpose boundaries, as indicated with arrows in Fig. 6.9, ensure that the culture is amenable to continuous evaluation by its environment.[54] This type of evaluation means that the culture not only learns inside and within its own dynamics and based on its leaders, but also in relation to its internal and external environment. To make sure the promoted culture is in alignment with the organizational objectives and promote control effectiveness, Stansbury and Barry (2007) emphasize the need to establish external and internal mechanisms that continuously evaluate the culture of the organization. Open purpose boundaries address this need and ensure that the culture does not estrange from its environment. Ashforth and Anand (2003, p. 36-37) state that "... events that blur the line between the particularism of work [social system] and the universalism of society [environment] may make this clash of normative systems far more salient and cause ambivalence".

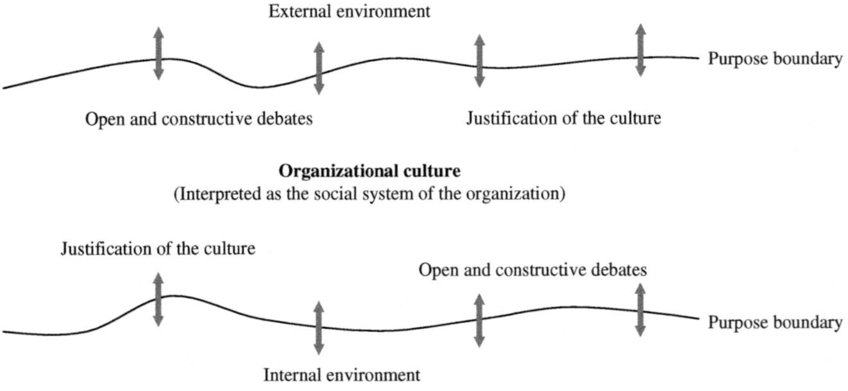

Fig. 6.9 Open purpose boundaries

[52] Ashforth and Anand (2003, p. 3).

[53] See Scherer and Palazzo (2007).

[54] Steinmann and Schreyögg claim that efficient strategic control requires that organizations are open to question their culture (Steinmann and Schreyögg 1986, p. 760).

Thus, if constructive debate between various hierarchical levels can take place in an organization, leaders (and any organizational members) need to justify their behavior to others in the organization. Open boundaries support democratic processes which force leaders to convince their employees about their directions, and ensure that the culture maintains openness towards its external environment (representing stakeholders and other external parties). Thus, open purpose boundaries blur the line between system and environment. They reflect Stansbury and Barry's evaluation because they make certain that culture is evaluated by organizational members' backgrounds as internal environment and by society as external environment. Most importantly, these open boundaries ensure that the culture can learn and develop over time. Existing closed boundaries can be evaluated and changed over time.[55] Nevertheless, Steinmann and Schreyögg (1986, p. 762) clarify that achieving openness in the culture is challenging because openness continuously questions the existing behavioral patterns and organizational structures. Moreover, openness can challenge existing power and resource allocations, and even risk possible career opportunities. In the figure these open boundaries are indicated with the arrows that stand for open and constructive debates and that the culture needs to be justified by senior-level people.

6.3.4 Mix between Closed and Open Boundaries

It is now evident that both closed and open boundaries are necessary for establishing a culture that enhances effective controls (see Fig. 6.10). Closed purpose boundaries, on the one hand, are necessary for organizational members to know what is accepted and expected and what is not. These closed boundaries define the accepted control behavior within the culture. Open purpose boundaries, on the other hand, are necessary in order to ensure that the culture is open to criticism, evaluation, and dissenting voices from both the internal environment (representing the employees) and the external environment. These open purpose boundaries ensure that the organization learns and develops and stays open to feedback. To establish a culture that bars unacceptable behavior from the culture, and is still open for evaluation by its environment, a mix between closed and open purpose boundaries is necessary. Such a culture will open and not estrange from its environment, but still can keep ineffective behavior outside.

Whatever the optimal mix is, each boundary (whether open or closed) needs to be strong in order to be effective. A weak closed boundary will not be able to keep unacceptable behavior outside and a weak open boundary can mean that active debate happens only pro-forma. In this latter case, opinions from organizational members and external groups are considered, but actually only on the surface.

---

[55] Derived from Schreyögg and Steinmann's (1987, p. 92) feedback control.

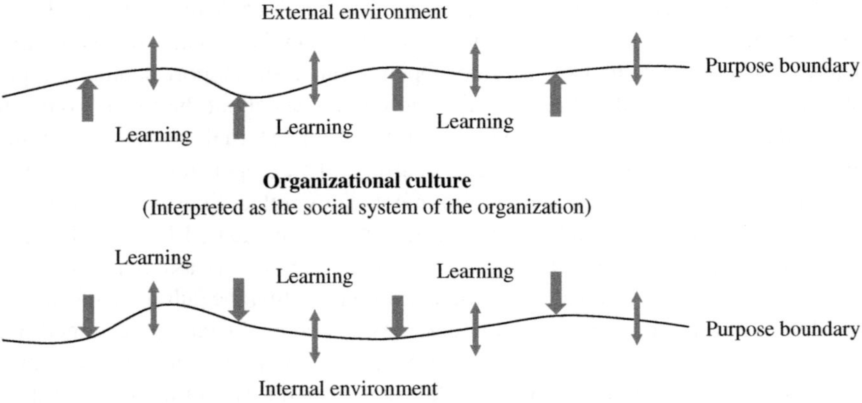

Fig. 6.10 Mix between closed and open boundaries

6.4 Implications

Combining the separate literatures on the theory of social systems, on organizational culture, and on corruption in organizations provides important implications for establishing a culture that supports effective controls. The chapter illustrated that purpose boundaries define what part of the culture is and what is not. These purpose boundaries are primarily defined by leaders since leaders have a significant impact on culture.[56] This theory supports the premise that these boundaries need to be strong in order to be effective in defining the culture. Thus, a culture with strong as opposed to weak purpose boundaries is more likely to define what behavior is part of the culture and what is not, and is more likely to establish consistent behavior among organizational members. A strong culture also has limitations. Examples of corrupt and otherwise ineffective organizations demonstrate that a strong culture can lead to ineffective behavior. As a remedy, this study distinguishes between closed and open purpose boundaries. A closed boundary makes it clear to organizational members what type of control behavior is accepted in the culture and what is not. These closed boundaries are necessary to keep cohesiveness in the culture, develop consistent behavior and keep ineffective behavior outside the culture. However, the chapter discussed the possibility that a culture that builds solely on closed purpose boundaries is likely to estrange from its environment. As such, a culture also needs to establish open purpose boundaries. Open purpose boundaries make the culture amenable to constructive debates between organizational members (e.g., leaders and followers). They support the premise that leaders are forced to convince their followers about their directives, and open the culture to democratic processes. Open purpose boundaries ensure that existing closed

[56]For example, Schein (1985).

boundaries can be questioned by organizational members and become the subject of debate and change. Open purpose boundaries are not only necessary for keeping the culture evaluated by its environment, but beyond that they assure that the culture can learn from the environment and does not estrange itself from it.

The chapter applied the theory of social systems to analyze how behavior can become part of the culture. However, even if a culture has commonly accepted behavior that seems to support control effectiveness, in an organization particularly a large one – it is still possible that some individuals are likely to perform controls that are ineffective, or even conduct fraudulent behavior. Consequently, the question arises – what leaders can do to motivate each individual in performing controls properly. This is subject of the next chapter, which focuses on the individual level of culture.

Chapter 7
The Individual Level

7.1 Setup

While the last chapter examined culture at the organizational level, this chapter focuses on how culture influences an individual in performing control.[1] This chapter reveals under what conditions organizational members follow organizational interests rather than personal ones. For example, under what conditions does culture reinforce that people give their best effort for the organization and do not sleep on the job? How can culture assure that people do not steal assets or otherwise behave in a way that does not support the organization's long-term interests? This chapter provides theoretical patterns in order to analyze the tension between individual and organizational interests. More specifically, the analysis turns towards possible reasons to explain under what conditions people follow their individual interests and under what conditions they follow organizational interests in their control behavior (see Fig. 7.1).

To explain culture at the individual level, this chapter sets culture equal to shared values and norms.[2] Adapting the value theories to analyze the individual level is adequate for two major reasons. First, value theories can explain psychological processes that match the aim of investigating how culture affects individual behavior. Second, value theories represent culture defined as shared values and social norms.[3] Hence, while the prior chapter built on adaptation and integration, this chapter complements with focusing on shared values and social norms. Together,

---

[1] Discussing first the organizational level and then the individual level is based on the assumption that an individual typically enters an organizational culture that already exists (except that he or she is the organizational founder).

[2] See Sect. 2.2.3.

[3] The emphasis in this approach is on values and not on social norms. However, values and norms interrelate and their functions are partially interchangeable. Therefore the chapter also covers aspects of social norms.

J. Pfister, *Managing Organizational Culture for Effective Internal Control*, Contributions to Management Science,
DOI: 10.1007/978-3-7908-2340-0_7, © Springer Physica-Verlag Berlin Heidelberg 2009

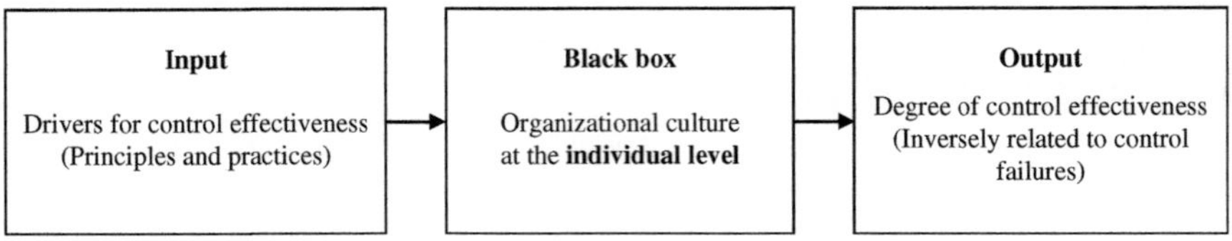

Fig. 7.1 Examining culture at the individual level

the two approaches provide a holistic view of organizational culture such as defined in Part I.

To provide an understanding of the tension between individual and organizational interests, the chapter discusses both personal and organizational values. The discussion starts with a brief overview of personal values and their relation to control behavior. Next, the discussion looks at values at the organizational level in order to analyze how they influence the behavior of each individual. The central question throughout the chapter is: If individual values differ from the organizational values, how can the organization assure that people follow the organizational interests and perform internal control properly? In order to examine this point, the discussion continuous with values at the individual level.

7.2 Values at the Individual Level

7.2.1 Individual Differences

Based on their personality, job history, and national, cultural, religious and other backgrounds, people bring unique characteristics to the organization. Personal values are one way to capture these influences that people bring into an organization and provide a basis for analyzing the relation between personal and organizational interests. There are numerous explanations for the similarities and differences in the values held by individuals.[4] It is important to recognize that individuals have different receptivity to influences on their respective value systems such as cognitive style, self-esteem, and specific attitude structure.[5] One fundamental hypothesis is that values are "founded, in part, upon the fundamental biological similarities of all human beings".[6] Another way to explain similarities and differences among

[4]Meglino and Ravlin (1998, p. 354).

[5]Meglino and Ravlin (1998, p. 355), Simon (1990), Wanous and Colella (1989).

[6]Kluckhohn (1951, p. 418). A study from Keller et al. (1992, p. 79) concluded that, based on a study of twins who grew up apart from each other, 40% of work values could be explained by genetic factors.

people is to observe how their values are influenced by personal experiences.[7] People learn, formally and informally, how to behave in an appropriate way in their social environment. General social values are learned early in life, while socialization processes of values of specific groups such as an organization are principally learned from the time an individual enters the organization.[8] One individual may be part of many social groups and share values with all these group members. In this context Rescher (1969, p. 14) writes: "We correspondingly obtain such classificatory groupings as personal values, professional (profession-wide) values or work values, national (nationwide) values, etc". For instance, a marketing specialist shares values with people from his organization (organizational values). Also, he shares values with people that are also marketers but may work in another organization (professional values).[9] Whether it is the organization or the profession, the individual learns what is expected in his groups and adapt to behave in conformity with those values which, while they are different from his values, operate in the function of social norms. To better understand how values influence control behavior, the next section exemplifies the influence of values in specific control situations.

7.2.2 *Values at Work*

One way to distinguish personal values is to divide them into instrumental and terminal values.[10] While *instrumental values* such as being "intelligent", "honest," or "accurate" represent what one sees as desirable modes of conduct, *terminal values* represent what a person believes to be desirable end-states of existence such as "freedom" and "wealth".[11] Instrumental values such as being "logical" and "responsible" are a mode of conduct for the realization of terminal values like "happiness" and a "sense of accomplishment". Although the theory does not rule out the possibility that these two value categories can influence each other in both directions, the main proposition is that instrumental values help towards the achievement of terminal values.[12] Terminal values are motivating because they express the super goals that people want to achieve in the long run. They seem not

[7] Bern (1970, p. 14), Jones and Gerard (1967, p. 181).

[8] Meglino and Ravlin (1998, pp. 353-354).

[9] Ouchi (1979, p. 837).

[10] This application of personal values is based on Rokeach (1973), which has been widely replicated and discussed until today. See for example: Agle and Caldwell (1999), Bardi and Schwartz (2003), Meglino and Ravlin (1998), Van Rekom et al. (2006). Another commonly accepted value framework offer Schwartz (see Schwartz and Bilsky 1990).

[11] See Rokeach (1973).

[12] Meglino and Ravlin (1998, p. 353).

to be periodic in nature, nor do they seem to be ultimately reachable. Rokeach writes: "We seem to be forever doomed to strive for these ultimate goals without quite ever reaching them".[13] While terminal values represent what people want to reach as super goals, instrumental values stand for the means to achieve those goals. Although on first impression this discussion appears to stray far from internal control, it is actually close to the topic. Drawing on the relationship between control and culture, internal control and instrumental values are a means to an end, but each is not an end in itself.[14] Thus, the nature of instrumental values and internal control is close because both support the achievement of goals.[15] These instrumental values can therefore explain behavioral patterns in the context of internal control.

Kinney (2000b, p. 95) states that the quality of internal control is directly related to the competence and integrity of people: "Competence influences their ability to carry out responsibilities, and integrity determines how they are carried out". With regard to competence and integrity, one classification of instrumental values is that they can be classified into competence and moral values. A person who is being logical and intelligent feels that he or she is acting competently. If these competence values are violated, they bring up feelings of inadequacy.[16] For example, an accountant at a publicly held company who is not current with generally accepted accounting principles (GAAP) may feel inadequate in fulfilling his or her duties. In contrast to the values of competence, there are values of morality. A person who is acting in accordance with moral values, such as being honest or dutiful, feels that he or she is behaving morally. If these moral values are violated, they in turn bring up feelings of guilt.[17] For instance, a division manager who intentionally reports performance-adjusted numbers to headquarters could have a feeling of guilt for wrongdoing. Because values typically interact, issues can arise if values stand in conflict to each other.

[13]Rokeach (1973, p. 8).

[14]COSO (1992, p. 13), Rokeach (1973, p. 12).

[15]This goes together with Meglino and Ravlin (1998, p. 353) who find in their literature review on organizational behavior that a greater amount of research has been spent on instrumental values as opposed to terminal values. In general, instrumental values are more common to describe organizational culture than terminal values (Schein 1985, p. 2).

[16]Rokeach (1973, p. 8).

[17]Guilt needs to be distinguished from shame, which is a related emotion. Shame and guilt have often been used as synonyms even though many researchers agree they are different emotions, for example, in the degree of focus on the self. Shame is related to discrepancies between one's beliefs about the self and beliefs about what the self ought to be or what the ideal self would be. In contrast, guilt refers to a specific behavior and is therefore less focused on the self (see Eisenberg 2000).

7.2.3 Conflicts of Values

Behaviors are rarely based on a single value; rather they are the result of a classification of values that act in concert with one another.[18] England (1967, p. 54) introduces the personal value system as "a relatively permanent perceptual framework which shapes and influences the general nature of an individual's behavior". A value system develops by competing between values and the decision about which of the conflicting values is the more important. According to Rokeach and Ball-Rokeach (1989, p. 775) people naturally resolve such conflicts by a cognitively driven process of paired comparisons between two values. Conflicts may occur between two moral values, two competence values, or between a moral and a competence value. A conflict between two moral values would be when someone who has been taught to be helpful and honest may be requested to help another by lying.[19] For example, an account manager who is told to adjust the numbers illegally will be in a dilemma to either fulfill his function or to talk to other people in the company about the incident. Or, to give an example of two competence values in conflict, someone who needs to meet a deadline must choose between being pragmatic and timely or being accurate. This would be the case if a financial manager who is in charge of one country within a multinational corporation needs to choose between skipping certain reviews in order to meet the worldwide consolidation deadline, or to delay the process for more accuracy. So values at the personal level play a key role in the determination and resolution of ethical dilemmas.[20] A value system helps one choose among alternatives, resolve conflicts, and make decisions.[21] These value conflicts are not only solved by the individual alone. The social environment in which the individual acts has an impact on these decisions, and on whether the individual will decide about one or the other value that will be followed. This argumentation brings back to organizational values and their influence on individual's behavior.

7.3 Tension between Organizational and Individual Interests

7.3.1 Organizational Values

In order to explain the discrepancies between organizational and individual interests, the analysis continuous with the organizational values and relates their role to

---

[18] Liedtka (1989, p. 806); Williams (1968, p. 287).

[19] Meglino and Ravlin (1998, p. 358).

[20] Glover et al. (1997, p. 13).

[21] Rokeach (1973, p. 14).

the individual's behavior. In the same way the values of individuals differ, values of organizations differ as well. Organizational culture – defined as shared values of organizational members – must enhance the organization's ability to deal with its environment and enhance internal stability. Organizational values[22] have an impact on organizational goals, strategies and policies[23] and guide group members in their actions and in their understanding and interpretation of the world around them. Moreover, the organizational value system offers a "unique meaning and perspective to the understanding of organizational phenomena".[24] Organizational values underlie all organizational actions and are a defining factor for why one group's actions diverge from another group's actions.[25] Collins and Porras (2000, p. 73) use "core values" as "central and enduring tenets of the organization" and describe them as the "glue that holds an organization together as it grows, decentralizes, diversifies and expands". These core values prevail over most other values in the organizational value system and have a major influence on people's behavior.[26] These core values remain constant while business strategies have to adapt to the changing environment.[27]

The literature of organizational culture defines that the value system of the organization is defined based on three criteria:

- Dimension
- Sharing
- Intensity

First, the values that an organization promotes must have the appropriate dimensions (e.g., pragmatic vs. detail-oriented, risk-taking vs. conservative) to support internal control effectiveness. In other words, management must evaluate the appropriate values that help an organization succeed in its environment and that ensure internal stability.[28] While this chapter will only briefly discuss the dimension criteria, of primary relevance for the analysis of the individual level are the second and third criteria, which reflect cultural strength. Wiener states that organizational value systems "span a continuum from weak, in which key values are not broadly

[22]The literature distinguishes between values in a general sense and work values. Pine and Innis (1987, p. 280) define these work values as "an individual's needs and priorities and consequent personal dispositions and orientations to work roles that have the perceived capability to satisfy those needs and priorities". Thus, some studies on organizational values are criticized as investigating work instead of general organizational values. These difficulties with consistently defining and measuring of organizational culture have contributed to the inclusiveness of the research (Lim 1995, p. 20).

[23]Wiener (1988, p. 536).

[24]Wiener (1988, p. 544).

[25]Van Rekom et al. (2006, p. 180).

[26]See Pant and Lachman (1998), Van Rekom et al. (2006, p. 176).

[27]Collins and Porras (1996, p. 66).

[28]Schein (1985, p. 9).

and intensely shared by members, to strong, in which they are".[29] Thus, the second criterion is that organizational values need to be shared broadly. That is to say, people from an organization have a wide range of values in common.[30] Third, values need to be intense. Values are intense when people in the organization hold to them strongly.[31] These three criteria dimension, sharing and intensity are discussed in the subsequent sections and are related to the individual in order to extract implications for the further course of study.

7.3.2 Dimensions

The dimensions of organizational values influence how people perform any activity relating to internal control.[32] For instance, people working in an organization that primarily encourages conservative risk taking interact differently than people in an organization that is characterized by innovation and growth.[33] In the former organization people may perceive control as inflexible, bureaucratic and slow because the risk aversion leads to high formalization and control procedures. In a worst-case scenario this conservative type of organization fails to adapt to changing conditions because of inflexibility and outdatedness. In contrast to the risk-averse culture, an innovative and risk-taking culture might operate in an industry with high technological development, in which projects often imply non-routine tasks that require collaboration among people.[34] In this fast-paced work environment people feel overwhelmed to deal not only with daily activities but also with intensive change. They need to be pragmatic and concentrate on outcome.[35] In the risk-taking organization's worst-case scenario, instability of organizational structures and processes and inability to focus on details are likely to raise internal control issues.[36] These examples show the importance of adequate dimension for the

[29]Wiener (1988, p. 535).

[30]O'Reilly (1989, p. 17).

[31]Chatman and Jehn (1994, p. 524).

[32]To give an idea of different value dimensions and their possible influences on the individual, the value dimensions of the organizational culture profile (OCP) are discussed. The OCP is a widely accepted measurement method that assumes every organizational culture is measurable through the dimensions of innovation, stability, respect for people, outcome orientation, detail orientation, team orientation, and aggression (O'Reilly et al. 1991, p. 494-495).

[33]Chatman and Jehn (1994, p. 527).

[34]Pennings and Harianto (1992, p. 357-358).

[35]Chatman and Jehn (1994, p. 527), Kanter (1988, p. 98). See also the, flexible' firm according to Mouritsen (1999).

[36]This echoes the finding of Ashbaugh-Skaife et al. (2007, p. 3), Doyle et al. (2007, p. 5), Ge and McVay (2005, p. 138). Firms in industries such as computers, services, retail, pharmaceuticals and medical products have a higher relative incidence of material weaknesses in internal control. These industries usually require more innovation and risk taking and are more competitive because product lifetimes are relatively short compared to those in more traditional industries.

organizational setting. The dimensions of organizational values are crucial for the organization to survive in its environments. To explain the tensions between individual and organizational interests, which is the focus of this chapter, the next two criteria are more relevant: sharing and intensity.

7.3.3 Sharing

If personal and organizational objectives are identical, the enthusiasm for pursuing an organization's goals will be high.[37] In this sense shared values contribute to internal control because they help individual, group, and team decision-, action-, and policy-making.[38] A culture with shared values simplifies the interaction between the organizational members necessary to achieve their common goals.[39] As values influence behavior and perception, they are important for interpersonal interactions. People who share similar values receive external stimuli in the same ways, and classify and interpret them in similar matters. This simplifies the interpersonal communication.[40] Additionally, researchers agree that shared values support strategy implementation, organizational change, and the perception of the organization from the outside.[41] When people work in an organization, however, their personal values can conflict with the organizational values and norms. Value conflicts contribute to labor–management strife, poor morale, and poor communications.[42] Value conflicts are also negatively associated with performance,[43] retaliation for whistle-blowing,[44] and are positively associated with job search behavior and intent to leave the organization.[45] Therefore operating in an environment that is consistent with one's values has a positive effect on organizational goals. People with similar values can also better predict the behavior of others and are more efficient in coordinating their actions.[46]

[37] Ouchi (1979, p. 842).

[38] CoCo (1995b, p. 14).

[39] Kluckhohn (1951, p. 395).

[40] Meglino and Ravlin (1998, p. 356).

[41] Becker et al. (1996, p. 481), Chatman and Jehn (1994, p. 523), Deal and Kennedy (1982, p. 8), Kotter and Heskett (1992, p. 8), Wilkins and Ouchi (1983, p. 364).

[42] McMurray (1963, p. 144).

[43] Becker et al. (1996, p. 481), Lee and Mowday (1987, p. 144).

[44] Miceli and Near (1994, p. 773).

[45] Cable and Judge (1996, p. 294), Lee and Mowday (1987, p. 421).

[46] Meglino and Ravlin (1998, p. 356) On the other hand, variations in the values held by organizational members can also be positive for creativity and innovation.

7.3.4 Intensity

As Wiener states above, values need not only be shared broadly among organizational members, they also should be intense, which is most important for the analysis of this chapter. Intensity is about how strongly people in the organization stick to the shared values. The more intensely the values are held, the less likely people are to follow other interests than the shared values.[47] With regard to intensity of values, rationalization is important. A value is a standard that helps an individual rationalize attitudes and actions that would otherwise be personally and socially unacceptable. Because values have a social factor in the sense that individuals may experience guilt when they do not behave in accordance to social expectations they will believe in,[48] values can be used to rationalize these feelings. In other words, personal feelings of morality and competence, which maintain and enhance self-esteem, can be defended through values that rationalize inappropriate behavior.[49] That is why values are often interpreted as "oughtness," indicating how the person believes he or she "should" or "ought to" behave.[50] Rokeach (1973, p. 13) explains rationalization as the following:

> An unkind remark made to a friend, for example, may be rationalized as a life guided by self-control; an act of aggression by a nation may be justified on the basis of one human value or another such as national security or the preservation of liberty.

Thus, the intensity of values is important for internal control because people will be less likely to rationalize a following of personal rather than organizational interests. Rationalization is part of the fraud triangle. The fraud triangle, illustrated in Fig. 7.2, explains that the roots of fraud consist of three elements: motive, opportunity and rationalization. The motive, as the first element of the fraud triangle, stands for the reason why people commit fraudulent behavior. Biegelman and Bartow (2006, p. 33) explain that the motive often relates to greed and can be traced back to motivations such as "living beyond one's means, an immediate financial need, debts, poor credit, a drug or gambling addition, and family pressure, to name a few". Opportunity, as the second element, is about the possibility that a person allows conducting fraud, which is usually determined by his or her position of authority in the company and access to assets and records. Rationalization, as the third element of the fraud triangle, is the way a person justifies fraudulent behavior.

---

[47] For example, Chatman (1991) and O'Reilly et al. (1991).

[48] Kluckhohn (1951, p. 394).

[49] Rokeach (1973, p. 13).

[50] Meglino and Ravlin (1998, p. 354), Rokeach (1973, p. 11), Williams (1968, p. 15).

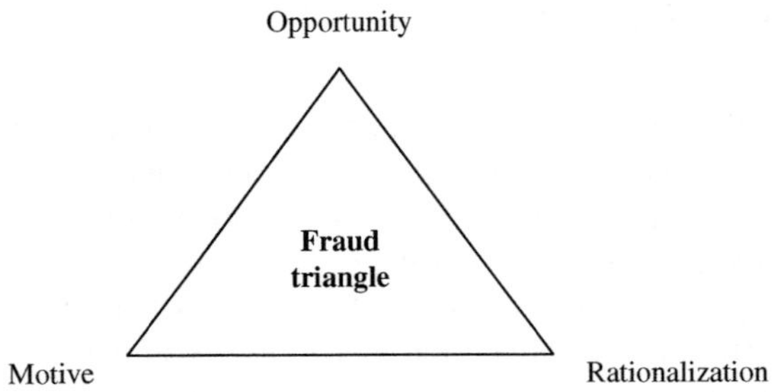

Fig. 7.2 The fraud triangle
Soruce: ACFE (2004, p. 1).

In the literature of organizational corruption rationalization is defined as one of three major reasons that corruption can become normalized in the culture. For example, as illustrated in Table 7.1, denial of responsibility, as the first category, represents actors who rationalize corrupt behavior because they perceive that they have no other choice than to participate in corrupt activities. Another example, social weighting, occurs when actors rationalize their behavior by comparing themselves with others. If competitors do the same why should "we" not do it? This study argues that these reasons for rationalization can be transferred to any control behavior that does not – knowingly – follow the organizational values properly. For example, if people do shoddy work and appear lazy they might rationalize their behavior by comparing themselves to their leaders that also do not perform controls accurately.

Referring back to the value theories, strong values can avoid a situation in which organizational members easily rationalize ineffective (including corrupt) behavior. The stronger the promoted and taught values are in the organization, the more difficult it is for the individual to rationalize the organizational values if the organizational values are threatened. Accordingly, the more intense the shared values of an organization are, the less they will be threatened through personal interests and the more likely they will be of concern to organizational members.[51] This conclusion can relate to any behavior of the organizational members. For example, when people would like to be lazy and do not perform their control tasks properly because they are having a "bad day," strong values can motivate people to work more effectively. Likewise, when people have the tendency to conduct fraud, strong values can make them refrain from doing that. Thus, organizational values most not only have the right dimensions and be shared broadly, but also need to be held intensely. The organization must reach a broad agreement on the organizational values throughout the entity in order to have members pushing in the same direction. People must adhere to the organizational

[51] Van Rekom et al. (2006, p. 179).

Table 7.1 Types of rationalization[52]

Strategy	Description	Examples
Denial of responsibility	The actors engaged in corrupt behaviors perceive that they have no other choice than to participate in such activities	"What can I do? My arm is being twisted". "It is none of my business what the corporation does in overseas bribery"
Denial of injury	The actors are convinced that no one is harmed by their actions; hence the actions are not really corrupt	"No one was really harmed". "It could have been worse"
Denial of victim	The actors counter any blame for their actions by arguing that the violated party deserved whatever happened	"They deserved it". "They chose to participate"
Social weighting	The actors assume two practices that moderate the salience of corrupt behaviors: 1. Condemn the condemner, 2. Selective social comparison	"You have no right to criticize us". "Others are worse than we are"
Appeal to higher loyalties	The actors argue that their violation of norms is due to their attempt to realize a higher-order value	"We answered to a more important cause". "I would not report it because of my loyalty to my boss"
Metaphor of the ledger	The actors rationalize that they are entitled to indulge in deviant behaviors because of their accrued credits (time and effort) in their jobs	"We've earned the right". "It's all right for mc to use the Internet for personal reasons at work. After all I do work overtime"

values so they are less likely to rationalize pursuing personal rather than organizational interests.

7.4 Implications

Combining the literature of personal and organizational values, organizational culture, and corruption in organizations in this chapter provides important implications for a culture that supports effective internal control. The theories confirm the importance of adequate value dimensions for internal control. Thus, an organization needs to promote adequate values in order to be successful in its environment. Which dimension is promoted is part of the organizational level. However, what is important in this theoretical analysis at the individual level is the discrepancy and interplay between personal and organizational interests. Cultural strength is defined as

[52]Anand et al. (2005, p. 11).

sharing and intensity of values among organizational members. If values are broadly shared among members, it brings consistency in behavior. Shared values mean that if members are asked what values are important in the culture, they will share many values. The values, however, not only need to be shared broadly, but they also must be held intensely by organizational members. When people strongly hold organizational values, it becomes more difficult for organizational members to rationalize a following of other than organizational values. Thus, from the approach taken in this chapter, it becomes clear – whatever the cultural dimension – that values promoted need to be strong in order that organizational member will follow them. To establish strong organizational values, the organization can reinforce the values by:

- Leadership
- Selection
- Socialization

These three factors are generally seen as contributing to establishing organizational culture. To begin with, establishing and maintaining an organizational culture that consists of strong values is primarily influenced by executives and senior management. Research indicates that only top managers are in a position to influence identity and change of organizational values.[53] Consequently, top management must be aware of its role as gatekeeper for the organization in much the same way as educators, military leaders or priests are gatekeepers for other organizational, institutional or societal entities.[54] Management must establish procedures to identify and select the optimal values to deal with the organizational environment as well as to promote and manifest those values throughout the organization.

Another implication is that management needs to identify new members that are predisposed to adapt to the organizational values.[55] It is important that an organization hires appropriate personnel that commit to the organization and are able to fulfill internal control requirements competently. Clear communication of the organizational values to potential employees is therefore necessary because people whose personal values are similar to the organization's values are more likely to feel attracted to the organization.[56] Managers should also build procedures to understand how well an individual fits the organizational context[57] so that individuals with similar values as those of the organization are selected.[58] In this way it is more likely that the organization establishes personnel that pursue the organizational goals.

---

[53] Barlow et al. (2003, p. 567), Sarros et al. (2005, p. 160).

[54] Rokeach and Ball-Rokeach (1989, p. 777).

[55] Wilkins and Ouchi (1983, p. 498).

[56] In this context Rokeach and Ball-Rokeach (1989, p. 777) argue that a good way to assess organizational values is to evaluate the values of people that aspire to having membership in an organization.

[57] Kirsh (2000, p. 111).

[58] Freedman and Fesko (1996, p. 49).

Table 7.2 Results from Part III

	Chapter 6	Chapter 7
Level of analysis	Organizational level	Individual level
Applied theory	Theory of social systems	Value theories
Cultural dimension	Purpose content	Dimensions of values
Implications	Need for a mix of closed and open purpose boundaries	Selection of dimensions that help surviving in the environment
Cultural strength	Strength and clarity of purpose boundaries	Sharing and intensity of values
Implications	Keeps inadequate behavior outside the culture	No easy rationalization of a following of other than organizational interests

Finally, although for a large and complex organization it is more difficult to establish shared values than for a one-unit organization or a subgroup of an organization,[59] at least some core values can be promoted throughout any type of organization.[60] Management must establish socialization processes to transmit the organizational values to new members and to reinforce the values to existing members. It is important that management sets clear expectations about people's conduct on a continuous basis. A common way is to establish and maintain rites and rituals that support and reemphasize the existing organizational values.[61]

Table 7.2 summarizes the results from the theoretical analysis in Part III. The table shows that the two theories confirm and complement each other. Both theories provide explanations for the analysis of cultural dimensions and cultural strength. From the analysis in Part III two driver criteria for the synthesis in Part IV have been derived. The drivers (from the field) should

- Establish an adequate mix between closed and open purpose boundaries within the culture
- Build strong boundaries in order that members follow the organizational long-term interests and do not rationalize other interests

The first criterion, derived from the theoretical approach taken to analyze culture at the organizational level, stands for an adequate mix between closedness and openness towards the culture's environment. Culture can be seen like a house with doors and managers decide what control behavior they let come into the house and what not. Closedness assures that it is clear to organizational members what the culture stands for and what behavior is unacceptable in the culture. It also gives the culture consistency and cohesion because it is clearly defined how

[59] Van Rekom et al. (2006, p. 180).

[60] Chatman and Jehn (1994, p. 524).

[61] Wiener (1988, p. 541).

controls need to be performed. Conversely, some openness enhances that the culture can be evaluated from its external and internal environment and can be modified if necessary. Thus, openness assures that the culture does not estrange itself from its environment and develops dynamics inside the culture that contradict its environments.

As a second criterion, the analysis at the individual level demonstrated that when the culture is strong, individuals are less likely to pursue other than organizational interests because it is more difficult for them to rationalize such behavior. Hence, a strong culture makes it clear to organizational members that following other interests than the organizational ones is not accepted in the culture. Managers can establish cultural strength by leadership, selection and socialization. While through leadership managers can provide an example to their followers how controls need to be performed, selection and socialization processes assure that predisposed people are selected and new and existing members are continuously socialized to the culture.

Now that the two criteria have been explained, this study's resulting framework can be presented in Part IV.

Part IV
Synthesis

Chapter 8
A Framework for Control and Culture

8.1 The Framework

8.1.1 The Theory-Building Process

The literature review in Part I has confirmed that influence of culture on control is typically covered in management accounting and control research, but less emphasis is given the opposite: the influence of control on culture. This study supports the latter stance: not only does culture influence control, but so does control influence culture. By integrating all prior results from field and theory, this chapter attempts to address this gap in the literature. A unique framework that explains how managers can establish a culture for effective controls is presented.

Before introducing the framework, a brief look back is necessary to show how the framework has been derived from prior study results. The framework rests on two pillars. On the one hand, the framework is based on the empirical grounding presented in the field study in Part II. The field brings a wide collection of principles and practices (drivers) that managers perceive as supportive to a culture for effective controls. In contrast to other control terminologies, which look at "controls" or "systems",[1] "drivers" are more broadly defined in this study. The drivers not only contain formal and informal control mechanisms, but can also include other factors influencing behavior that can be more unintentional in nature (e.g., leadership behavior). Taking this broad view helps to capture more influences impacting a culture that supports the overall effectiveness of internal control.

While the field study provides the empirical grounding, Part III, the second pillar, contributes with two interdisciplinary theories for the role of culture in the context of control. Looking at the organizational and individual levels of culture, the theories provide explanations not only for how culture influences control

---

[1] In more detail, the terminologies are explained in Sects. 3.3.3 and 3.3.4. Also, the terminologies from Merchant and Simons will be compared in more detail in Sect. 8.3.2.

J. Pfister, *Managing Organizational Culture for Effective Internal Control*, Contributions to Management Science,
DOI: 10.1007/978-3-7908-2340-0_8, © Springer Physica-Verlag Berlin Heidelberg 2009

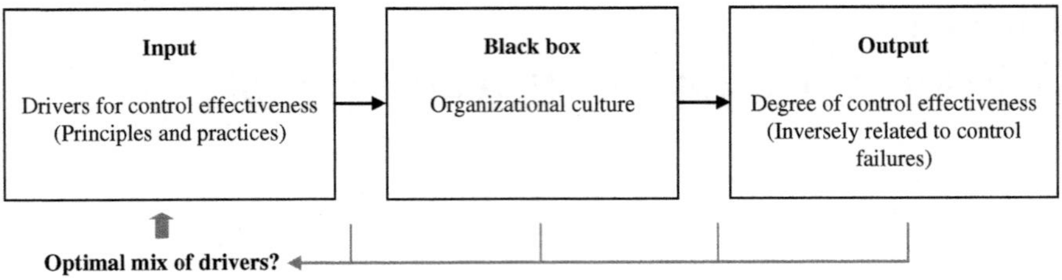

Fig. 8.1 Finding the optimal mix of drivers

effectiveness, but also how cultural conditions that support control effectiveness can be reached.

Based on an iterative process between examining and re-examining these empirical and theoretical inputs, the framework is the product of the synthesis of these two pillars. As will be shown in this chapter, the framework is clearly unique because it treats cultural aspects significantly differently than other frameworks, by interpreting culture as a variable that can be actively influenced. The integration of Part IV within the entire study is illustrated in Fig. 8.1. The thin gray arrow indicates the combination of prior insights in order to examine how the drivers can be mixed optimally. Thus, this chapter addresses how managers can apply the drivers for control effectiveness[2] so that organizational culture[3] is influenced in a way that supports internal control effectiveness.

8.1.2 Framework Overview

Based on prior insights, the drivers for control effectiveness are divided into closing, opening and reinforcing drivers. *Closing drivers*, the first category, define how controls need to be performed and set clear limits for organizational members. Closing drivers close the culture to specific behavior that is unacceptable in the culture. *Opening drivers*, the second category, give members freedom, to some extent, to perform controls and assure that the culture is evaluated by internal and external parties, and modified if necessary. These drivers open the culture because they allow some transfer between environment and culture. *Reinforcing drivers*, the third category, manifest and disperse the content of closing and opening drivers throughout the culture via leadership, selection and socialization processes. These reinforcing drivers make the culture strong by reinforcing the other two types of drivers. As illustrated in Fig. 8.2, these three types of drivers are integrated within a framework, which will be referred to as the *control-and-culture framework* for effective control.

[2] For an overview of the drivers see Sect. 4.3.1.

[3] For the theoretical explanations see Chaps. 5, 6 and 7.

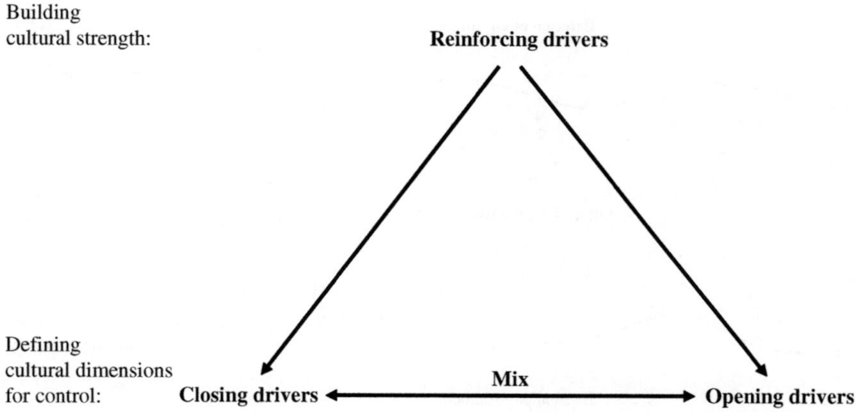

Fig. 8.2 The control-and-culture framework for effective control

As illustrated in the figure (and discussed below), the three types of drivers interrelate. While closing and opening drivers primarily define how controls are performed and how much openness exists in the culture, the role of reinforcing drivers is to reemphasize and manifest the content of closing and opening drivers.

To give a brief illustration of how the drivers interrelate, a hypothetical example of implementing a new system is discussed based on the driver examples from the field study:

- "Take appropriate time"[4] is a *closing driver* because it closes the culture to rushing the implementation of a new system. Thus, when implementing a new system, the driver "take appropriate time" means that people test the system adequately before implementing it into the business, and people do not risk control failures as a result of inadequate testing.
- "Encourage constructive debate"[5] is an *opening driver* because it leads to a discussion between managers and employees. These debates can lead to the result that in a particular case early implementation of a new system in the business is adequate. For this particular case, no significant risks of control failures have been identified if the system is tested while running it in the business. Thus, the openness assures flexibility in the application of *closing drivers* because of open debates.

[4]See driver 5-4 in Chap. 4.

[5]See driver 3-4 in Chap. 4.

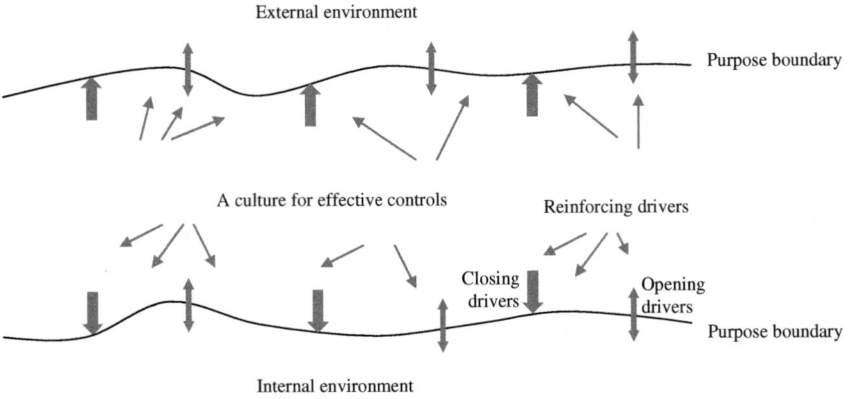

Fig. 8.3 Three types of drivers

- "Lead by example"[6] is a *reinforcing driver* because it can show employees that managers take adequate time for implementing a new system, but if there are good reasons (for example, derived through constructive debate), the implementation can be rushed. This behavior is demonstrated to employees and as a consequence builds an example for handling further such situations in their role as leaders themselves.

Hence, closing and opening drivers form cultural dimensions in regard to performing controls, whereas reinforcing drivers build cultural strength by dispersing and manifesting the other two drivers throughout the culture. The closing driver "take appropriate time" builds some consistency in the culture by giving direction, while the opening driver "encourage constructive debate" provides some flexibility if there are adequate reasons. Finally, "lead by example" assures that these drivers are dispersed throughout the culture. By doing that, any reinforcing driver can influence and promote both closing as well as opening drivers. The three types of drivers and their interrelations in the culture are illustrated in Fig. 8.3.

Because every organization has its individual characteristics and environment, the exact composition of the drivers for control effectiveness that managers need to apply will vary from one organizational setting to another. What this study claims, however, is that in any organization these three types of drivers need to be adequately mixed in order to establish a culture for effective controls. Thus, if a culture does not consider, underemphasizes or overemphasizes one of these types of drivers, the culture might be less likely to support control effectiveness and the organization's long-term performance. The following two sections will demonstrate the three types of drivers in more detail and illustrate them based on the drivers from the field study.

[6]See driver 1-1 in Chap. 4.

8.1.3 Closing Drivers and Opening Drivers

Closing drivers and opening drivers stand for the degree of openness of the culture. While closing drivers close the culture from specific behavior, opening drivers open the culture to influence from its internal and external environments. To decide on the degree of openness of a culture is a decision that senior-level people make – whether intentionally or unintentionally. Before discussing more on the interrelation between closing and opening drivers, each is discussed and illustrated.

8.1.3.1 Closing Drivers

Closing drivers define clearly how controls need to be performed and set organizational members' limits. Closing drivers offer advantages that they:

- Give guidance to organizational members on how controls need to be performed
- Establish consistency in control behavior throughout the culture
- Define what behavior is unacceptable in the culture

The field study offered several examples of closing drivers. These are summarized in Table 8.1. In that table, the drivers themselves stand for accepted control behavior, while the examples on the right side of the table illustrate behavior that these drivers oppose and keep outside of the culture. The middle column indicates the number of the driver in the field study.

For example, managers that ingrain sustainability[7] make it clear to their followers that controls need to support the organization's long-term interests. Applying this driver ensures that the culture is more likely to keep short-term thinking (e.g., winning at all costs, bribing) outside of the culture. Dealing with reality[8] means that control issues should not be postponed. Rather, issues should be addressed immediately. Making specialists available[9] makes clear in the culture that control issues should not arise due to inadequate expertise. Promoting effective communication[10] ensures that for a particular control issue the relevant people within the organization are informed. These examples illustrate that closing drivers explain how controls need to be performed, and make clear what type of behavior is unacceptable.

Closing drivers are fundamental for the culture because they define a common understanding of how controls need to be performed. They build consistency in behavior and contribute to the cohesion of the culture. However, an overemphasis on closing drivers can make the organization inflexible as organizational members are confronted with a large amount of formal and informal rules. Organizational

[7] See driver 1-2 in Chap. 4.

[8] See driver 1-3 in Chap. 4.

[9] See driver 2-4 in Chap. 4.

[10] See driver 3-2 in Chap. 4.

Table 8.1 Examples of closing drivers

Closing drivers	Field study no.	Examples: these drivers close the culture to
Ingrain sustainability	1-2	Solely short-term thinking (e.g., winning at all costs)
Deal with reality	1-3	Procastinating of addressing control issues
Make specialists available	2-4	Inadequate access to expertise
Promote effective communication	3-2	Inadequate communication channels
Keep a holistic view	4-1	Disregard of control gaps and overlaps
Focus on risks	4-2	Misallocating resources for control
Measure processes	4-3	Inadequate management attention
Establish consistency	4-4	Inconsistent and inefficient controls
Embed controls	4-5	Performing controls as something extra at the end of the day
Monitor continuously	5-1	Becoming complaisant and ignoring necessary changes
Capture change	5-2	Inadequate processes for capturing changes
Standardize change	5-3	Inefficient dealing with changes
Take appropriate time	5-4	Rushing the implementation of changes

members might even perceive these drivers as a sign of mistrust or poor workmanship because an extensive number of closing drivers minimizes their autonomy in designing and executing controls.[11] Moreover, a culture that is based solely on closing drivers can develop its own dynamics and estrange itself from its environment as its leader can define the culture, much like a dictator in a dictatorship. For example, in a corrupt culture leaders can often influence that bribery is the common practice in the culture without a need to justify this closing driver to his or her followers. That is why the literature on corruption supports that cultures which are closed are often more likely to lead to corruption.[12]

On the other hand, having just a few closing drivers gives the culture less cohesion and consistency since little guidance is given to organizational members on how to perform controls. Also, a small number of closing drivers is likely to make the culture look weak because members share fewer behavioral patterns.[13] Consequently, a fair number of closing drivers will be necessary to establish a culture for effective controls. As the theoretical framework above indicates, these closing drivers need to be dispersed and manifested by reinforcing drivers to be effective. Moreover, in order to be evaluated and modified adequately over time they need to co-exist with opening drivers.

[11] Derived from O'Reilly and Chatman (1996, p. 161).

[12] See Ashforth and Anand (2003).

[13] See O'Reilly et al. (1991), Wiener (1988).

8.1.3.2 Opening Drivers

Opening drivers assure that the opinions of organizational members are considered in designing and executing control within their area of responsibility. These drivers assure that a culture is open to constructive criticism and reevaluation by its members and stays open to feedback from the external environment. Opening drivers have the advantage that:

- Constructive debate takes place, which can continuously evaluate and improve controls.
- More opinions are considered and, as a result, internal control can become more effective.[14]
- Leaders and followers cannot easily rationalize ineffective (i.e., corrupt) behavior because they need to justify these behaviors to internal and external parties.[15]

Table 8.2 illustrates four examples of opening drivers that were identified from the field study. In the middle column the table shows the number of driver in the field study. The right column provides examples how these drivers open the culture.

Defining process ownership[16] cascades the responsibility to the lower hierarchical levels in the organization. This gives individuals, within the boundaries of closing drivers, the opportunity to design and execute controls with some autonomy. Thus, defining process ownership is an opening driver because it allows members to bring in their personal ways of dealing with controls and enhance the open debate between leaders and followers, as both have related control responsibilities. Likewise, explaining benefits[17] considers the backgrounds of the individuals because senior-level people do not simply dictate how controls need to be

Table 8.2 Examples of opening drivers

Opening drivers	Field study no.	Examples: these drivers open the culture to
Define process ownership	1-4	Employees by giving them autonomy of controls within their control area
Explain benefits	3-3	Debates between managers and employees about the benefits of specific controls
Encourage constructive debate	3-4	Criticism, knowledge sharing and sensitivity within and towards the outside of the organization
Enhance a positive attitude	5-5	Debates when managers need to convince their subordinates that change is something positive

[14]Derived from interviews with Lisa Lee, Google and Phil Greybas, SureWest.

[15]Derived from Ashforth and Anand (2003).

[16]See driver 1-4 in Chap. 4.

[17]See driver 3-3 in Chap. 4.

performed. Instead, they must explain to organizational members why specific controls need to be performed and, consequently, managers' ideas are left open to debate by their followers in order to convince the followers of the necessity of certain controls. Explaining benefits leads directly to encouraging constructive debate,[18] possibly the most crucial opening driver. A culture in which organizational members can speak up when there are control issues assures that the culture is constantly being evaluated by organizational members. It also makes the culture open to criticism by external parties. Enhancing a positive attitude[19] towards change, as the fourth example shows, makes leaders explain to followers why changes are necessary. Therefore, leaders need to consider the followers' background in order to convince them that change is positive.

While closing drivers provide organizational members relatively little freedom by clearly defining how controls need to be performed, opening drivers consider the opinion and personal motivation of each individual as a performer of controls. To establish these opening drivers can be challenging for managers because managers need to balance the concerns of the organization, its employees, customers, competitors, and the public at large. As these various interests can often be oppositional, balancing these concerns is a complex effort. However, opening drivers are crucial for the culture because they ensure that the culture does not estrange itself from its environments (e.g., corrupt organization). On the other hand, as with closing drivers, an overemphasis on opening drivers can lead to disadvantages. Too many opening drivers can make the organization seem sluggish because too many opinions need to be considered. Moreover, in a worst case scenario, an overemphasis on these opening drivers is likely to bring inconsistencies in controls and can undermine leaders' authority. Therefore, as was discussed in Sect. 8.1.3.1, these opening drivers need to be performed contingent upon an adequate set of closing drivers.

8.1.3.3 Mix between Closing and Opening Drivers

Closing drivers and opening drivers represent opposing extremes. Closing drivers stand for control, while opening drivers stand for autonomy. Closing drivers are applied more top-down within the organization, while opening drivers promote a bottom-up direction. Closing drivers stand for consistency and centralization; opening drivers can provide flexibility and decentralization.[20]

This mix of closing and opening drivers is in alignment with existing control frameworks and literature. In the literature these balances of extremes are referred to as "tensions", "tight versus loose control", or "paradoxes of governance". For example, Merchant and Van der Stede (2007) use the concept of "tightness of

---

[18] See driver 3-4 in Chap. 4.

[19] See driver 5-5 in Chap. 4.

[20] See in more detail Appendix C.

controls", and discuss whether and in which situation controls should be designed as loose or tight. Simons (1995) discusses the four types of systems as opposing forces such as "yin and yang" from Chinese philosophy. While belief systems and interactive control systems resemble positive and inspirational forces (yang), boundary systems and diagnostic control systems stand for the negative – constraints and compliance with rules (yin).[21] In 2005, Simons relates his theories to those tensions that relate to strategy and structure, accountability and adaptability, or self-interest and mission success.[22] In the governance literature these tensions between "control and collaboration" are discussed as paradoxes of governance. For example, Sundaramurthy and Lewis (2003) address these paradoxes and state that management needs to manage both control *and* collaboration. What these approaches all have in common is that they are, to varying degrees, concerned with the extremes of control and empowerment. Additionally, all the above researchers propose that for the overall effectiveness of the (control or governance) system, the "tensions" or "paradoxes" of control and empowerment need to be managed by balancing the extremes.

This framework differs from the other approaches on two main points. First, this *control-and-culture framework* addresses tensions in regard to how control can influence the closeness/openness of the culture. This is a different approach from others which are primarily concerned with control or governance. Second, the approach here differs from the examples in the literature because the closing and opening drivers here rely on reinforcing drivers. Closing and opening drivers can only be effective if they are reemphasized throughout the culture by reinforcing drivers.[23] Reinforcing drivers are discussed in more detail in Sect. 8.1.4.

8.1.4 Reinforcing Drivers

Reinforcing drivers disperse and manifest the content of closing and opening drivers throughout the culture via leadership, selection and socialization. Based on their own behavior, leaders can make visible how closing and opening drivers need to be performed.[24] Selection ensures that new people coming into the organization are predisposed to follow the closing and opening drivers of the organization,[25] and socialization assures that new and existing members are continuously

---

[21] Simons (1995, p. 7).

[22] Simons (2005, p. 8–12).

[23] These are two major differences from other approaches in the literature. In more detail, the differences between the *control-and-culture framework* to Merchant and Simons will be discussed at the end of the chapter.

[24] Barlow et al. (2003, p. 567) and Sarros et al. (2005, p. 160).

[25] Wilkins and Ouchi (1983, p. 498).

socialized to the drivers that are important for the culture.[26] Thus, with reinforcing drivers come the advantage that both closing and opening driver become stronger and, hence, more effective.

Reinforcing drivers do not provide content themselves (e.g., how controls need to be performed). Rather, they primarily assure that opening and closing drivers are promoted throughout the culture. Each reinforcing driver can promote any closing or opening driver. Thus, they can relate to various opening and closing drivers and reinforce the content of these drivers. Table 8.3 contains examples of reinforcing drivers from the field. The right column lists the reinforcing functions of these drivers. Similar to the prior table, the middle column lists the commensurate number of the particular field driver.

As the table demonstrates, leaders need to set an example[27] and illustrate with their behavior what they expect from their employees in regard to closing and opening drivers. Also, the right people should be selected[28] to become part of the culture in order to assure that the culture can be maintained. The drivers demonstrate that new people are brought in, not just appropriate qualifications need to be considered but also the social skills[29] that fit with the closing and opening drivers.

Table 8.3 Examples of reinforcing drivers

Reinforcing drivers	Field study no.	Examples: these drivers reinforce the culture by
Lead by example	1-1	Role modeling the application of closing and opening drivers
Ensure accountability	1-5	Using accountability in order to ensure closing and opening drivers are applied
Select appropriate qualification	2-1	Selecting people that bring the qualification to apply the closing and opening drivers
Consider social skills	2-2	Selecting people that bring the necessary social skills for applying the closing and opening drivers
Offer continuous training	2-3	Providing training that disperses the closing and opening drivers
Establish an attractive work environment	2-5	Attracting people that are predisposed to the closing and opening drivers of the organization
Set clear and continuous messages	3-1	Setting clear messages about the closing and opening drivers of the organization
Announce actions	3-5	Clarifying that actions are taken if people do not behave in accordance with the closing and opening drivers

[26] For example, O'Reilly and Chatman (1996) and Wiener (1988).

[27] See driver 1-1 in Chap. 4.

[28] See driver 2-1 in Chap. 4.

[29] See driver 2-2 in Chap. 4.

Establishing an attractive work environment[30] attracts an adequate pool of potential employees from which the organization can choose the best individuals. Even when adequate people are selected they need to be "socialized" in keeping with the closing and opening drivers. One of these aspects is to project strong, ongoing messages,[31] which reminds employees that closing and opening drivers stand for the work culture. Another way to socialize people to the culture is to offer continuous training.[32] Training is a way to ensure that people understand and learn how they should perform controls. Finally, ensuring accountability[33] and announcing actions[34] are two additional drivers that socialize people to the closing and opening drivers of the culture because people come to understand that there are sanctions or rewards according to how their behavior relates to the closing and opening drivers.

These reinforcing drivers rely on the content of closing and opening drivers. If the prior two drivers do not reflect the adequate dimensions for a culture that enhances control effectiveness in the organization, these reinforcing drivers will be useless in supporting a culture for effective controls. Conversely, if these reinforcing drivers promote the adequate mix of closing and opening drivers they become a major driver for the effectiveness of the other two drivers.

8.2 Application

8.2.1 Overview

In the preceding sections the *control-and-culture framework* was introduced in order to provide a theory that explains how managers can establish a culture for effective controls. The framework provides theoretical patterns that can be useful in research and in practice. To illustrate possible opportunities for how the framework can be applied, this section provides ideas for the application of the framework in research and in practice. This section looks at three possible application areas:

- Qualitative research
- Quantitative research
- Practice

[30] See driver 2-5 in Chap. 4.

[31] See driver 3-1 in Chap. 4.

[32] See driver 2-3 in Chap. 4.

[33] See driver 1-5 in Chap. 4. With regard to reinforcing the opening drivers through accountability, Steinmann and Schreyögg clarify that the incentive and sanctioning system of the organization should support openness. For example, organizations should not sanction transmitters of bad news and critical comments by isolating these people or not promoting them (e.g., the role of whistle-blowers in companies) (Steinmann and Schreyögg 1986, p. 761).

[34] See driver 3-5 in Chap. 4.

These three areas and how the framework can be applied to them are discussed briefly in the following three sections. After possible applications have been demonstrated, the chapter continuous with a critical reflection of the framework and a comparison to well-established frameworks from management accounting and control research.

8.2.2 *Qualitative Research*

In order to facilitate the application of the *control-and-culture framework* in qualitative research, a possible setting for a case study is discussed.[35]

As mentioned in the introduction, Siemens, a conglomerate of more than 450,000 people, has maintained covert funds in the amount of €1.3 billion used as bribes to win contracts worldwide.[36] These funds were maintained in an organization of front firms and bank accounts that enhanced the payments. Siemens is accused of bribery that took place over a time period between 1998 and 2006, with one exception in 1996.[37] Despite the existence of formal compliance systems which led people to confirm a code of conduct, the scandal involved large parts of Siemens' senior managers throughout various business units.[38]

An interesting focus to illustrate the *control-and-culture framework* is the executive-level management at Siemens.[39] After the scandal surfaced Siemens hired a new CEO whose task it was to change the culture. Changing the culture would imply that the closing, opening and reinforcing drivers from the new CEO and his predecessor differ significantly. Therefore a possible setup for an in-depth case study could distinguish between the time period before (with the old CEO) and after the bribing affair was revealed (with the new CEO). The following briefly discusses the two time periods. The Siemens bribery affair provides a possible case study that can illustrate the interrelations between closing, opening and reinforcing drivers in practice.

[35] According to Yin (1994, p. 13) a case study is defined as: "an empirical inquiry that investigates a contemporary phenomenon within its real-life context, especially when the boundaries between phenomenon and context are not clearly evident".

[36] Among the destinations of alleged bribery in the Siemens scandal are Azerbaijan, Brazil, Cameroon, China, Egypt, Greece, Hungary, Indonesia, Israel, Italy, Kuwait, Libya, Malaysia, Nigeria, Norway, Poland, Russia, Saudi Arabia, Spain and Vietnam (Heimann and Dell 2008, p. 45).

[37] Heimann and Dell (2008, p. 45).

[38] The allegations concern the payment of bribes by high-level Siemens employees in connection with Siemens telecommunications, power generation, power transmission, transportation systems, health care and industrial solutions groups. Siemens' bribings were allegedly transferred through a network of intermediaries, front companies and bank accounts in Austria, the British Virgin Islands, Cyprus, Hong Kong, Italy, Liechtenstein Monaco, Puerto Rico, Switzerland, and the US (Heimann and Dell 2008, p. 45).

[39] A case study would also need to clarify which level it focuses on (e.g., executives, senior managers, employees).

8.2.2.1 The "Bribing" Culture (1998–2006)

Investigators confirm that Siemens' senior managers maintained and reinforced a culture of paying bribes from slush funds in order to win contracts.[40] Siemens admitted that these payments were made but neglected to mention that they were made based on authorized company policy. Instead, the company asserts the transfers were made by "the actions of rogue employees".[41] In fact, the former CEO, Klaus Kleinfeld, and the former Chairman, Heinrich von Pierer, both denied having any knowledge of the corrupt activities and resigned under pressure from shareholders.[42] Independent of whether they knew about the bribes or not, the Siemens' culture obviously lacked reinforcing drivers and possibly a lack of opening drivers as well. The executives failed in reinforcing from the top that bribing is unacceptable in the culture (at least because of the risk to reputation), and that people who bribe need to be sanctioned.[43] A more detailed analysis in a case study would provide a better understanding what these leaders promoted, in particular how they apply closing, opening and reinforcing drivers.

8.2.2.2 The "New" Culture (2007–Present)

To put the scandal behind it, for the first time in its 160-year history, in 2007 Siemens appointed an outsider as CEO.[44] The new CEO, Peter Löscher, himself said: "One thing is clear: this company failed based on leadership responsibility and culture".[45] To change the culture, he restructured the complex and numerous business units into three major divisions and forced organizational members that were part of the bribery scandal to collaborate with investigators.[46] *The Economist* writes of Peter Löscher: "He then dropped a bombshell, warning top managers in a letter that ignorance and loyalty were no excuses for having broken the law. Managers were offered an amnesty until January 31st – later extended by a month – to encourage them to spill the beans. And they have been doing so: 110

---

[40] *Economist*, March 6 2008: Stopping the rot.

[41] Heimann and Dell (2008: 45-46).

[42] *Economist*, March 6 2008: Stopping the rot.

[43] Paine (1994, p. 108) explains: "Managers who fail to provide proper leadership and to institute systems that facilitate ethical conduct share responsibility with those who conceive, execute, and knowingly benefit from corporate misdeeds". About the role of executives for the effectiveness of ethics control systems, see also Weaver et al. (1999).

[44] Löscher had previously headed divisions at Siemens' competitor General Electric and Merck, a pharmaceutical giant (*Economist*, March 6 2008: Stopping the rot).

[45] *Financial Times*, January 20 2008: Scandal puts Siemens to the test.

[46] *Economist*, July 8 2008: Time to fix Siemens.

came forward, giving investigators dozens of new leads".[47] An employee states about the new CEO: "There is now clarity of action and no doubt of consequences".[48]

Although Mr. Löscher still needs to prove that he can change the Siemens culture, the new CEO seems to make clear that the *closing driver* "bribery is unacceptable" is not only pro-forma, but he reinforces this closing driver by saying that there is "no excuse" for illegal behavior. While before bribing was a common practice at Siemens, Mr. Löscher, who is about to change Siemens' culture, applies strong *reinforcing drivers* so that organizational member understand that bribery is unacceptable in the culture. Whether Mr. Löscher keeps adequate *opening drivers* in the culture could be the subject of an in-depth case study. A culture that supports more critical debates from top to bottom and vice versa might support that bribing will be less likely to become part of the "new" culture. This requires that many people involved would personally prefer that bribing is not part of the culture. From the external environment, the Siemens's culture is now subject to much more public surveillance and, as a result, will need to maintain some openness towards the outside as well.

Table 8.4 provides an overview of possible questions to be solved in a case study focusing on the executive level.[49] The Siemens illustration demonstrates that a change in leadership (after a scandal has been revealed) provides a good setting to investigate these three types of drivers and how they influence internal control effectiveness in more depth.

8.2.3 Quantitative Research

While Sect. 8.2.2.2 discussed a possible application of the *control-and-culture framework* in qualitative research, this section turns towards possible quantitative research applications. Simons (1995, p. 71) states that there are "two accepted truisms" in management accounting and control research:

> First, measurement is critical to management control. Second, participants focus a disproportionate amount of attention on any variable that is measured. These observations, which have important organizational implications, have led to their own familiar set of catch-phrases such as, "what you measure is what you get", "what gets measured gets managed", or "you get what you inspect, not what you expect".

Continuing, Simons explains that "nebulous concepts" such as "success" and "changes in business culture" are difficult to monitor because they are difficult to measure. While this study does not posit that it is possible to measure organizational culture in its entirety, applying the *control-and-culture framework* offers key indications that can be measured. Based on the terminology of closing, opening and reinforcing drivers, theoretical patterns are developed that explain how managers

[47] *Economist*, March 6 2008: Stopping the rot.

[48] *Financial Times*, January 20 2008: Scandal puts Siemens to the test.

[49] The division in different time periods is adapted from Alt (2006).

Table 8.4 Siemens as an example

		Closing drivers	Opening drivers	Reinforcing drivers
The "bribing" culture (1998–2006)	Facts	Formal code of conduct in place and signed periodically by employees; winning contracts at all costs (Siemens admitted that payments were made for bribes)	Culture has estranged from external environment (e.g., German legal environment)	Lack of leadership (300 high-level employees from various departments were involved); lack of sanctions for employees that use bribes
	Examples of questions to be solved in a case study	What type of closing drivers did the CEO promote in public speeches and documents? What were his public statements in regard to bribing and winning contracts?	Was the CEO open to his employees? Did the CEO promote a culture of speaking up? What kind of statements were expressed in regard to the legal environment?	Was the CEO well-known for taking actions if people did not behave with common standards of business conduct? Was there continuous messaging against bribing?
The "new" culture (2007–present)	Facts	Formal code of conduct in place and formally signed periodically by employees; bribing is prohibited and linked to the reputation risk	Debates inside and outside the organization on how Siemens will get out of the crisis; Siemens is closely observed by public attention and needs to keep openness	New CEO makes clear that sanctions will be taken; many former managers have been fired
	Examples of questions to be solved in a case study	What type of closing drivers does the new CEO promote in public speeches and documents? What are his public statements in regard to bribing and winning contracts?	Is the new CEO open to his employees? Does the new CEO promote a culture of speaking up? What kind of statements are expressed in regard to the legal environment?	Is the new CEO well-known for taking actions if people do not behave with common standards of business conduct? Is there continuous messaging against bribing?

Table 8.5 Examples of possible research hypotheses

Example 1:	Organizational settings, in which opening drivers are adequately (weakly) applied, will be less (more) likely to have control failures
Example 2:	Organizational settings, in which strong (weak) reinforcing drivers are applied, will be less (more) likely to have control failures
Example 3:	Organizational settings, in which small (large) discrepancies exist between the perception of managers and their followers on how the mix of drivers is applied, will be less (more) likely to have control failures
Example 4:	Organizational settings, in which small (large) discrepancies exist in the relative mix of drivers across levels and/or units, are less (more) likely to have control failures
Example 5:	Organizational settings, in which the relative amount of opening drivers at the top of the organization is low (adequate), will be more (less) likely to be corrupt

can establish a culture for effective controls. The theory provides multiple hypotheses, which could be tested in future research. Table 8.5 provides examples of possible hypotheses.

In order to investigate such hypotheses, a measurement tool needs to be able to measure these three types of drivers in an organizational setting.[50] To build a measurement tool that supports the testing of these hypotheses, the tool would need to measure how:

- Closing, opening, and reinforcing drivers are ingrained in the culture
- Individuals perceive the drivers in their roles as leader, coworker, and follower
- The average responses differ among hierarchical levels and units within the organization

There are many ways of measuring culture. One way would be to develop a "control and culture profile" measurement instrument. To develop such a measurement tool, knowledge from other disciplines could be useful. In particular, the literature on organizational culture provides a huge amount of measurement techniques. Lim (1995, p. 17) remarks that the huge amount of classification frameworks makes it difficult for researchers to choose the appropriate type. Thus, building a measurement tool that fits to internal control and organizational culture could be developed by applying successful frameworks from other disciplines.[51]

Another way to measure these drivers would be to rely on the terminology from existing control frameworks such as the one from Merchant and Simons. To reinterpret their terminologies based on the *control-and-culture framework*, Table 8.6 relates the existing terminologies to the framework from this study.

As the table indicates, Merchants' result controls would be divided into three parts. The result itself would be a closing driver because it defines for the employee a clear result to achieve. The action leading to the result would be an opening driver

[50]Michela and Burke (2000, p. 229).

[51]For various measurement techniques for organizational culture, see Alexander (1978), Cooke and Lafferty (1983), Denison et al. (2006), O'Reilly et al. (1991).

Table 8.6 Relation to common management control terminologies

	Closing drivers	Opening drivers	Reinforcing drivers
Merchant (result controls; action controls; personnel/cultural controls)	Result controls without accountability (close the culture in regard to a specific result); action controls without accountability (close the culture in regard to the action)	Result controls (open the culture in regard to the action leading to the result)	Personnel controls; cultural controls; action accountability; result accountability
Simons (belief systems; boundary systems; diagnostic control systems; interactive control systems)	Belief systems that give direction; boundary systems; diagnostic control systems without accountability	Belief systems that give openness; diagnostic control systems (if outcome-oriented, provide freedom in regard to the process); interactive control systems	Belief and boundary systems (the way they are dispersed); accountability of diagnostic control systems

because the employee is given autonomy for this part. Finally, whether or not accountability would be taken if the employee achieves the result or not would be a reinforcing driver. To also give an example from Simon's terminology, interactive control systems correspond to opening drivers because they provide open discussion between managers and employees about strategic uncertainties. The *control-and-culture framework* will be compared in more detail to the frameworks from Merchant and Simons in Sect. 8.3.2. The table provides some indications how the framework can be applied in theory-testing studies based on these existing terminologies.

8.2.4 Practice

The *control-and-culture framework* also provides important implications for professionals. The following two paragraphs discuss the relevance of the framework for managers and employees as well as for auditors and consultants.

8.2.4.1 Managers and Employees

For managers the *control-and-culture framework* indicates that three important questions need to be resolved by senior-level people in order to establish a culture for effective controls:

- Do I clearly define to subordinates what is expected from them in regard to the design and execution of controls?

- Do I listen adequately to my subordinates and be open to debates and necessary changes in regard to controls?
- Do I reinforce strongly enough how controls need to be performed and that open debate can take place?

These three questions simplify the framework and do not capture all aspects. However, they illustrate the essence of the framework which contributes to practice by explaining how the drivers for control effectiveness (identified in the field study) need to be mixed. In order to establish a culture for effective controls, managers need to mix closing and opening drivers, and manifest those drivers throughout the culture by reinforcing drivers. The framework therefore provides a better understanding for the cultural processes "underneath". Likewise, the framework provides employees with a better understanding for analyzing the cultural setting of the organization.

8.2.4.2 Auditors and Consultants

For auditors and consultants the framework also offers some possible applications. A framework cannot keep corrupt leaders from entering an organization and establishing an ineffective and corrupt culture. Nevertheless, what this theoretical framework can do is contribute a piece of the puzzle to explain the complexity of the relationship between control and culture. Culture could become more systematically integrated into auditing, assurance and consulting services by providing an early indicator based on the *control-and-culture framework*, which would show if a culture was on a wrong track. It would raise awareness within organizations and could bring leaders to the position that they need to adjust their behavior based on the measured "control and culture profile". Such an indicator could have an important preventative role because auditors and consultants would be given the opportunity to systematically evaluate the cultural aspects of internal control. When managers let auditors and consultants measure their culture, this cultural indicator could send a quality signal inside and outside the organization. Managers could not only improve their culture if it is lacking, but also testify in the form of ratings that they meet the criteria that support a culture for effective controls.

Consequently, this subchapter demonstrates that results from this framework have both important implications for research and in practice. The relevance of the framework and possible applications for research and practice are shown.

8.3 Critical Reflection

8.3.1 General Comments

Section 8.2.4 demonstrated that the *control-and-culture framework* can be applied in research and in practice. Before evaluating the framework against the research theses and comparing it with the control frameworks from Merchant and Simons, this section discusses some general comments.

First, the framework differs clearly from common research in management control by interpreting culture as being influenced by control (instead focusing on the other direction). The framework was developed from a field study with 21 companies and by combining the internal control discipline with literatures from other areas such as strategic control, management control, organizational culture, organizational corruption, theory of social systems, and value theories.[52] By synthesizing these various insights, the framework provides an innovative approach.

Second, the framework primarily relates to internal control because the drivers from the field have been gathered by interviewing senior-level people on the subject of internal control (and organizational culture). However, as there are many overlaps between internal control and management control,[53] the framework seems to be transferable to the broader field of management control research as well as to broader discussions on organizational control.

Third, a surprising result of the framework is that for the overall effectiveness of internal control, the distinction between formal and informal mechanisms[54] seems to have little primary relevance. Rather as Table 8.7 illustrates, each of the three types of drivers (closing, opening, reinforcing) contains formal and informal drivers. Therefore, the question of the degree of formalism seems to be less important for culture as the research might indicate. Nevertheless, at a second level of analysis, the distinction between formal and informal mechanisms gives additional insights.

Another question is what the optimal relative amount for each type of driver is in an organizational setting. By discussing the concept of loose versus tight controls, Simons (1995, p. 161) states that: "In any organization, at any point in time, and at any level, managers will report varying degree of 'tightness'". Likewise, the mix of closing, opening and reinforcing drivers will distinguish one situation from the other based on the point in time and the organizational setting. For example, having many closing drivers, few opening drivers, and no reinforcing drivers will give rise

Table 8.7 Formal versus informal drivers

	Closing drivers	Opening drivers	Reinforcing drivers
Example of a formal driver	Standardize change (driver 5-3)	Define process ownership (driver 1-4)	Offer continuous training (driver 2-3)
Example of an informal driver	Deal with reality (driver 1-3)	Encourage constructive debate (driver 3-4)	Lead by example (driver 1-1)

[52] Simons states that in order to address organizational design issues, research needs to be interdisciplinary (Simons 2005, p. vii).

[53] See Sect. 2.1.2.

[54] For example, Collier (2005) and Nixon and Burns (2005).

to a particular control situation. Exactly these situational differences in composition of closing, opening and reinforcing drivers offer the opportunity to analyze and compare settings according to functions, hierarchical level, industry, and control effectiveness. Thus, an exact mix that would provide the most effective controls is subject to further studies that apply different methods (e.g., survey).[55] This study theorizes that in most organizational settings all three types of drivers need to be considered to achieve long-term effective internal control.

Finally, the framework can easily give the impression that a strong culture is posited. This is true. The framework, however, distinguishes itself from the typical critique on strong cultures (e.g., the Mafia has also a strong culture) by defining that the culture needs to keep openness. A strong culture is most dangerous when it is closed. In contrast, this study proposes that if the culture keeps an adequate "openness" towards the internal and external environments, a strong culture can contribute fundamentally to control effectiveness and the long-term performance of the organization.[56]

8.3.2 Distinction from Merchant and Simons

Section 8.2.3 discussed how the *control-and-culture framework* relates to the terminologies from Merchant and Simons. To provide a better understanding for how this framework distinguishes from Merchant's and Simon's frameworks,[57] this section discusses fundamental differences between the three control terminologies.[58]

Table 8.8 provides an overview of the three basic setups of the control frameworks. When considering the overall objective, the three frameworks differ significantly. For example, Merchant takes the typical management control perspective[59] and attempts to control the behavior of people so they follow organizational objectives. In contrast, Simons is concerned about how strategy can be successfully implemented in control systems. Again, in contrast, the *control-and-culture framework* aims to establish (and maintain) a culture for effective controls.

[55]The relative amount of drivers from the field study may give an indication as to how the drivers should be mixed in order to establish a culture for effective controls. This statement, however, is subject to further investigation and is not supported by this study here.

[56]For more detail about this discussion on strong cultures and their negative effects see Chap. 1.

[57]See Sects. 3.3.3 and 3.3.4.

[58]The framework from Ouchi, which was introduced in the literature review, is excluded here. Ouchi's framework was an important contribution to the study of culture and control. However, as a research framework it provided relatively little empirical support. Moreover, the framework from Merchant builds on Ouchi's terminology and implicitly includes Ouchi's concepts (see Merchant and Otley 2007).

[59]For example, the definition of management control by Anthony (Sect. 2.1.2).

Table 8.8 Basic distinctions from Merchant and Simons

	Control-and-culture framework	Merchant	Simons
Objective	Establishing a culture that enhances effective controls	Control employee's behavior in order to achieve organizational objectives	Strategy implementation in control systems
Focus on	Drivers (formal and informal control mechanisms; can also include unintentional influences)	Controls (formal and informal control mechanisms)	Systems (formal controls, discussed with social and behavioral aspects, e.g., use of systems)
Typology	– Closing drivers – Opening drivers – Reinforcing drivers	– Action controls – Result controls – Personnel/cultural controls	– Belief systems – Boundary systems – Diagnostic control systems – Interactive control systems
Classification criteria	Cultural meaning (closing, opening, and reinforcing the culture)	Control objective (input, process, outcome)	Four levers (core values, risks to be avoided, strategic uncertainties, critical performance variables)

These different objectives are also reflected in what the three frameworks focus on. While Simons focuses the most of the three frameworks by discussing "formal systems", Merchant takes a broader approach and looks at formal *and informal* control mechanisms. The *control-and-culture framework* is even broader than Merchent's and includes not only formal and informal control mechanisms, but also unintentional influences on control effectiveness such as leadership behavior.

Not only do the three frameworks differ according to objective and focus, but also in regard to the classification criteria. While Merchant's terminology builds on a distinction according to the control objective, Simons identifies four constructs, which he defines as being important to address. Again in contrast, the *control-and-culture framework* is based on the cultural meaning (function) of the drivers.

Although focusing on closely related organizational phenomena, these basic distinctions between frameworks demonstrate their different purposes. Depending on the specific research objective, one or the other framework may be more or less adequate. To further illustrate these differences the next paragraphs discusses more specific distinctions.

Table 8.9 shows an overview of specific distinctions between the three control frameworks in order to illustrate for what purpose the *control-and-culture framework* provides assistance.

First, the *control-and-culture framework* differs from the other two frameworks by interpreting culture as being involved in any type of control. Hence

Table 8.9 Specific distinctions from Merchant and Simons

	Control-and-culture framework	Merchant	Simons
Consideration of culture	Integrated in all drivers	One type of control (personnel/cultural controls)	Primarily addressed in two types of systems (belief systems and boundary systems)
Interrelation of controls	Explained and integrated	Emphasis on distinction of controls (explained that they work simultaneously)	Explained and integrated
Accountability	Action/results definition and action/result accountability are separated in closing drivers and reinforcing drivers	No distinction	No distinction
Tone at the top/ leading by example	Integrated in reinforcing drivers	Weakly integrated	Weakly integrated (discusses management attention)
Bottom-up control (employees control managers)	Opening drivers	Weakly integrated	Partially integrated (implicitly discussed in interactive control systems)
Major advantage	Explains how culture can be influenced through controls	Clear and simple distinction between types of controls	An integrative approach to address complexity of large organizations
Major disadvantage	Categorization requires interpretation	Weak consideration of how controls interrelate (incomprehensive consideration of culture)	Focus on formal control systems (incomprehensive consideration of culture)

the cultural meaning of the drivers is the criteria to distinguish the different types of drivers. In contrast, in Merchant and Simons' frameworks culture is typically integrated as one or two types of controls, standing next to other more technical controls. This study takes the stand that all these controls have cultural meaning and reflect and influence the culture. Although in Merchant and Van der Stede's personnel and cultural controls this view is implicitly considered, those authors do not take an integrated view of culture in all types of controls.

Another aspect of comparison is whether the control frameworks consider how controls interrelate when applied simultaneously. One surprising result from this study is that the cultural meaning offers explanations for how different types of controls interrelate, and how and why specific drivers need to be performed simultaneously in order to achieve overall control effectiveness. Interrelations between controls are explained in Simon's terminology of diagnostic and interactive control systems.[60] In Merchant's terminology the emphasis is on the distinction between the different types of controls and mentions that they interrelate, but not much insight is provided as to how the types of controls interrelate except that they address different parts of the process (input, action, result).

Another distinction between the three frameworks is how accountability is integrated in the framework. The *control-and-culture framework* clearly distinguishes the action/result and action/result accountability. From a cultural perspective these two concepts need to be separated because one clearly defines the direction, while the other ensures sanctions and rewards. These are therefore two different cultural concepts. Seeing the action/result as a closing driver and noting accountability as a reinforcing driver is a major difference to the other two frameworks.[61] Merchant and Simons do not distinguish between result and accountability in their terminologies.

A fourth aspect is leadership and tone at the top. The *control-and-culture framework* argues that these leadership aspects are crucial for control effectiveness. If leaders do not stand behind internal control (or any other control activity in the organization), there is a huge impact on the culture and whether organizational members recognize the importance of these controls. Leadership and tone at the top are discussed by Merchant and Simons. However, from a cultural perspective, these, very important aspects for control effectiveness are weakly integrated in their frameworks.

Fifth, control effectiveness often fails as a result of bad leadership. If managers are themselves corrupt, the chance that this behavior may transfer throughout the culture is relatively high.[62] The typical management accounting and control perspective, such as is applied by Merchant, is that managers need to control their employees. In the *control-and-culture framework* another view considers that employees can control their managers as well. If managers need to debate with their employees (opening drivers) then, to some extent, managers will need to justify their behavior. This view is important in regard to accounting scandals where top executives may engage in corrupt behavior. In Simons' terminology

[60] See the discussion about the interrelations of systems in Sect. 3.4.

[61] Accountability (as a reinforcing driver) can reemphasize not only closing but also opening drivers. For example, if constructive debate within the culture of a sub-unit is not given even through the overall culture promotes open debates, the higher managers could held the responsible sub-unit manager accountable for not promoting constructive debates.

[62] See Anand et al. (2005), Ashforth and Anand (2003), Lange (2008).

this argument is implicitly considered in interactive control systems, which promote active debate between organizational members in order to address strategic uncertainties.[63]

In sum, the comparison between the *control-and-culture framework* and the other two frameworks shows major differences among the three concepts. All three frameworks have their benefits and limitations. The section offers information about which framework can provide optimal assistance for specific research questions. The analysis shows that for any research question regarding the relation between control and culture, this study's framework provides an innovative contribution to research.

8.3.3 Review of Research Theses

This section refers to the research theses that were defined at the end of Part I and discusses how the framework relates to them. Table 8.10 summarizes the five theses and how they have been addressed in the framework.

The first research thesis proposes that culture should be seen as a dependent variable rather than an independent variable. As the examples from Merchant's and Simon's frameworks illustrate, control frameworks typically only partially integrate culture. In contrast, the *control-and-culture framework* interprets culture as variable that can be influenced by management. The framework builds on aspects that are commonly accepted in defining organizational culture.[64] While closing and opening drivers define the cultural dimensions, reinforcing drivers enhance the establishment of cultural strength.

The second research thesis argued that culture should be interpreted as meaning (cultural function of controls) and not as a type of control (category). In contrast to standard control terminology, which often considers culture as one (e.g., cultural controls by Merchant) or two types of controls (e.g., belief systems and boundary systems by Simons), the framework here considers culture as an integrated part of all types of controls. Any type of control reflects and influences the organizational culture. Culture provides the meaning to distinguish the different types of drivers and is not simply one type or one part of a type of control itself.

A third research thesis stated that the degree of perceived explicitness is at least equally important as the degree of formalism for any control system. As has been shown above,[65] the primary question derived from the framework is not the degree of formalism in order to achieve control effectiveness, but how closing, opening

---

[63] In the management accounting and control area exists research on involvement (e.g., sub-unit's controller involvement), which addresses these types of questions (for example, Rouwelaar 2007).

[64] Culture is often defined through the dimensions, sharing and intensity of organizational values. For more detail on the role of culture and how it is established, see Chaps. 1 and 7.

[65] See Sect. 8.3.1.

Table 8.10 Review of the five research theses

	Content	Addressed in *control-and-culture framework*
Thesis 1	Culture as a dependent variable (instead as an independent variable)	Closing, opening and reinforcing drivers represent three basic mechanisms that influence culture
Thesis 2	Culture as meaning (instead as one type of control)	All three types of drivers are based on cultural meaning (culture is ingrained)
Thesis 3	The degree of perceived explicitness (instead of the degree of formalism)	Particularly reinforcing drivers address the degree of perceived explicitness
Thesis 4	Focus the process between culture and action (instead the topics themselves)	The framework is based on in-depth interdisciplinary theory that provides explanations for the relation between culture and action
Thesis 5	Interrelations between controls (instead distinguishing between controls)	The framework explicitly builds on the interrelations between three types of drivers

and reinforcing drivers interrelate. Closing and opening drivers need to be enhanced by reinforcing drivers (e.g., leadership, selection and socialization) in order to be strongly perceived. Hence, reinforcing drivers are important for perceived explicitness because they clarify how seriously senior-level people work with specific closing and opening drivers.[66]

The fourth research thesis claimed that the process between culture and action needs to be focused on. The *control-and-culture framework* is based on a broad range of literature from other disciplines in order to explain how culture and action interrelate. This process has been divided into an organizational and an individual level of analysis. While the organizational level showed how a culture can transform over time and impact commonly accepted behaviors, the individual level provided explanations for why culture needs to be strong in order to impact people's behavior. Combining the two views in Part III provided insights into how best to interpret the drivers from the field.

Finally, the fifth research thesis recommended that research should primarily focus on explaining the interrelations between controls, and give less emphasis to the distinction between different types of controls. As has been illustrated at the beginning of this chapter, the framework is clearly based on the interrelation between controls. For example, if closing drivers only relate to an adequate number of opening drivers, the culture can balance direction and continuous evaluation.

[66]Nevertheless, the study of Birnberg and Snodgas discusses other factors such as national culture, which has a fundamental impact on the perceived explicitness of the control system. Therefore, reinforcing drivers are one part of a larger story (see also Sect. 3.3; Birnberg and Snodgrass 1988).

Moreover, in order to become effective, these closing and opening drivers need to be manifested by reinforcing drivers. Explaining these interrelationships is a major contribution of this framework, which can also help explain typical control issues.[67]

8.3.4 Strengths and Limitations

The last three sections discussed the framework regarding the literature, other frameworks and the research theses. Finally, this section concludes with a brief overview of the major strengths and limitations of the *control-and-culture framework*.

Starting with strengths, the framework provides an innovative contribution to research on internal control and management control research because it provides an explanation for how drivers can establish a culture that supports effective controls. Viewing culture as a dependent variable that can be influenced by drivers (which are broadly defined control mechanisms) provides huge opportunities for research. Surprisingly, this direction of research has garnered relatively little attention to date, even though the news provides repeating scandals and company failures that illustrate how important a change of the culture is for any control system.

This alternate view of control has resulted in a conceptualization different from common research. For example, because drivers include formal and informal control mechanisms in addition to unintentional influences, the framework captures important aspects for control effectiveness such as the support from the top of the organization (so called tone at the top), and that leaders lead by example. Practical internal control frameworks and the field study results clearly underline the importance of these leadership aspects. In common research frameworks, however, these aspects have found relatively little consideration. Another aspect is the bottom-up control, which finds explicit consideration in opening drivers: Not only do managers control employees, but so also do employees control managers (assuming adequate openness is given in the culture). These aspects have all been included in this framework because drivers consider a broad set of controls and influences that need to be considered for overall control effectiveness.

Furthermore, as has been previously discussed, dividing drivers according to their cultural meaning provides explanations for how they interrelate. This is important in order to analyze control issues. For example, it can help explain the reasons why formal control mechanisms are informally circumvented. One reason is that the closing driver (which stands for the content of the formal control mechanisms) is not adequately reinforced by senior-level people. Another reason could be that the culture is closed towards its external environment and ignores, for

[67] For example, understanding interrelations between drivers (or controls) can help explain why formal control mechanisms are informally undermined (for example, Sect. 8.2.2).

example, legal rules, which in the case of noncompliance provide huge reputation risks. Consequently, the framework addresses ethical and cultural issues in the management control literature, which, according to Merchant and Van der Stede (2007), is an important research gap.

Last but not least, the framework separates actions from action accountability, as well as results from result accountability. While defining actions and results are closing drivers, whether or not accountability is maintained, has a different cultural meaning and is part of the reinforcing drivers. Separating actions/results from accountability is an important aspect that provides a huge set of research opportunities.

As with any concept, this framework is an abstraction of reality and therefore also has its limitations. One is that distinguishing according to the cultural meaning requires some extent of interpretation. While it is simple to distinguish the drivers into closing, opening and reinforcing drivers, in some cases a specific type of driver seems to belong to one or the other category. As with any other framework, the researcher needs to decide and classify accordingly.

Another aspect of this framework represents a strengths and limitation at the same time. Because the framework takes a broader focus (drivers instead of controls/systems), the framework allows the researcher to include typical aspects associated with culture (e.g., leadership). This broad view, however, also provides more complexity when measuring the drivers. Therefore, researchers are required to clearly scope the research setting (e.g., which drivers for each type are relevant for a specific question) in order to focus the broadness of the framework to a measurable level.

Finally, the framework needs to prove its relevance for theory-testing studies. For example, Ouchi's terminology of market, bureaucracy and clan mechanisms introduced culture in the control literature. Empirical studies, that attempted to measure the clan mechanism, however, found relatively weak empirical evidence.[68] By integrating insights from other disciplines, this study attempts to identify issues in management control research and possibly misleading concepts. Whether the resulting *control-and-culture framework* proves viable in a larger population and can be broadly generalized relies on future theory-testing research.

The contribution of this study is to provide a clear, distinguishable framework in research that is based on an in-depth empirical field study and interdisciplinary theories. Therefore, the setup of this study provides some indication that the framework might have relevance in a more general sense as well.

8.4 Summary

This final part has synthesized all prior results to provide a holistic framework that can explain how managers might establish a culture with effective controls. The

[68] See the literature review in Sect. 3.3.

framework distinguishes between closing, opening and reinforcing drivers. Closing drivers, the first category, represent drivers with which management, define how controls need to be performed, and establish clear limits for organizational members. Opening drivers, the second category, make the culture open to its internal and external environment. The third category, reinforcing drivers, reemphasizes the other two types of drivers throughout the culture. Based on the framework, managers need to find an adequate mix between closing and opening drivers, and disperse and manifest these two drivers using reinforcing drivers.

The application of the framework in research and practice has been illustrated. The Siemens bribery scandal was discussed to demonstrate a possible setting for a case study. From the distinctions among these three types of drivers, a variety of possible hypotheses can be derived for future theory-testing studies. Responding to this, several possible measurement techniques were proposed. Finally, possible applications for managers and employees, as well as auditors and consultants were discussed to demonstrate how the framework enables practical relevance.

Finally, Sect. 8.3.4 critically reflected the contribution of the framework in the existing literature. The framework was compared with well-established frameworks from Merchant and Simons in management control research in order to show how this *control-and-culture framework* differs. Furthermore, the five research theses[69] were reviewed to explain how they have been addressed in this study. Finally, a summary of the benefits and limitations of the framework was presented.

In summary, the analysis demonstrates that the *control-and-culture framework* provides fundamentally distinct features from other frameworks in management control. Consequently, the framework contributes to research efforts with an innovative viewpoint on the relationship between control and culture in general, and internal control and organizational culture in particular.

[69] See Sect. 3.4.

Chapter 9
Conclusion

9.1 Key Results

Repeating business failures bring the importance of effective internal control to the forefront. This study has examined the link between internal control and organizational culture in order to better understand how managers can establish a culture that enhances effective controls. In contrast to existing research in accounting and control, which typically studies culture as a contextual variable, this study has examined culture as a variable that can be influenced by senior-level people.

9.1.1 The Control-and-Culture Framework

The objective of this study was to investigate how senior-level people's principles and practices can *actively* influence organizational culture in such a way that the culture enhances effective controls. Studying this research objective in-depth resulted in a framework. This *control-and-culture framework* builds on drivers, which represent a broad set of management principles and practices that can influence control outcomes. According to their cultural meaning, the framework distinguishes three types of drivers:

- *Closing drivers* close the culture to specific behavior that is unacceptable in the culture and define how controls need to be performed. They give organizational members direction and constrain their autonomy.
- *Opening drivers* open the culture by considering the opinion of internal and external parties. They give organizational members freedom in regard to controls and ensure that controls are continuously evaluated and modified if necessary.
- *Reinforcing drivers* make the culture strong by dispersing and manifesting the content of closing and opening drivers throughout the culture via leadership, selection and socialization processes.

J. Pfister, *Managing Organizational Culture for Effective Internal Control*, Contributions to Management Science,
DOI: 10.1007/978-3-7908-2340-0_9, © Springer Physica-Verlag Berlin Heidelberg 2009

The framework explains how these three types of drivers interrelate. It proposes that senior-level people should mix closing and opening drivers and reemphasize them with reinforcing drivers in order to establish and maintain a culture for effective controls.[1]

The framework is the result of theory-building based on two pillars. The first pillar was a field study consisting of semi-structured interviews with 31 senior-level people from 21 companies. The field study gathered principles and practices senior-level people perceive as contributors to a culture for effective controls. It provided the empirical grounding for studying internal control and organizational culture. The second theory-building pillar applied interdisciplinary theories in order to explain the role of organizational culture for internal control. These theoretical explanations addressed the organizational[2] and individual levels to provide an understanding of how control influences culture in a way to achieve cultural conditions that enhance control effectiveness. These theory-building pillars were examined and re-examined in order to find the best fit between empirical data and theoretical explanations. The result is the summarized *control-and-culture framework* referenced above.

9.1.2 Distinction from Common Control Frameworks

The framework clearly distinguishes between common management control frameworks such as Merchant and Van der Stede (2007)[3] and Simons (1995). The *control-and-culture framework* differs from these two frameworks primarily in regard to objective, typology, degree of informalism captured in the framework, and criteria for classifying the different types of controls.[4]

More specifically, the *control-and-culture framework* distinguishes itself from other frameworks by interpreting organizational culture as a variable being influenced by the *entire driver mix* that senior-level people apply. The framework is founded on the assumption that every control mechanism as well as unintentional behaviors reflect on and influence the culture. In contrast, Merchant and Van der Stede include culture in their personnel/cultural controls, but provide less understanding of how result controls and action controls relate to organizational culture. Likewise, Simons considers culture in his theory. As his primary focus is strategy implementation, however, the concept says little about how the mix of "systems" influences organizational culture. Thus, a major difference is that the *control-and-culture framework* interprets any control (drivers) by its cultural meaning.

---

[1]For more details see Chap. 8.

[2]The organizational level in this study reflects any organizational instance such as team, group, unit, country, or the organization as whole.

[3]The framework was originally developed by Merchant (1985).

[4]For more detail on these general distinctions see Sect. 8.3.2.

Also, the *control-and-culture framework* distinguishes significantly from common frameworks in how important accounting and control aspects are treated. For example, the framework separates action accountability from action definition, and result accountability from result definition. From a cultural point of view, defining results and actions closes the culture by giving direction. In contrast, whether people are held accountable for behaving accordingly or reaching the results is a reinforcing aspect of culture. Consequently, the *control-and-culture framework* proposes to distinguish these aspects of defining behavior or outcomes from holding people accountable for behaving accordingly or achieving results.[5]

Another aspect the *control-and-culture framework* integrates is tone at the top and leadership, which other frameworks capture only marginally. Interviewees from the field study repeatedly mentioned how fundamental tone at the top and leadership is for control effectiveness. If the top of the organization, particularly the executives, as well as leaders at any level of the organization do not support internal control, the risk of ineffective controls is said to rise significantly.[6] These aspects of tone at the top and leadership are integrated in reinforcing drivers.

Furthermore, the *control-and-culture framework* includes bottom-up control mechanisms, which can include that not only managers control their employees, but to some extent and under specific cultural conditions[7], employees control also their managers. Repeating accounting scandals show that top managers often play an important part in corrupt activities. Drawing from the literature of organizational corruption and the field study results, a culture can become dangerous if it is closed and leaders have unrestricted freedom in decision-making. Therefore, the existence of (intentional or unintentional) bottom-up control mechanisms is important. If a manager keeps some openness to his or her employees, he or she needs to convince followers about the direction taken. From a cultural point of view, this is a positive aspect and supports the hypothesis that the culture will be less likely to become corrupt.[8]

The framework also addresses current issues in the literature[9] by strongly integrating how various control mechanisms (drivers) interrelate. These aspects are particularly important in explaining ethical issues in internal control. For example, the interrelation of drivers can support investigating how (and why) formal control mechanisms are informally undermined. A discussion on how to analyze these types of issues was presented based on the example of Siemens.[10]

For all these reasons, the *control-and-culture framework* provides fresh perspectives in the accounting and control area. It represents an alternative terminology that

---

[5] For a literature review on control and accountability, see Merchant and Otley (2007).

[6] See the field study results in Chap. 4. Tone at the top and leading by example is also strongly considered in practical-oriented frameworks such as COSO, CoCo, and Turnbull (see Sect. 3.2).

[7] These conditions particularly rely on the openness of leaders.

[8] For more detail see the discussions in Chap. 6.

[9] See literature review in Chap. 3.

[10] See Sect. 8.2.2.

can be useful in studying control and culture and how various controls (drivers) interrelate.

9.2 Contribution

This study contributes to research efforts and practice by (1) offering a broad range of principles and practices that senior-level people perceive as drivers for control effectiveness[11]; (2) by explaining how control and culture interrelate at the organizational and individual levels[12]; and (3) by providing a framework that syntheses prior results in order to explain how managers can mix the drivers in a way to establish and maintain cultural conditions that enhance effective controls.[13] The following section discusses the academic and practice-oriented contribution of this study.

9.2.1 Academic Contribution

Claiming that this study addresses a research gap seems surprising. Failures of internal control, based on a lack in the organizational culture, possibly accompany the business world since businesses exist. Nevertheless, connecting the more "technical" areas of internal control with the more "behavioral" areas of culture in a relatively holistic way has found limited consideration in research beforehand. This study represents an innovative contribution to management accounting and control research for three major reasons.

First, in management accounting and control research, internal control is a relatively unexplored area.[14] Quality of information and safeguarding of assets were traditionally discussed in the auditing area, but management control research has given little attention to the topic.[15] Nevertheless, accounting researchers support the importance of effective internal control. Simons (2000), for example, emphasizes that effective internal control provides integrity for any other control system that implements strategy within an organization. Kinney (2000b) remarks that internal control affects not only the organization, but the welfare of the public at large, yet it is still a minimally researched area.

---

[11] See Chap. 4 and Appendix C.

[12] See Chaps. 5, 6, and 7.

[13] See Chap. 8.

[14] See Sect. 3.2.

[15] See Sect. 3.2.1.

Second, the relation between internal control *and organizational culture* has been considered in practical-oriented reports and internal control frameworks,[16] but was not considered in-depth in research efforts. For example, the report of the Treadway Commission from 1987[17] explains:

> A strong corporate ethical climate at all levels is vital to the well-being of the corporation, all of its constituencies, and the public at large. Such a climate contributes importantly to the effectiveness of company policies and control systems, and helps influence behavior that is not subject to even the most elaborate systems of controls.[18]

In contrast to these practical-oriented statements, the topic has not attracted much research attention. One reason for this lack of research on internal control and organizational culture might be the thinking in disciplinary frames, which does not promote cross-border research.[19]

Third, while the study of organizational culture in the accounting and control area has a long tradition, the typical viewpoint in existing research is that culture provides the context that influences accounting and control practices and outcomes.[20] The other direction, which this study addresses, namely how control influences culture (in order to achieve effective controls), is a fundamentally different viewpoint to common research. How culture can be influenced is discussed in other disciplines, but, with some exceptions,[21] in accounting and control research this aspect has garnered little attention.

The combination of these three arguments supports that this study offers new perspectives for accounting and control research.

9.2.2 Practice-Oriented Contribution

The study contributes to practice by offering a unique overview of practical statements from senior-level people of large, renowned organizations.[22] A particular benefit of this study is that not only is a checklist-like approach of principles and practice given in order to establish a culture for effective controls, but how these principles and practices (drivers) relate to cultural mechanisms is explained. A better understanding of the interplay between drivers, how cultural processes work, and

---

[16] See Sect. 3.2.

[17] Cited after COSO (1992, p. 24).

[18] The quote addresses climate which is related to culture. Climate is generally seen as more temporal than culture. However, both address the same social phenomena. For example, Michela and Burke (2000) and Schein (2001).

[19] For example, Osterloh and Frost (2007) and Simons (2005).

[20] See Chap. 3.

[21] For example, Merchant and Simons both include aspects of culture, which implicitly influence the culture.

[22] See Appendices A and B.

what implications can be derived for management allows professionals to better assess how to establish a control environment that is conducive to organizational characteristics. As much as professionals study portfolio growing techniques, investment plans, accounting standards, and other compliance issues, professionals should also have a better understanding for the cultural mechanisms surrounding internal control. This helps them manage their control environment in a way that enhances effective controls. This is true for any manager as well as employee at any level of the organization. Also, the study offers implications for auditors and consultants. For these professions a tool such as the *control-and-culture framework* can provide assistance in evaluating the control environment. Moreover, the framework can be used as a basis to develop a measurement tool for culture in regard to internal control. In the long run, such a tool could provide information as to whether a culture is on a misleading track and, as a result, could serve as a preventive function.[23]

Building bridges between different disciplines (e.g., accounting, business, sociology, psychology), the study builds theory for internal control to explain the cultural processes that relate to internal control. To what extent these results can be used for a broader population is discussed in the following section.

9.3 Generalization

To interpret the results in an adequate light, the reader needs to be aware of the study's limitations and to what extent the framework can possibly be generalized.

As has been discussed in the introduction, a constructivist epistemology implies that the knowledge gathered relates to the researchers that conduct the study.[24] Another researcher with a different background and other interests might have results in a different framework.[25] Also, the empirical input builds on a limited number of interviewees from a limited amount of companies.[26] Interviewees from other hierarchical levels, functions, companies, industries and countries could have resulted in a different framework. Although the cultural interpretation of the drivers from the field is supported by insights from interdisciplinary theories, the usefulness of the framework in providing a better understanding for the phenomena of control and culture relies on future research applying other methods which can address a broader population (e.g., survey). Such research needs to prove that the framework is able to distinguish various organizational settings depending on different degrees of control effectiveness.

---

[23] Such a tool would need to be built over time and gather benchmark information. Then such a tool could compare specific cultures with benchmark cultures in order to stimulate the discussion on the organizational direction and leadership.

[24] See Sect. 1.3.

[25] Argumentation adapted from Mikes (2005b).

[26] See Sect. 4.2.

A particular question that remains unclear is how the *control-and-culture framework* applies to other nationalities. Principles and practices for internal control from Swiss and US managers might be more closely related than, for example, similar principles and practices employed by Asian managers. As the study from Birnberg and Snodgas (1988) demonstrates, Japanese and US employees can perceive different degrees of formalism is similarly explicit. The generalization of closing, opening, and reinforcing drivers for other cultures therefore needs further clarification. A more in-depth connection to research on national cultures such as that conducted by Hofstede[27] could provide more evidence for the generalization of the framework to different nationalities.

Although the *control-and-culture framework* was developed by interviewing *senior-level* people, the framework seems to be applicable at any level of the organization in which managers as gatekeepers have an influence on a cultural setting (team, group, unit, organization as a whole). Most interviewees have worked at lower hierarchical levels in organizations earlier in their career. Therefore, by interviewing senior-level people, the empirical input contains knowledge gathered from various levels and settings of organizations.

The research setup (exploratory, based on semi-structured interviews) was not designed to focus on specific cases in more depth or to measure control effectiveness. The study builds on perceptions from senior-level people. All interviewees were at this senior level and therefore brought that experience, so they had an understanding of what was important for control to be effective. Other studies, which take a different method, are necessary to see if these results can be applied to broader populations.

Another open question is the huge variety of cultural aspects that can be focused on. This study was built on two commonly accepted (yet distinct) definitions of organizational culture in order to capture a broad range of "culture".[28] Nevertheless, focusing on other concepts of organizational culture could lead to different interpretations of the drivers. How relevant the patterns found are needs to be proven by future empirical studies.

As the focus of the study was on how managers at any level can *actively* influence their cultural setting, how their mix of drivers is *passively* influenced by the cultures themselves would need further investigation as well. The discussion on how senior-level people themselves have been selected and socialized by their cultural environment and how that influences their respective mix of drivers would be a possible research question that can be addressed by the *control-and-culture framework*.[29]

---

[27] For example, Hofstede (1991) and Hofstede (2001).

[28] See Sect. 2.2.1.

[29] See Sect. 9.4, which addresses possible research opportunities. Indices on whether senior-level people are influenced by the culture or how they influence the culture (for controls) could be investigated by longitudinal studies based on the *control-and-culture framework*.

Finally, as was introduced at the beginning of this study, internal control is closely related to management control. In particular, a research setup that studies what managers can do to achieve effective internal control is closely related to management control (despite clearly focusing on internal control). Hence the resulting *control-and-culture framework* from this study is part of the broader field of management control and can provide research opportunities for management accounting and control research.

9.4 Research Opportunities

The discussion about the generalization of the study leads to future research opportunities. Researching internal control in general, and researching internal control and organizational culture in particular, offers many open questions and research opportunities for exploration into the field of management accounting and control.[30] On the basis of this study, several more specific research opportunities can be proposed:

- As the last section discussed, the generalization of the *control-and-culture framework* for broader populations needs to be proven in theory-testing studies. In particular, research needs to demonstrate whether the framework is able to distinguish organizational settings with more control effectiveness from organizational settings with less control effectiveness (or whether the framework is able to provide new insights into other topics such as budgeting, strategy, performance, etc.).
- In order to conduct theory-testing studies, future research needs to develop a measurement tool that is able to capture the three types of drivers. This study provides the basic terminology and examples from the field. In a measurement tool, the insights from this study would need to be refined and combined with successfully applied measurement tools from management control research or other disciplines.[31]
- Another current opportunity would be to measure an organizational setting (particularly a financial department) based on the *control-and-culture framework* and examine its correlation with disclosed material weaknesses in internal control over financial reporting such as introduced by Section 404 of the Sarbanes-Oxley Act of 2002.[32]
- Measuring the mix between closing, opening and reinforcing drivers would allow comparing the driver mix of individuals with one from the organizational setting. Such measurement could, for example, provide explanations for the strength of organizational culture in regard to control, the "fit" of individuals

[30] See also Sect. 8.2, which discusses possible applications of the *control-and-culture framework*.

[31] Some suggestions for measurement are provided in Sect. 8.2.3.

[32] For this type of study, see Ashbaugh-Skaife et al. (2007), Doyle et al. (2007).

into the culture, and how individuals influence and are influenced by the culture in regard to controls over time.[33]

- A longitudinal study could provide indices for how much the overall culture (average driver mixes through all levels) and the key gatekeepers (e.g., such as a CEO) influence each other.
- The study discussed the external and internal environment and how transfers can take place. Further research could clarify in more depth how opening drivers relate to the external environment and how this relationship affects control effectiveness.
- While the basic interrelations between closing and opening drivers have been discussed in this study, more knowledge is needed for specific settings. For example, under what conditions are closing drivers modified by the influence of opening drivers. Such a question could be subject to future in-depth case study research or empirical surveys.
- As was illustrated with the Siemens example, the terminology of reinforcing drivers offers explanations for why formal control mechanisms are informally undermined. More in-depth understanding of how aspects of leadership, selection and socialization impact control systems is an important research area and possible case study.
- The *control-and-culture framework* can also be connected to other research fields in management accounting and control research such as the study of control and trust, norms, and incentive systems.[34]
- The framework could be related to auditing research, which is traditionally concerned with internal control. As was suggested earlier, developing an indicator that measures how supportive the culture is for internal control would provoke the discussion on whether a culture is adequate and, at best, would change the culture before failing.
- The study developed based on a broadly designed field study. Future research could conduct field study research on internal control on more specific aspects that have been derived in this field study.[35]
- The theoretical explanations for organizational culture provide opportunities to further theorize internal control with other disciplines (sociology, social psychology, the literature of organizational corruption and organizational culture).

These are some suggestions for how this research could be the starting point for future research efforts.

[33] The person-organizational fit is typically studied in the field of organizational behavior. See, for example, O'Reilly et al. (1991).

[34] For example, Das and Teng (1998), Sitkin and George (2005), and Whitener et al. (1998).

[35] See Appendix C.

9.5 Final Remarks

This study was built on the belief that organizational culture is a phenomenon that can and needs to be captured – not only in behavioral disciplines, but also in the accounting, control and auditing areas. It does not make sense that everyone who is asked knows a story to tell about control and culture if "culture" would not be an existing phenomenon that has some key features. How can people debate, write or protest against the culture of organizations, if that concept is really just a "fata morgana"? More insight about how control and culture relate provide the necessary core variables that managers, auditors, consultants, researchers and the public at large can focus on. If the topic does not become more concrete, it will remain below the surface and less likely to be proactively addressed. Past business scandals and failures indicate what that means. If the relation between control and culture does not become more concrete, managers will pay less attention to it for the simple reason that they have other priorities. Simons (2000, p. 9) states:

> Businesses must deliver financial performance – not tomorrow, or the year after, but today. The stock market, representing shareowners, rewards managers who can produce earnings in the current period. ... Managers must also manage for the long term. They must renew production facilities, enter new markets with new products, and invest in research and development to stay current with competitors and meet changing customer needs.

Having this plethora of responsibilities, both internal control and organizational culture can easily come from management attention. Consequently, concepts that simplify control and culture to key features support that managers can, with relatively little attention, achieve a high outcome in establishing a culture for effective controls. Thus, the *control-and-culture framework* is an attempt to provide simple patterns that can be used not only in research but also in practice. This is important because both internal control and organizational culture are fundamental for any business. As long as their relationship remains a mystery and few attempts are made to provide possible measures, other priorities will take precedence and will remain in the forefront of management attention. The seriousness of failures such as Enron, WorldCom, Siemens, UBS, Lehman Brothers (and list to be continued in the future) show that professionals and researchers should give adequate attention on how to establish a culture for effective controls: not tomorrow, or the year after, but today in order to deliver *long term* financial performance.

Appendix A

List of Interviewees

No.[a]	Name	Function	Company	Location	Interview date
1	Baer, Jakob	Chairman of the Audit Committee	Adecco	Zurich, Switzerland	12/20/2005 (in person)
2	Adel, Amin	Group Controller	AMD	Austin (TX), USA	07/19/07 (conference call)
3	Dick, Ryan	Director of Internal Audit	AMD	Austin (TX), USA	7/12/2007 (conference call)
4	Tellini, Marc	Senior VP and Deputy General Counsel	Charles Schwab Corporation	San Francisco (CA), USA	19/07/07 (in person)
5	Heri, Erwin	Chairman of the Audit Committee	Ciba Specialty Chemicals	Winterthur, Switzerland	12/21/2005 (in person)
6	Hauser, Daniel	Chief Auditor Private Banking	Credit Suisse Group	Zurich, Switzerland	1/4/2006 (in person)
7	Van Oppen, Timothy	Director of Professional Practice	Deloitte	San Francisco (CA), USA	5/30/2007 (in person)
8	Ceran, Jennifer	Vice President and Treasurer	eBay	San Jose (CA), USA	6/7/2007 (conference call[b])
9	Studer, Martin	Head ERM Central Europe	Ernst & Young	Zurich, Switzerland	12/19/2005 (in person)
10	Lee, Alvin	Project Manager Quality Business Systems	Genentech	South San Francisco (CA), USA	9/13/2007 (conference call[b])
11	Fuchs, Mark	Vice President of Finance and Chief Accountant	Google	Mountain View (CA), USA	8/2/2007 (in person)
12	Lee, Lisa	Director of Internal Audit	Google	Mountain View (CA), USA	7/31/2007 (in person)
13	Schmidt, Eric	Chairman and Chief Executive Officer	Google	Mountain View (CA), USA	8/26/2007 (via email)
14	Pashley, Robert	Director of Enterprise Financial Reporting	Hewlett Packard	Palo Alto (CA), USA	6/12/2007 (conference call)
15	Downing, Maxwell	Shared Services Controller	Intel	Hillsboro (OR), USA	6/26/2007 (conference call[b])
16	Shea, Gus	Senior Audit Manager, Head SOX Office	Intel	San Jose (CA), USA	7/6/2007 (in person)
17	Marti, Simon	Senior Manager, Internal Auditing Switzerland	KPMG	Zurich, Switzerland	12/23/2005 (in person)
18	Pfyffer, Hans-Ulrich	Head Risk Management Advisory Switzerland	KPMG	Zurich, Switzerland	12/23/2005 (in person)
19	Allen, John	Chief Financial Officer	Leadis	Sunnyvale (CA), USA	6/13/2007 (in person)
20	Beckman, Jeffrey		Levi Strauss & Co.	San Francisco (CA), USA	3/23/2007 (in person)

		Director of Worldwide and US Communication			
21	Ploos van Amstel, Hans	Chief Financial Officer	Levi Strauss & Co.	San Francisco (CA), USA	3/23/2007 (in person)
22	Thorbecke, Rik	Vice President, Head Global Audit and ERM	Levi Strauss & Co.	San Francisco (CA), USA	3/23/2007 (in person)
23	Byers, Marilee	Director of Financial Compliance	Microsoft	Redmond (WA), USA	8/25/2007 (conference call)
24	Winters, Rod	General Auditor	Microsoft	Redmond (WA), USA	9/18/2007 (conference call)
25	Garber, Michael	Director of Assurance Management	Motorola	Schaumburg (IL), USA	8/24/2007 (conference call[b])
26	Barlow, Steven	Head Internal Auditing	Novartis	Basel, Switzerland	11/17/2005 (in person)
27	Noetzold, Wieland	Quality Assurance Manager	Novartis	Basel, Switzerland	12/19/2005 (in person)
28	Van Oerle, Jaap	Deputy Head Internal Audit, Regional Manager	Novartis	Basel, Switzerland	11/17/2005 (in person)
29	Johns, Chris	Chief Financial Officer	Pacific Gas & Electric Company	San Francisco (CA), USA	6/29/2007 (in person)
30	Ribar, Geoff	Chief Financial Officer	Sirf Technologies	San Jose (CA), USA	8/14/2007 (in person)
31	Grybas, Phil	Chief Financial Officer	SureWest	Sacramento (CA), USA	6/7/2007 (conference call[b])

[a]Listed by company
[b]Met in person beforehand

Appendix B

Company Information

No.[a]	Name	Industry	Group sales (in million USD)		Net income (in million USD)		Worldwide employees	
			2006	2007	2006	2007	2006	2007
1	Hewlett Packard	Computer peripherals	91,658.00	104,286.00	6,198.00	7,264.00	156,000	172,000
2	Microsoft	Software & programming	44,282.00	51,122.00	12,599.00	14,065.00	71,000	79,000
3	Intel	Semiconductors	35,382.00	38,334.00	5,044.00	6,976.00	94,100	84,600
4	Novartis	Major drugs	37,020.00	38,072.00	6,825.00	6,540.00	94,241	98,000
5	Motorola	Communications equipment	42,900.00	36,622.00	3,661.00	(49)	66,000	66,000
6	Credit Suisse Group	Investment services	30,882.40	33,127.50	9,061.60	6,466.67	44,871	48,700
7	Deloitte	Business services	20,000.00	23,100.00	–	–	132,400	146,600
8	Ernst & Young	Business services	18,400.00	21,100.00	–	–	114,279	130,000
9	Adecco SA	Business services	20,417.00	21,090.00	611.00	743.00	37,000	36,514
10	KPMG	Business services	16,880.00	19,810.00	–	–	112,795	123,322
11	Google	Computer services	10,604.92	16,593.99	3,077.45	4,203.72	10,674	16,805
12	Pacific Gas & Electric Company	Energy	12,539.00	13,238.00	985.00	1,024.00	20,500	20,400
13	Genentech	Biotechnology & Drugs	9,284.00	11,724.00	2,113.00	2,769.00	10,533	11,174
14	eBay	Retail (Specialty)	5,970.00	7,672.33	1,126.00	348.25	13,200	15,500
15	Ciba Speciality Chemicals	Chemical manufacturing	6,352.00	6,523.00	(41.00)	237.00	14,000	13,319
16	Advanced Micro Devices	Semiconductors	5,649.00	6,013.00	166.00	(3,344.00)	16,500	16,420
17	Charles Schwab Corporation	Investment services	4,309.00	4,994.00	1,227.00	2,407.00	12,400	13,400
18	Levi Strauss & Co	Clothing	4,106.50	4,266.10	239.00	460.40	10,680	11,550
19	Sirf Technology Holdings	Communications equipment	247.68	329.38	2.40	(10.40)	445	753
20	SureWest Communications	Communications services	222.74	206.82	5.74	1.79	863	803
21	Leadis Technology	Semiconductors	101.20	39.58	(11.90)	(30.93)	141	184

[a]Listed by group sales 2007

Appendix C

Data Analysis

In order to provide transparency of the field study process, this appendix presents the data analysis of the drivers for control effectiveness (see Chap 4). The tables represent the working documents that led to the evaluation of the empirical data. The columns represent the 31 interviewees. The numbers in the columns relate to the coding of the transcripts. Each number reflects how many times a specific interviewee mentioned a specific topic. The total observations for each category are listed in the columns to the right side of the topics. The total data derived from the field study can be clustered as following:

Total observations		1,347
Excluding	Roots of control failures	163
Excluding	Discussions about Sarbanes-Oxley related issues	134
Excluding	Other issues	80
Drivers for control effectiveness (presented in the Appendix)		970

Category	Topics (examples, statements)		Interviewee (number of interviewee does not relate to Appendix A)																													
			1	2	3	4	5	6	7	8	9	10	11	12	13	14	15	16	17	18	19	20	21	22	23	24	25	26	27	28	29	30	31
Commitment																																	
1 Tone at the top	Promotion of internal control by board and top management; Personality of CEO	33			2	4	1		1	1		1		1	2	2	2	2	5					1		2	1			3	1	1	
2 Lead by example	Role modeling by leaders at all levels; Philosophy, style, and values of leaders; Visibility of leaders; Believe in necessity of controls by leaders	24	2	3	1	1	4			1			1	1	1							4				1		2		1			1
3 Ingrain sustainability	Building of long-term systems; Long-term thinking; Reputation risk; Integrity of the brand name; Confidence that unproper activities will come to light over time (e.g., bribing for short term opportunities)	19		1			1			1					1		1		5			1									6	2	
4 Establish discipline	Deal with reality; Commitment to perform specific controls by employees; Compliance activities by specific date;	7				1												2			2		1							1			

		Establish systems that enhance procedures and controls for reporting in a timely and reliable manner																															
5	Define process ownership	Cascading and decentralizing responsibility; Creating an ownership mentality; Ownership is bottom-up	24	1	2	2	3						3	1	2	3	2		1		1	2			1								
6	Code of business conduct	Reading and signing code of conduct periodically	5										1				2					1				1							
7	Ensure accountability	Clear sanctions and punishments; Firing people if necessary in order to encourage others to understand; Reward if controls are properly executed	24	1		2				1				1		1	2		2	2	2			3		3				1		2	1
8	Reward compensation plan	Linking controls with reward compensation plan	3													1			1												1		
9	Cultural empathy internationally	Different expectations among different countries; Consider that some cultures prefer checklist approaches (e.g., China); Establish relationships and partnerships worldwide	22	1			1											1		2		4		1	4			2	1		2	2	1

(*continued*)

Category	Topics (examples, statements)		Interviewee (number of interviewee does not relate to Appendix A)																													
			1	2	3	4	5	6	7	8	9	10	11	12	13	14	15	16	17	18	19	20	21	22	23	24	25	26	27	28	29	30	31
10 External pressures	Law used to enhance controls; Play the SOX card; Pressures from analysts and government bodies	4		1							1									1							1						
Competence																																	
11 Establish an adequate hiring procedure	Have a reasonable hiring process; Interviews for skill sets; Multi-step interview process; Phone screening; Checking references; Background checks; Hire people that have no conflicts of interests; Identify people internally and externally; Review hiring philosophy of the department; Give particular attention to key positions	17								1					1	2	4	3	2					1	1	1							1
12 Select adequate qualification	Require experience (e.g., internally with business knowledge, 5–10 year work experience); Require analytical skills (particularly	30		6	3					1		1	1		1	3	1	1	2				1	4		3	1						1

		for top positions; critical thinking); Require specific education (e.g., CPA); Define clear job descriptions and requirements																														
13	Consider social skills	Hire people who can say "no"; Select ethical, enthusiastic, motivated, and team oriented people	8	2		1				1						3	1															
14	Offer continuous training	Well-organized training program (keeps people up-to-date, tops-down, centralized, systematic); External and internal training (e.g., third party provider); Online education (e.g., multiple choices of training); Educate people's role, standards of business conduct, compliance with rules, communication, leadership development, team building etc.; Specific training for newcomers (make people aware of importance of controls)	41	1	5	1	2			1			5		1	3	7	2		3	3	4				1						2

(*continued*)

Category	Topics (examples, statements)		Interviewee (number of interviewee does not relate to Appendix A) 1	2	3	4	5	6	7	8	9	10	11	12	13	14	15	16	17	18	19	20	21	22	23	24	25	26	27	28	29	30	31
15 Promote rotation programs	Gaining business experience by working in various departments; Understanding the business risks	3															1							1								1	
16 Make specialists available	Provide advice for complicated areas such as treasury, tax, revenue, risk identification and evaluation, disclosure, MD&A	11															6	2				1	1		1								
17 Experts for change	Provide subject matter experts (e.g., acquisitions, internal transactions, customer arrangements, supplier arrangements, finance, operations, legal, visibility of acquisition); Evaluate changes and give feedback to business	7											1				2	1				2	1										
18 Establish an attractive work environment	Work-life balance; Flexibility in dress code; Enthusiastic, motivated, and competitive environment	10		1					2							2			5														

19	HR development	Tracking and grading of employees' progress; Certification; Mandatory training	8						1					1	1	4	1															
	Communication																															
20	Communicate clear goals, expectations and responsibilities, raise control awareness	Set continuous messages about the importance of controls; Make clear process advancements; Give clear direction and time frame; Messaging from the executives	36	2	3	3	4	1	1	1	1	1	4			6	2	2	1		3				1							
21	Communicate clear standards of business conduct	Messages about doing the right things; Promote a strong culture of ethics and integrity; Encourage good standards of conduct; Communicate policies and procedures to acquired company	11			1						2				3	1		1					1					1			1
22	Communicate seriousness of consequences	Make clear that there is zero tolerance; Compliance newsletter (e.g., "what were they thinking"); Communicate sanctions taken	12	1		1	1									3	2								1						1	2
23	Provide necessary information and assure information quality	Set meetings to inform people (e.g., conference calls, live meetings); Make	13		1	3										3			1	1		1		3								

(*continued*)

Category	Topics (examples, statements)		Interviewee (number of interviewee does not relate to Appendix A)																														
			1	2	3	4	5	6	7	8	9	10	11	12	13	14	15	16	17	18	19	20	21	22	23	24	25	26	27	28	29	30	31
	sure everyone understands the requirements; Give benchmark information; Provide information to evaluate risks; Communicate for consistent execution; Confidentiality, integrity, availability and accuracy of information; Build trust in information (consistency from period to period, location to location)																																
24 Promote effective communication	Give emphasis on the importance of communication throughout the organization; Organize communication flows carefully; Make clear to process owners that they need to communicate expectations to people in their cycles; Meetings to align expectations	27		2	2					2	1			1		2	2			2	3	3	1	2	1					2		1	

		among people; Make decisions in groups (in order to grasp change and complexity); Encourage communication horizontally (e.g., similar things in many time zones, business and accounting)																	
25	Make people accountable for communication	Confirmation that communication is taken place; Confirmation that person read and understood specific control and that person will execute control; Define process ownership for communication	3										1	2					
26	Establish a collaborative environment	Promote collaboration across organization, units, teams, individuals (e.g., between internal auditing and business, between executives and audit committee); Build respect and teamwork	10		2	1			1		1	1			1	2		1	
27	Explain benefits	Explain why controls are necessary; Establish purpose for controls; Develop proactive thinking for controls also from	16	1	4		1	1		1	1	2			1	2	1		1

(*continued*)

Category	Topics (examples, statements)		Interviewee (number of interviewee does not relate to Appendix A)																														
			1	2	3	4	5	6	7	8	9	10	11	12	13	14	15	16	17	18	19	20	21	22	23	24	25	26	27	28	29	30	31
	less control oriented functions (e.g., technicians); Explain the need of specific functions (e.g., internal auditing is supportive to the business and not a police); Mediation processes on control issues																																
28 Encourage constructive debate	Establish an open culture (with open debate and discussion); Have employees with the rights and responsibilities to question and challenge issues; It is not good if: the head is telling the legs what to do, but the ground is much different than the head is thinking; Consider tone at the bottom; Mix and match teams (cross-pollenization) in order to create open debates	18			2		2	1		2	2						1						3	1						2			2
29 Promote escalating of issues	Establish a structure for escalating issues; Highlight problems to the	24			1	1							1		1	3		3	1			1	2	1		1				4	1	1	2

		audit committee; Frequent update of management (e.g., major new environment, new changes); Escalate significant events and transactions; Communicate issues from subunit to central; Put information at the right level of the organization together; Employee satisfaction surveys; Highlight issues to subject matter experts; Whistleblower hotlines																										
30	Willingness to listen from the top	Take adequate responses to issues; Senior people need to be willing to listen; Willingness to listen internationally (e.g., in some cultures trust is more important than in others); Opinion of employees; Comments from hotlines are received at the top	5			1								2						1	1							
31	Asking critical and the "right" questions	Asking questions as an education process; Questions for management	11	1	1							1		1	1			1					2		1			2

(*continued*)

Category	Topics (examples, statements)		Interviewee (number of interviewee does not relate to Appendix A)																														
			1	2	3	4	5	6	7	8	9	10	11	12	13	14	15	16	17	18	19	20	21	22	23	24	25	26	27	28	29	30	31
	inquiry; Top-down effect; Details can be important																																
32 Benchmarking	Participate at conferences; Talk to companies from the same industry and colleagues from outside	4					1						1		1										1								
33 Reporting structure	Dual reporting lines (e.g., internal auditing to CFO and to audit committee chairman); Give focus on reporting structure (e.g., centralized, getting information back); Quarterly board meetings (internal control agenda); Annual summary (of internal controls); Central reporting and central oversight of implementation of controls	9			1			1					2				2			1										1	1		
34 Consider cultural differences in communication	Translation to local languages; Challenge of making clear that certain customs are not okay (e.g.,	8																	1	1			1	1	1					1	1		1

	bribing, jewelry for governor's wife); Getting the culture alive in every region; Standardize code of conduct worldwide (clear rules centrally for bribing); Multinational companies often have a culture based on their home country																														
Complexity																															
35 Keep a holistic view	Understanding, documenting and validating the business activity behind each reporting process; Control needs to respond to business; Take into account operations and compliance and not only finance; Mapping out of controls; Understanding of how numbers come together	20	1	3							3	1		1			1		1	1		1	1		1	1			4		
36 Integrate functions and activities	Manage gaps and overlaps (e.g., risk management, Sarbanes-Oxley requirements, governance, monitoring, compliance management);	6								1												1			1				1	1	1

(*continued*)

Category	Topics (examples, statements)		Interviewee (number of interviewee does not relate to Appendix A)																													
			1	2	3	4	5	6	7	8	9	10	11	12	13	14	15	16	17	18	19	20	21	22	23	24	25	26	27	28	29	30	31
	Enhance compliance for less experienced people by providing shared services																																
37 Adequate organizational complexity	Certain degree of internal complexity is necessary; Build an organization that can handle complexity; Appropriate amount of procedures and reviews relative to the complexity; Checks through matrix organization	4																1							1						1		1
38 Give attention to goal setting process	Manage the goal setting process; Set the right goals (e.g., integrating controls into goals, consider ethics); Reach agreements on control objectives; Align controls with strategy; Achieve and execute the product roadmap; Make controls part of job; Set objectives that can be met	13					1	1						2							3	1			1			3		1			

39	Focus on risks	Identify risks; Evaluate risks (quantitatively and qualitatively); Focus on materialty; Manage interrelation between risks and controls; Monitor closely critical functions; Strengthen key roles (e.g., corporate controller, internal auditing); Direct management attention; Track key controls; Manage key control matrix; Focus on entity-level controls	41	3	1	3	2	3		2	5	3	2			1		1		3				1	1	4		3	2		1
40	Segregation of duties	Give attention that duties are segregated; Find alternative assurance solutions (e.g., segregation of duties in small companies)	6					1		1			1			2		1													
41	Define process and responsibilities	Define responsibilities and processes (e.g., who does the testing and who does the checking of testing); What is the right level of information to be escalated	7								1							1	2									3			

(continued)

Category	Topics (examples, statements)		Interviewee (number of interviewee does not relate to Appendix A)																														
			1	2	3	4	5	6	7	8	9	10	11	12	13	14	15	16	17	18	19	20	21	22	23	24	25	26	27	28	29	30	31
42 Formal documentation	Provide evidence; Give attention to audit trails; Formalization can help simplifying; Skip redundancies; Clarify central documentation of testing; Transparency of the process	17			1	1	3			1	1	2	1				3			1					1	1						1	
43 Measure processes	Set the right measures; What gets measured will be done; Set tolerances of measures; Measure information protection; Key performance indicators; Support integrity and code of conduct	12					1						2	2			1		1	2			1				1			1			
44 Simplify control structure and build consistency	Establish consistency; Standardize (e.g., financial reporting); Simplify even when costs for controls are cheap (e.g., emerging countries); Centralize assessments and conclusions; Centralize	40		2		1	1					2	3		1	1	4			1	1	4	3	2		1	1	1	1	6	2	2	

		policies and procedures (e.g., common definitions, one global answer to specific accounting standards, exception policies); Compliance and self-regulation; Develop a common language for controls (e.g., manual); Reconciliation requirements and standards; Simple business lines and structures; Avoid complex transactions (e.g., stock options, leasing)																													
45	Embed controls	Controls as part of the actual process; Make ownership for efficiency; Compliance requirements; Embed structures; Controls as part of day to day activities	18			1	2	1	1					2				2	3			3	1						1		1
46	Build automation	Enterprise resource planning; Automate as much as possible; Systems can enhance controls (e.g., alarm systems as detective controls,	11					1			2			1		1		2			2				1					1	

(continued)

Category	Topics (examples, statements)		Interviewee (number of interviewee does not relate to Appendix A)																													
			1	2	3	4	5	6	7	8	9	10	11	12	13	14	15	16	17	18	19	20	21	22	23	24	25	26	27	28	29	30	31
	built-in compliance); Importance of IT controls (e.g., need for IT benchmark controls, password controls, IT-based applications); Reengineer documentation and design																																
47 Provide tools and methodology	Risk control matrix; Role matrix; Monitoring matrix; Templates; Work-flows; Planning memorandum; Cause and effect analysis; Six sigma, COSO framework; Control self assessments; Certifications, SOX 302; MD&A; Reconciliation of accounts; Outsourcing; Walk throughs; Check details; Control procedures design and implementation	55		2	2	5	9	1		2		3	3		2	2	2	2		4	5	2	1		1	1			1	3	1	1	

48	Reviews and monitoring	Internal control approved by board; Balance sheet reviews; Review forecasts and budgets in low detail; Review of processes, systems, numbers and transactions; Specific expertise (e.g., understand business risks)	14			3			1			1	1	1	1			2	1		1	1							1	
49	Auditing and quality assurance	Internal auditing needs to be high in the organization; Establish culture through audit process; Substantive versus formal controls (Quality vs. compliance); ISO certification; Quality management; Quality assurance functions	9				1													2					3					3
Change																														
50	Monitor continuously	Monitor continuously; Be suspicious; Keep internal control up-to-date; Maintain visual flexible documentation (keep it up-to-date); Organize for change; Have	9	3						1	1			2			1							1						

(*continued*)

Category	Topics (examples, statements)		Interviewee (number of interviewee does not relate to Appendix A)																														
			1	2	3	4	5	6	7	8	9	10	11	12	13	14	15	16	17	18	19	20	21	22	23	24	25	26	27	28	29	30	31
	sufficient rigor and discipline in systems development; Frequent update and release of new solutions; Routine with adequate change management																																
51 Capture change	Capture unordinary information flows; Quarterly surveys for capturing changes; Good two-way communication between business and support functions; New areas and business opportunities with financial and legal impact; Get understanding how change impacts the organization (e.g., acquisitions); Manage leadership development; Deal with lawsuits; Response to changes from the business	12		1	1								2	1		1	2	1		1	2												
52 Standardize change	Routine changes (encourage people to do the same); Collective	8		1	2	1							1				1	1													1		

		decisions on changes among process owners; Have processes and people in place that can react to changes; Reference structures and procedures; Avoid implementing bad structures																												
53	Importance of due diligence	Avoid surprises; Have a full book of all the expenses of the acquired company; Review financial history; Analyze processes; Be aware of cultural issues in case of an acquisition or merger; Run out on old system; Map out control structures in an acquisition (current set of controls with acquired)	3													1									2					
54	Use synergies when acquiring	Take best practices; Eliminate redundancies; Select the right people from acquired company	4									2	1						1											
55	Testing period (whether new system, acquisitions implementation)	Development cycle; Input from the user space (QA testing); Sign off for	16	1								1	4		2	1			1			4			1					1

(*continued*)

Category	Topics (examples, statements)		Interviewee (number of interviewee does not relate to Appendix A)																														
			1	2	3	4	5	6	7	8	9	10	11	12	13	14	15	16	17	18	19	20	21	22	23	24	25	26	27	28	29	30	31
	meeting requirements; Approvals process; Testing while implementing the system; Start with a risk based (principles based approach in testing); Keep separately and integrate in adequate time; Take appropriate time for a new system																																
56 Attention to change	Be agile instead rigid; Work hard to maintain information flow; Have a "healthy" paranoia; Push people to assess and report changes; Enforce rules; Seeing change as a good thing	19	3	3	1	1	2			1			4		1				2														1
Culture and control																																	
57 Creating values	Manage values; Live values and ethical standards; Consistent behavior of board and executives	14	1			3	3	1										2	1							1		1					1

		with values; Company values go ahead of country values; Promote organizational compared to individual value; Values attract people; People self-select themselves out of a culture they not fit; Value statements; Values as foundation for business and control														
58	Culture supports controls	Importance of culture for controls (e.g., culture needs to support controls); Culture is important for systems; Culture is important for how to deal with stakeholders; Culture is a cost factor; Need to be clear where culture may create risk; Ethical culture is important for financial services; Strong values are important; Less need for detective controls; Values are the foundation	27	1	1	1	2	1	2	1	7	1	2	1	4	3

(*continued*)

Category	Topics (examples, statements)		Interviewee (number of interviewee does not relate to Appendix A)																													
			1	2	3	4	5	6	7	8	9	10	11	12	13	14	15	16	17	18	19	20	21	22	23	24	25	26	27	28	29	30	31
	for the internal control system																																
59 Types of values	Examples of values: trust, respect, integrity, professionalism, honesty, doing the right thing, accountability, excellence, teamwork, keeping it human, communication, opinion of employees, ethics, self-critical thinking, learning organization, discipline, keeping it legal, open debate, open discussion, open culture, openness, controllership	38				9				5	3					1	6	1					6				1					4	2
Trade-offs																																	
60 Top-down versus bottom-up	Risk management can be bottom-up or top-down	4						1																						2		1	
61 Pragmatism versus detail-orientation	Is it always necessary to standardize for the sake of standardizing? Organize control without overkill (technical means, databases, issues tracking)	4					1			1																1		1					

62	Localization versus global standards	Considering local laws and cultures; Delegation versus global standards; Functionality, centralization, control environments varies across business units in multinational (styles, histories, charter)	7														1		2	1					1		1		1		
63	Autonomy versus control	Innovation (and creativity, flexibility, trust, reasonable assurance process) versus standardization (e.g., centralization, bureaucracy, conservatism, "full" assurance process)	6				1				1		1						1													2
64	Cost versus quality and time	Cost-benefit trade-offs; Time consuming internal controls; Cost versus reducing the level of precision	9	2						1	2		1	1		1						1											
65	Formalism versus informalism	But only reasonable formality is necessary; Nice to have documentation but bribery might still be in place; Keep it reasonably	3																						1							2

(*continued*)

Category	Topics (examples, statements)		Interviewee (number of interviewee does not relate to Appendix A)																													
			1	2	3	4	5	6	7	8	9	10	11	12	13	14	15	16	17	18	19	20	21	22	23	24	25	26	27	28	29	30	31
66 Proactive versus reactive	Proactive versus reactive (message: be proactive); Need for detective controls for human errors; Detective controls (for speeding up); Prevent things; Detective versus preventive controls; Define controls for past failures; Define ownership for past failures	7			1	1							2				1			1												1	
Total		970	7	37	48	49	53	11	6	32	15	20	58	19	29	41	82	48	37	36	33	45	27	25	27	29	9	15	7	45	25	28	27

Appendix D

Interview Questions

The selection of interview questions was adjusted depending on the stage of the research project and the interviewee's function, company and industry. The questions also changed and were specified over time in order to confirm or reexamine prior results from the field. The following presents questions sorted by topic.

1. General Questions

1. What function does internal control (operations, financial reporting and compliance aspects) have at ... and how do you interpret your role as ... for internal control?
2. What do you understand under internal control? How do you see the relation of internal control and corporate governance? What is your responsibility in regard to internal control?
3. What would you recommend as the most important issues a researcher should give weight on in a holistic study of internal control?

2. Understanding for Internal Control (From Preliminary Interviews)

4. At ..., how are the following risk assessments related: enterprise risk management – risk assessment for internal control - risk for internal audit planning?

5. What are the major control, compliance and assurance functions at ...? How do you make sure that these various functions are aligned with each other? How are synergies and gaps managed?
6. How do you measure effectiveness and efficiency in a consistent way across your individual business units?
7. Who is in charge of ensuring that the reported financial figures are reliable?
8. Which functions at your company are checking compliance with laws and regulations?
9. How does your company ensure that the code of ethics is lived in all business units across the world?
10. How do you assess the risks and determine appropriate control activities?
11. What role plays information and communication in your company? Is it recognized as a separate function?
12. Who is in charge for the monitoring of the internal control processes?
13. What do you think are the five most influencing functions (e.g., persons, groups, and positions) in regard to the design and functioning of internal control in your company?
14. What impact has the company's complexity on the internal control design and functioning? How much formalism is needed?
15. Are differences of the business environment's quality and the regulatory influences relevant in respect of the internal control design and functioning in an international company? If yes, what are the most important issues?
16. What are the cultural challenges for internal control when operating globally (e.g., U.S., Asia, and Europe)? Can you give some specific examples?

3. *Roots of Control Failures*

17. When looking at your field, what do you think are the typical roots of control deficiencies?
18. Where do you see the most problematic aspects of internal control in your company?
19. What are the main issues that you would address to change in the internal control system of your company?
20. Can you give some examples of entity-level and account-specific control issues that ... had to deal with or that you are generally concerned about?
21. What are your major personal concerns as part of the management of a global organization?

4. *Drivers for Control Effectiveness*

22. How do you address the roots of control deficiencies?
23. What do you think are the key success factors for control effectiveness?

24. How do you make sure that you have the right people in place in your area of responsibility?
25. How does ... address complexity in accounting and control (e.g., regulatory requirements, complex accounting standards)? Can you give some industry-specific examples?
26. How do you address change (e.g., acquisitions, IT-systems) in your area of responsibility?
27. How can one be sure to succeed in responsibly managing a large organization – What are your major personal concerns as part of the executive team of ...?

5. Control, Culture and Values

28. What do you think is the role of organizational culture with regard to internal control?
29. What do you think is the effect of strong values on people's behavior? Do you promote specific organizational values that have an impact on the quality of internal control?
30. From your perspective, do organizational values have an impact on internal control? If so, how do organizational values influence internal control?
31. What types of organizational values are important for internal control?
32. Would you say that Sarbanes–Oxley had an influence on some of ...'s values?

6. Sarbanes-Oxley Related Questions

33. How are you involved in internal control over financial reporting as ... of ...?
34. From your point of view, how did/does the implementation of the Sarbanes–Oxley Act influence ...'s management?
35. How does/did the Sarbanes-Oxley Act affect ... with regard to (a) the company as a whole, (b) internal control, (c) the CEO, (d) the CFO, (e) Internal Auditing, (f) External Auditing, (g) the Board and the Audit Committee, and (h) other important groups?
36. How do you interpret the difference between the practical realization of Sections 302 and 404 of the Sarbanes-Oxley Act?
37. What do you think are costs and benefits of the Sarbanes-Oxley Act to ...?
38. Where do you see internal control, accounting and Sarbanes-Oxley in 10 years?

References

Abernethy MA, Brownell P (1997) Management control systems in research and development organizations: The role of accounting, behavior and personnel controls. Account Org Soc 22(3/4):233–248

ACFE (2004) Report to the nation on occupational fraud and abuse. Association of Certified Fraud Examiners, Austin, TX

Agle BR, Caldwell CB (1999) Understanding research on values in business: A level of analysis framework. Bus Soc 38(3):326–387

Ahrens T, Chapman CS (2004) Accounting for flexibility and efficiency: A field study of management control systems in a restaurant chain. Contem Account Res 21(2):271–301

Ahrens T, Chapman CS (2006) Doing qualitative field research in management accounting: Positioning data to contribute to theory. Account Org Soc 31:819–841

Ahrens T, Dent JF (1998) Accounting and organizations: Realizing the richness of field research. J Manage Account Res 1–39

AIA (1948) Internal control: Elements of a coordinated system and its importance to management and the independent accountant: A special report by the Committee on Auditing Procedure. American Institute of Accountants, New York

AICPA (1958) Statement on auditing procedure no. 29: Scope of the independent auditor's review of internal control. American Institute of Certified Public Accountants, New York

AICPA (2006) A section 325 communication of internal control related matters noted in an audit. American Institute of Certified Public Accountants, New York

Akaah IP, Lund D (1994) The influence of personal and organizational values on marketing professionals' ethical behavior. J Bus Ethics 13:417–430

Alexander M (1978) Organizational norms opinionnaire. In: Pfeiffer JW, Jones JE (eds) The 1978 annual handbook for group facilitators. University Associates, La Jolla, CA, pp 81–88

Alt JM (2006) Organisationswandel und Unabhängigkeit in Professional Service Firms. Dissertation, University of Zurich, Rainer Hampp Verlag

Alvesson M (1989) Concepts of organizational culture and presumed links to efficiency. Int J Manage Sci 17(4):323–333

Alvesson M (2002) Understanding organizational culture. Sage Publications, London

Anand V, Ashforth B, Joshi M (2005) Business as usual: The acceptance and perpetuation of corruption in organizations. Acad Manage Exec 19(4):9–23

Anderson U (2003) Assurance and consulting services. In: Bailey A, Gramling A, Ramamoorti S (eds) Research opportunities in internal auditing. The Institute of Internal Auditors Research Foundation, Altamonte Springs, pp 97–129

Anderson SW, Christ MH, Sedatole KL (2006) Managing strategic alliance risk: Survey evidence of control practices in collaborative inter-organizational settings. The Institute of Internal Auditors Research Foundation, Altamonte Springs

Anthony RN (1965) Planning and control systems: Framework for analysis. Harvard University Press, Boston

Anthony RN, Govindarajan V (2006) Management control systems, 12th edn. McGraw-Hill, New York

Arens AA, Elder RJ, Beasley MS (2007) Essentials of auditing and assurances services: An integrated approach, 12th edn. Upper Saddle River, Prentice Hall, NJ

Ashton RH (1974) An experimental study of internal control judgments. J Account Res 12(1):1143–1157

Ashbaugh-Skaife H, Collins DW, Kinney WR (2007) The discovery and consequences of internal control deficiencies prior to SOX-mandated audits. J Account Econ 44(1–2):166–192

Baecker D (2006) The form of the firm. Organization 13(1):109–142

Bailey CA (2007) A guide to qualitative field research, 2nd edn. Pine Forge Press, Thousand Oaks, CA

Ballinger C (2006) Demonstrating rigour and quality? In: Finlay L, Ballinger C (eds) Qualitative research for allied health professionals: Challenging choices. Wiley, Chichester

Bardi A, Schwartz SH (2003) Values and behavior: Strength and structure of relations. Pers Soc Psychol 29(10):1207–1220

Barlow CB, Jordan M, Hendrix WH (2003) Character assessment: An examination of leadership levels. J Bus Psychol 17(4):563–584

Barney J (1986) Organizational culture: Can it be a source of sustained competitive advantage? Acad Manage Rev 11:656–665

BCBS (1998) Framework for internal control systems in banking organizations. Basle Committee on Banking Supervision, Basle

Becker TE, Billings R, Eveleth DM, Gilbert NL (1996) Foci and bases of employee commitment: Implications for job performance. Acad Manage Rev 39:464–482

Berle AA, Means GC (1932) The modern corporation and private property. The Macmillan Company, New York

Bern DJ (1970) Beliefs, attitudes and human affairs. Brooks/Cole, Belmont, CA

Bhimani A (1999) Mapping methodological frontiers in crossnational management control research. Account Org Soc 24:413–440

Biegelman MT, Bartow JT (2006) Executive roadmap to fraud: Prevention and internal control: Creating a culture of compliance. Wiley, Hoboken, NJ

Birnberg J, Snodgrass C (1988) Culture and control: A field study. Account Org Soc 13(5):447–464

Bititici US, Mendibil K, Nudurupati S, Garengo P, Turner T (2006) Dynamics of performance measurement and organisational culture. Int J Oper Prod Manage 26(12):1325–1350

Bower JB, Schlosser RE (1965) Internal control: Its true nature. Account Rev 40(2):338–344

Brickey KF (2006) In Enron's wake: Corporate executives on trial. J Crim Law Criminol 96(2):297–434

Bromann P, Piwinger M (1992) Gestaltung der Unternehmenskultur. Stuttgart, Schäffer-Poeschel

Brown RG (1962) Changing audit objectives and technique. Account Rev 37(4):696–703

Brunnson N, Sahlin-Andersson K (2000) Constructing organizations: The example of public sector reform. Org Stud 21(4):721–746

Bruns WJ, Kaplan RS (1987) Field study in management accounting. In: Accounting & management: Field study perspectives. Harvard Business School Press, Boston, MA, pp 1–14

Bryan S, Lilien S (2005) Characteristics of firms with material weaknesses in internal control: An assessment of section 404 of Sarbanes-Oxley. Babcock Graduate School of Management, Wake Forest University (NC)

Bryman A, Bell E (2003) Business research methods. Oxford University Press, New York

Burton RM, DeSanctis G, Obel B (2006) Organizational design a step-by-step approach. Sage Publications, London

Cable DM, Judge TA (1996) Person-organization fit, job choice decision, and organization entry. Org Behav Hum Decis Process 67:294–311

Campbell PL (2003) An introduction to information control models, SAND2002–0131, Unclassified Unlimited Release
Chatman J (1991) Matching people and organizations: Selection and socialization in public accounting firms. Adm Sci Q 36(3):459–485
Chatman J, Jehn KA (1994) Assessing the relationship between industry characteristics and organizational culture: How different can you be? Acad Manage Rev 37:522–553
Chenhall RH (2003) Management control systems design within its organizational context: Findings from contingency-based research and directions for the future. Account Org Soc 28:127–168
Clegg SR (1981) Organization and control. Adm Sci Q 26:532–545
Coates JC (2007) The goals and promise of Sarbanes-Oxley Act. J Econ Perspect 21(1):91–116
CoCo (1995a) Guidance for directors. Guidance on Control Board, The Canadian Institute of Chartered Accountants, Toronto
CoCo (1995b) Guidance on control. Guidance on Control Board, The Canadian Institute of Chartered Accountants, Toronto
CoCo (2006a) Internal control 2006: The next wave of certification: Guidance for directors. Guidance on Control Board, The Canadian Institute of Chartered Accountants, Toronto
CoCo (2006b) Internal control 2006: The next wave of certification: Guidance for management. Guidance on Control Board, The Canadian Institute of Chartered Accountants, Toronto
CoCo (2007) Helping smaller public companies with certification and disclosure about design of internal control over financial reporting. Guidance on Control Board, The Canadian Institute of Chartered Accountants, Toronto
Collier PM (2005) Entrepreneurial control and the construction of a relevant accounting. Manage Account Res 16:321–339
Collins DW, Porras JI (2000) Built to last: Successful habits of visionary companies. Harper Collins, New York
Collins JC, Porras JI (1996) Building your company's vision. Harv Bus Rev 74:65–77
Conger JA (1998) Qualitative research as the cornerstone methodology for understanding leadership. Leadersh Q 9(1):107–121
Cooke RA, Lafferty JC (1983) Level V: Organizational culture inventory (Form I). Plymouth (MI): Human Synergistics
COSO (1992) Internal control: Integrated framework. Committee on Sponsoring Organizations of the Treadway Commission, Jersey City
COSO (2004) Enterprise risk management: Integrated framework. Committee of Sponsoring Organizations of the Treadway Commission, Jersey City
COSO (2006) Internal control over financial reporting: Guidance for smaller public companies. Sponsoring Organizations of the Treadway Commission, Jersey City
COSO (2008) Guidance on monitoring internal control systems: Exposure draft. Committee of Sponsoring Organizations of the Treadway Commission, Jersey City
Curall SC, Epstein MJ (2003) Lessons from the rise and fall of Enron. Org Dyn 32(2):193–206
D'Andrade RG (1984) Cultural meaning systems. In: Shweder RA, LeVine R (eds) Essays on mind, self, and emotion. Cambridge University Press, Cambridge, pp 88–119
Das TK, Teng BS (1998) Between trust and control: Developing confidence in partner cooperation in alliances. Acad Manage Rev 23(3):491–512
Deal T, Kennedy A (1982) Corporate cultures: The rites and rituals of corporate life. Addison-Wesley, Reading, MA
Denison DR, Mishra AK (1995) Toward a theory of organizational culture and effectiveness. Org Sci 6(2):204–223
Denison DR, Jenovics J, Young J, Cho HJ (2006) Diagnosing organizational cultures: Validating a model and method. International institute for management development
Dent JF (1991) Accounting and organizational cultures: A field study of the emergence of a new organizational reality. Account Org Soc 16(8):705–732
DeVaus D (2001) Research design in social research. Sage Publications, London

Dey I (1999) Grounding grounded theory: Guidelines for qualitative inquiry. Academic, San Diego, CA
Dicksee LR (1892) Auditing: A practical manual for auditors. London, Gee and Company, reprinted in 1976. Arno Press, New York
Doyle J, Ge W, McVay S (2007) Determinants of weaknesses in internal control over financial reporting and implications for earnings quality. J Account Econ 44(1–2):193–223
Efferin S, Hopper T (2007) Management control, culture and ethnicity in a Chinese Indonesian company. Account Org Soc 32:223–262
Eisenberg N (2000) Emotion, regulation, and moral development. Annu Rev Psychol 51:665–697
Eisenhardt KM (1985) Control: organizational and economic approaches. Manage Sci 31(2): 134–149
Eisenhardt KM (1989) Building theories from case study research. Acad Manage Rev 14(4): 532–550
England G (1967) Personal value systems of American managers. Acad Manage J 10:53–68
FEE (2005) Risk management and internal control: Fédération des Experts Comptables Européens
FEE (2006) Survey of financial control and expenditure approval in central governments across Europe: Fédération des Experts Comptables Européens
Fehr E, Fischbacher U (2004) Third party punishment and social norms. Evol Hum Behav 25:63–87
Fernald HB (1943) Internal auditing. Account Rev 18(3):228–234
Freedman IR, Fesko SL (1996) The meaning of work in the lives of people with significant disabilities: Consumer and family perspectives. J Rehabil 62:49–55
Gannon M (2000) Understanding global cultures: Metaphorical journeys through 23 nations. Sage Publications, Thousand Oaks, CA
Ge W, McVay S (2005) The disclosure of material weaknesses in internal control after the Sarbanes-Oxley Act. Account Horiz 19(3):137–158
Gerdin J, Greve J (2004) Forms of contingency fit in management accounting research: A critical review. Account Org Soc 29:303–326
Glaser B (1992) Basics of grounded theory analysis. Sociology Press, Mill Valley, CA
Glaser B, Strauss A (1967) The discovery of grounded theory: Strategies for qualitative research. Chicago, Aldine
Glover SH, Bumpus MA, Logan JE, Ciesla JR (1997) Re-examining the influence of individual values on ethical decision making. J Bus Ethics 16:1319–1329
Gomez P (1988) Die Organisation der Autonomie: Neue Denkmodelle für die Unternehmensführung. Zeitschrift für Organisation 1988(6):389–393
Govindarajan V, Fisher J (1990) Strategy, control systems, and resource sharing: Effects on business-unit performance. Acad Manage J 33(2):259–285
Gray DE (2004) Doing research in the real world. Sage, London
Habermas J (1981) Theory des kommunikativen Handelns 2nd edn. Suhrkamp, Frankfurt
Hampdon-Turner C (1990) Corporate culture for competitive edge. Economist, London
Harris JR (1990) Ethical values of individuals at different levels in the organizational hierarchy of a single firm. J Bus Ethics 9:741–750
Harrison R (1972) Understanding your organization's character. Harv Bus Rev 50(3):119–128
Hartmann FG (2005) The impact of departmental interdependencies and management accounting system use on subunit performance: A comment. Eur Account Rev 14(2):329–334
Heier JR, Dugan MT, Sayers DL (2005) A century debate for internal controls and their assessment: A study of reactive evolution. Account Hist 30(3):39–70
Heimann F, Dell G (2008) Progress report 2008: Enforcement of the OECD convention on combating bribery of foreign public officials. Transparency International
Heinemann B (2007) Avoiding integrity land mines. Harv Bus Rev 85(4):100–108
Hofstede G (1983) The cultural relativity of organizational practices and theories. J Int Bus Stud 14(2):75–89
Hofstede G (1991) Cultures and organizations. McGraw-Hill, New York

Hofstede G (2001) Culture's consequences: Comparing values, behaviors, institutions, and organizations across nations, 2nd edn. Sage, Thousand Oaks, CA

Hofstede G, Neuijen B, Ohayv DD, Saners G (1990) Measuring organizational cultures: A qualitative and quantative study across twenty cases. Adm Sci Q 35(2):286–316

Hopwood AG (1978) Towards an organizational perspective for the study of accounting and information systems. Account Org Soc 3–13

Hopwood AG (1983) On trying to study accounting in the contexts in which it operates. Account Org Soc 8(2–3):287–305

ICAEW (1999) Internal control: Guidance for directors on the combined code. Institute of Chartered Accountants in England and Wales, London

IFAC (2006) Internal controls: A review of current developments. International Federation of Accountants

IIA (2005) The professional practices framework. The Institute of Internal Auditors, Altamonte Springs, FL

ISACA. (2007) COBIT framework, 4.1. Information Systems Audit and Control Foundation, Rolling Meadows, IL

Jenal L (2006) Internal Control: Theoretisches und Empirisches zum ganzheitlichen Zusammenwirken der Control-Funktionen. Dissertation, University of St. Gall

Jensen MC, Meckling WH (1976) Theory of the firm: Managerial behavior, agency costs and ownership structure. J Financ Econ 3:305–360

Johnson M (1987) The body in the mind. Chicago University Press, Chicago, IL

Jones EE, Gerard HB (1967) Foundations of social psychology. Wiley, New York

Kanter R (1988) When a thousand flowers bloom: Structural, collective, and social conditions for innovation in an organization. In: Staw BM, Cummings LL (eds) Research in organizational behavior, vol. 10. JAI Press, Greenwich (CT), pp 169–211

Kaplan RS, Norton DP (1992) The balanced scorecard: Measures that drive performance. Harv Bus Rev 70:71–79

Keller LM, Bouchard TJ, Arvey RD, Segal NL, Dawis RV (1992) Work values: Genetic and environmental influences. J Appl Psychol 77:79–88

Kerlinger FN (1986) Foundations of behavioral research, 3rd edn. Holt, Rinehart Winston, New York

Keyton J (2005) Communication and organizational culture: A key to understand work experience. Sage Publications, Thousand Oaks, CA

Kiefel J (2003) Unternehmenssteuerung im Informationszeitalter: Gestaltung zwischen systematischer Machbarkeit und ökonomischer Realität. Köln: Eul

Kiefel J, Wille K (2002) Bausteine einer systemisch-ökonomischen Theorie der Unternehmung: Grundlagen: Modell: Implikationen. Gerhard-Mercator Universität Duisburg

Kinney WR (2000a) Information quality assurance and internal control: For management decision making. Irwin/McGraw-Hill, Burr Ridge, IL

Kinney WR (2000b) Research opportunities in internal control quality and quality assurance. Audit J Pract Theory 19:83–90

Kinney WR, Maher MW, Wright DW (1990) Assertions-based standards for integrated internal control. Account Horiz 4:1–8

Kirsh B (2000) Organizational culture, climate and person-environment fit: Relationships with employment outcomes for mental health consumers. Work 14(2):109–122

Kluckhohn C (1951) Values and value-orientations in the theory of action. In: Parsons T, Shils E (eds) Toward a general theory of action, pp 388–433. Harvard University Press, Cambridge MA

Kotter JP, Heskett JL (1992) Corporate culture and performance. Free Press, New York

Krishnan J (2005) Audit committee quality and internal control: An empirical analysis. Account Rev 80(2):649–675

Kristiansen CM, Hotte S (1989) Morality and the self: Implications for when and how of value-attitude-behavior relations. In: Seligman C, Olson JM, Zanna MP (eds) The Ontario symposium: Vol. 8. The psychology of values, Lawrence Erlbaum, Hillsdale, NJ, pp 77–106

Kroeber, Kluckhohn C (1952) Culture: A critical review of concepts and definitions. Harvard Business Press, Cambridge, MA
Kunz AH, Pfaff D (2002) Acency theory, performance evaluation, and the hypothetical construct of instrinsic motivation. Account Org Soc 27:275–295
Lange D (2008) A multidimensional conceptualization of organizational corruption control. Acad Manage Rev 33(3):710–729
Lee TW, Mowday RT (1987) Voluntarily leaving an organization: An empirical investigation of Steers and Mowday's model of turnover. Acad Manage J 30:721–743
Leone AJ (2007) Factors related to internal control disclosure: A discussion of Ashbaugh, Collins and Kinney (2007) and Doyle, Ge and McVay (2007). J Account Econ 44(1–2):224–237
Liedtka JM (1989) Value congruence: The interplay of individual and organizational value systems. J Bus Ethics 8:805–815
Lillis AM (1999) A framework for the analysis of interview data from multiple field research sites. Account Finance 39:79–105
Lim B (1995) Examining the organizational culture and organizational performance link. Leadersh Dev J 16(5):16–21
Lincoln J, Kalleberg AL (1990) Culture, control, and commitment: A study of work organization and work attitudes in the United States and Japan. Cambridge University Press, Cambridge
Lincoln YS, Guba E (1985) Naturalistic enquiry. Sage, Beverley Hills, CA
Luhmann N (1984) Soziale Systeme: Grundriss einer allgemeinen Theorie. Frankfurt am Main
Luhmann N (1986) The autopoiesis of social systems. In: Geyer F, Van der Zouwen J (eds) Sociocybernetic paradoxes: Observation, control and evolution of self-steering systems, Sage Publications, London, pp 172–192
Maijoor S (2000) The internal control explosion. Int J Audit 4:101–109
Maturana H (1981) Autopoiesis. In: Zeleny M (ed) Autopoesis: A theory of living organization North Holland, New York, pp 21–33
McClelland DC (1985) Human motivation. Scott, Foresman, Glenview, IL
McMurray RN (1963) Conflicts in human values. Harv Bus Rev 41:130–145
Meglino BM, Ravlin EC (1998) Individual values in organizations: Concepts, controversies, and research. J Manage 24(3):351–389
Merchant KA (1985) Control in business organizations. Marshfield, MA
Merchant KA (1998) Modern management control systems, text and cases. Prentice-Hall, Upper Saddle River, NJ
Merchant KA, Otley D (2007) A review of the literature on control and accountability. In: Chapman CS, Hopwood AG, Shields M (eds) Handbook of management accounting research, vol. 2. Elsevier, London, pp 785–802
Merchant KA, Van der Stede WA (2007) Management control systems: Performance measurement, evaluation and incentives, 2nd edn. Essex: Pearson Education Limited
Miceli MP, Near JP (1994) Relationship among value congruence, perceived victimation, and retaliation against whistle-blowers. J Manage 20:773–794
Michela JL, Burke WW (2000) Organizational culture and climate in transformations for quality and innovation. In: Ashkanasy NM, Wilderom CP, Peterson MF (eds) Handbook of organizational culture and climate, Sage, Thoudand Oaks, CA, pp 225–244
Mikes A (2005a) Enterprise risk management in action, *Discussion Paper No. 35*. London School of Economics and Political Sciences, London
Mikes A (2005b) Exploring the risk management mix: A field-study perspective.Harvard Business School
Mikes A (2008) Risk management and calculative cultures. Manage Account Res 20(1):18–40
Mintz SM (2005) Corporate governance in an international context: Legal systems, financing patterns and cultural variables. Corp Govern 13(5):582–597
Mintzberg H (1979) The structuring of organizations. Prentice Hall, Englewood Cliffs, NJ
Mitnick BM (1994) Public vs. private settings: An inclusive typology via systematics. In: Perry JL (ed) Research in public administration vol. 4. pp 105–136

Mock TJ, Turner JL (1981) Internal accounting control evoluation and auditor judgment, Audit research monograph #3, American Institute of Certified Public Accountants

Mouritsen J (1999) The flexible firm: Strategies for a subcontractor's management control. Account Org Soc 24(1):31–55

Nixon WA, Burns J (2005) Management control in the 21st century. Manage Account Res 16: 260–268

O'Reilly CA (1989) Corporations, culture and commitment: Motivation and social control in organizations. Calif Manage Rev 31:9–25

O'Reilly CA, Chatman JA (1996) Culture as social control: Corporations, cults and commitment. In: Staw BM, Cummings LL (eds) Research in organizational behavior, vol. 18, JAI Press, Greenwich, CT, pp 157–200

O'Reilly CA, Chatman JA, Caldwell DF (1991) People and organizational culture: A profile comparison approach to assessing person-organization fit. Acad Manage J 34:487–516

OECD (2004) OECD principles of corporate governance. Organization for Economic Co-Operation and Development, Paris

Osterloh M, Frost J (2007) Bad for practice: Good for practice: From economic imperialism to multidisciplinary mapping. University of Zurich, University of Hamburg

Otley D (1980) The contingency theory of management accounting: Achievement and prognosis. Account Org Soc 5(4):413–428

Otley D (1999) Performance management: A framework for management control systems. Manage Account Res 10(4):363–382

Ouchi WG (1979) A conceptual framework for the design of organizational control mechanisms. Manage Sci 25:833–848

Paine LS (1994) Managing for organizational integrity. Harvard Business Review, March–April

Pant PN, Lachman R (1998) Value incongruity and strategic choice. J Manage Stud 35:195–212

Parsons T (1937) The structure of social action. McGraw-Hill, New York

Parsons T (1951) The social system. The Free Press, New York

PCAOB (2007) Auditing standard no. 5: An audit of internal control over financial reporting that is integrated with an audit of financial statements. Public Company Accounting Oversight Board

Pennings J, Harianto F (1992) Technological networking and innovation implementation. Org Sci 3:356–382

Perrow C (1986) Complex organizations. McGraw-Hill, New York

Perrow C (1991) A society of organizations. Theory Soc 20(6):725–762

Pfaff D, Ruud TF (2007) Schweizer Leitfaden zum Internen Kontrollsystem (IKS). Zürich: Orell Füssli

Pfaff D, Ruud TF, Reichert F (2007) Interne Kontrolle. In: Jenny H (ed) Controller-Leitfaden, Zürich: WEKA, (pp 1–16, Teil 17, Kapitel 15)

Pine GJ, Innis G (1987) Cultural and individual work values. Career Dev Q 35:279–287

Porter ME (1985) Competitive advantage: Creating and sustaining superior performance. Free Press, New York

Power M (1997) The audit society: Rituals of verification. Oxford University Press, Oxford

Quattrone P (2000) Constructivism and accounting research: Towards a trans-disciplinary perspective. Account Audit Account J 13(2):130–155

Ramos M (2006) How to comply with Sarbanes-Oxley Section 404: Assessing the effectiveness of internal control, 2nd edn. Wiley, Hoboken, NJ

Rescher N (1969) Introduction to value theory. Prentice Hall, Englewood Cliffs, NJ

Rittenberg LE, Miller PK (2005) Sarbanes-Oxley Section 404 work: Looking at the benefits. The Institute of Internal Auditors Research Foundation

Rockness H, Rockness J (2005) Legislated ethics: From Enron to Sarbanes-Oxley, the impact on Corporate America. J Bus Ethics 57:31–54

Rockness H, Shields M (1984) Organizational control systems in research and development. Account Org Soc 9(2):162–177

Rokeach M (1973) The nature of human values. Macmillan, New York

Rokeach M, Ball-Rokeach SJ (1989) Stability and change in American values priorities, 1968–1981. Am Psychol 44(5):775–784

Ross SA (1973) The economic theory of agency: The principal's problem. Am Econ Rev 63:134–139

Rouwelaar H (2007) Theoretical review and framework: The roles of controllers. SSRN Working Paper Series

Rusch G (1987) Erkenntnis, Wissenschaft, Geschichte: Von einem konstruktivistischen Standpunkt. Suhrkamp, Frankfurt

Ruud TF (2003) The internal audit function: An integral part of organizational governance. In: Bailey A, Gramling A, Ramamoorti S (eds) Research opportunities in internal auditing, The Institute of Internal Auditors Research Foundation Altamonte Springs, CA, pp 73–96

Ruud TF, Jenal L (2005) Licht im Internal-Control-Dschungel: Begriffsdefinitionen sind unerlässlich. Der Schweizer Treuhänder 3(6):126–131

Ruud TF, Pfister J (2006) Ein adäquates Mittel zur finanziellen Berichterstattung: Best Practice: Umsetzung des Sarbanes-Oxley Act. io new management 11:30–36

Ruud TF, Sommer K (2006) Enterprise Risk Management: Das COSO-ERM Framework. Der Schweizer Treuhänder 6(3):126–131

Sarros JC, Gray J, Denston IL, Cooper B (2005) The organizational culture profile revisted and revised: An Australian perspective. Aust J Manage 30(1):159–182

Saunders M, Lewis P, Thornhill A (2000) Research methods for business students. Essex: Pearson Education

Schein E (1985) Organizational culture and leadership, Jossey-Bass, San Francisco, CA

Schein E (1990) Organizational culture. Am Psychol 45(2):109–119

Schein E (2001) Sense and nonsense about culture and climate. In: Ashkanasy NM, Wilderom CP, Peterson MF (eds) Handbook of organizational culture and climate, Sage Publications, Thousand Oaks, CA

Schein E (2004) Organizational culture and leadership 3rd edn., Jossey-Bass, San Francisco, CA

Scherer AG (2003) Multinationale Unternehmen und Globalisierung. Physica, Heidelberg

Scherer AG, Palazzo G (2007) Toward a political conception of corporate responsibility: Business and society seen from a Habermasian perspective. Acad Manage Rev 32(4):1096–1120

Scherer AG, Palazzo G, Baumann D (2006) Global rules and private actors: Towards a new role of the transnational corporation in global governance. Bus Ethics Q 16:505–532

Schreyögg G, Steinmann H (1987) Strategic control: A new perspective. Acad Manage Rev 12 (1):91–103

Schwandt TA (1994) Constructivist, interpretivist approaches to human inquiry. In: Denzin NK, Lincoln YS (eds) Handbook of qualitative research, Sage Publications London, pp 118–137

Schwartz SH, Bilsky W (1987) Toward a universal psychological structure of human values. J Pers Soc Psychol 53:550–562

Schwartz SH, Bilsky W (1990) Toward a theory of the universal content and structure of values: Extensions and cross-cultural replications. J Pers Soc Psychol 58(5):878–891

SEC (2007) Management's report on internal control over financial reporting. Release Nos. 33–8762; 34–54976; File No. S7–24–06. Securities and Exchange Commission, Washington, DC

Siehl C, Martin J (1990) Organizational culture: A key to financial performance? In: Schneider B (ed) Organizational climate and culture, Jossey-Bass, San Francisco, pp 241–281

Silverman D (2005) Doing qualitative research: A practical handbook, 2nd edn. Sage, London

Simon HA (1964) On the concept of organizational goal. Adm Sci Q 19:1–22

Simon HA (1990) A mechanism for social selection and successful altruism. Science 50:156–161

Simons R (1990) The role of management control systems in creating competitive advantage: New perspectives. Account Org Soc 15(1/2):127–143

Simons R (1995) Levers of control: How managers use innovative control systems to drive strategic renewal. Harvard Business School Press, Boston, MA

Simons R (2000) Performance measurement and control systems for implementing strategy. Prentice-Hall, Upper Saddle River, NJ

Simons R (2005) Levers of organizational design: How managers use accountability systems for greater performance and commitment. Harvard Business School Press, Boston, MA

Simons R (2008) Control in an age of empowerment. Harvard Business School Press, Cambridge

Sims RR, Brinkmann J (2003) Enron ethics (Or, culture matters more than codes). J Bus Ethics 45:243–246

Sitkin SB, George E (2005) Material trust-building through the use of legitimating formal and informal control mechanisms. Int Soc 20(3):307–338

Sørensen JB (2002) The strength of corporate culture and the reliability of firm performance. Adm Sci Q 47:70–91

Speklé RF (2001) Beyond generics: A closer look at hybrid and hierarchical governance. Dissertation Erasmus University Rotterdam

Stansbury J, Barry B (2007) Ethics programs and the paradox of control. Bus Ethics Q 17(2): 239–261

Steinmann H, Schreyögg G (1986) Zur organisatorischen Umsetzung der Strategischen Kontrolle. Zeitschrift für betriebswirtschaftliche Forschung 38(9):747–765

Stewart B (2006) The real reasons Enron failed. J Appl Corp Finance 18(2):116–119

Strauss A, Corbin J (1994) Grounded theory methodology. In: Denzin NK, Lincoln J (eds) Handbook of qualitative research, Sage, Thousand Oaks, CA, pp. 273–285

Sundaramurthy C, Lewis MW (2003) Paradoxes of governance: Managing control and collaboration. Acad Manage Rev 28:397–415

Sunder S (1997) Theory of accounting and control. South-Western Publishing, Cincinnati, OH

Thompson JD (1967) Organizations in action. McGraw-Hill, New York

Tichy NM (1982) Managing change strategically: The technical, political, and cultural keys. Org Dyn 10:59–80

Treviño LK, Brown M, Hartman FG (2003) A qualitative investigation of perceived executive ethical leadership: Perceptions from inside and outside the executive suite. Hum Relat 56(1):5–37

Treviño LK, Weaver GR, Reynolds SL (2006) Behavioral ethics in organizations: A review. J Manage 32(6):951–990

Ulrich H (1969) Die Unternehmung als produktives soziales System: Grundlagen der allgemeinen Unternehmenslehre. Haupt, Bern

Ulrich H (2001) Systemtheoretisches Management: Das Werk von Hans Ulrich. Haupt, Bern

Van Rekom J, Van Riel CB, Wierenga B (2006) A methodology for assessing organizational core values. J Manage Stud 43(2):175–201

Von Foerster H (1994) Prinzipien der Selbstorganisation im sozialen und betriebswirtschaftlichen Bereich. In: Schmidt SF, (ed) Wissen und Gewissen: Versuch einer Brücke, Suhrkamp, Frankfurt am Main, pp. 233–268

Wanous JP, Colella A (1989) Organizational entry research: Current status and future directions. In: Rowland K, Ferris G (eds) Research in personal and human resources management, vol 7. JAI Press, Greenwich (CT) pp 253–314

Weaver GR, Treviño LK, Cochran PL (1999) Corporate ethics programs as control systems: Influences of executive commitment and environmental factors. Acad Manage J 42:41–47

Weik K (2001) Sensemaking in organizations. Sage Publications, Thousand Oaks, CA

Whitener EM, Brodt SE, Korsgaard MA, Werner JM (1998) Managers as initiators of trust: An exchange relationship framework for understanding managerial trustworthy behavior. Acad Manage Rev 23(3):513–530

Whitley R (1999) Firms, institutions and management control: The comparative analysis of coordination and control systems. Account Org Soc 24:507–524

Wiener Y (1988) Forms of values systems: A focus on organizational effectiveness and cultural change and maintaince. Acad Manage Rev 13:534–545

Wilkins A, Ouchi WG (1983) Efficient cultures: Exploring the relationship between culture and organizational performance. Adm Sci Q 19:357–365

Williams RM (1968) Values. In: Sills E (ed) International encyclopedia of the social sciences, Macmillan, New York

Willke H (2001) Systemtheorie III: Steuerungstheorie 3rd edn.. Lucius & Lucius, Stuttgart

Willke H (2004) Einführung in das systemtheoretische Wissensmanagement. Carl-Auer Verlag, Heidelberg

Willke H (2005) Systemtheorie I: Grundlagen 7th edn. Lucius & Lucius, Stuttgart

Yin K (1994) Case study research: Design and methods vol. 3. Sage, Thousand Oaks

Zang IX (2005) Economic consequences of the Sarbanes-Oxley Act of 2002. AEI-Brookings Joint Center for Regulatory Studies

About the Author

Jan Pfister is a Lecturer in Accounting at Lancaster University Management School. He finished his doctoral studies at the University of Zurich and holds a Masters degree in Management from the University of Fribourg. Prior to joining Lancaster in 2009, Pfister was a Research and Teaching Fellow at the Institute for Accounting and Control at the University of Zurich and a Visiting Scholar at the Haas School of Business at the University of California at Berkeley. He was a speaker at several international conferences, and acted as advicer to national accounting and control associations in Switzerland. Pfister's doctoral research received financial support from the Swiss National Science Foundation and the Janggen-Pöhn Foundation, and he was awarded Best Paper by PhD Student at the 2007 Ethics Research Symposium of the American Accounting Association.

GPSR Compliance

The European Union's (EU) General Product Safety Regulation (GPSR) is a set of rules that requires consumer products to be safe and our obligations to ensure this.

If you have any concerns about our products, you can contact us on ProductSafety@springernature.com

In case Publisher is established outside the EU, the EU authorized representative is:

Springer Nature Customer Service Center GmbH
Europaplatz 3
69115 Heidelberg, Germany

Batch number: 10725798

Printed by Printforce, the Netherlands